Movie-Made Appalachia

Movie-Made Appalachia

History, Hollywood, and the Highland South

JOHN C. INSCOE

The University of North Carolina Press Chapel Hill

This book was published with the assistance of the Fred W. Morrison Fund of the University of North Carolina Press.

Set in Charis by Westchester Publishing Services
Manufactured in the United States of America

The University of North Carolina Press has been a member of the Green Press Initiative since 2003.

Library of Congress Cataloging-in-Publication Data

Names: Inscoe, John C., 1951– author.
Title: Movie-made Appalachia : history, Hollywood, and the highland South / John C. Inscoe.
Description: Chapel Hill : University of North Carolina Press, 2020. | Includes bibliographical references and index.
Identifiers: LCCN 2020022823 | ISBN 9781469660134 (cloth : alk. paper) | ISBN 9781469660141 (pbk. : alk. paper) | ISBN 9781469660158 (ebook)
Subjects: LCSH: Appalachians (People) in motion pictures. | Appalachians (People)—Social life and customs.
Classification: LCC PN1995.9.M67 I57 2020 | DDC 791.43/65874—dc23
LC record available at https://lccn.loc.gov/2020022823

Cover illustration: Margaret Wycherly and Gary Cooper in *Sergeant York*, directed by Howard Hawks (Burbank, California: Warner Bros., 1941). Used by permission of Warner Bros./Photofest, © Warner Bros.

Contents

Illustrations

Introduction

Teaching Appalachia through Film

An announcement in mid-2018 that J. D. Vance's controversial best-selling memoir, *Hillbilly Elegy*, would be made into a feature film by director Ron Howard prompted worrisome responses by numerous Appalachian residents as to how they'd be depicted onscreen. A lengthy editorial in the *Roanoke (VA) Times* expressed the reactions of many. It bemoaned the fact that "if Appalachia gets depicted at all, it's in a negative way. Think *Deliverance* or District 12 of *The Hunger Games*. Our fear is that the movie version of *Hillbilly Elegy* will simply add to those degrading portrayals . . . that this could be yet another retelling of the stupid, lazy, vicious hillbilly yarn."[1]

Reaction from scholars in and of the region was swift and harsh following the book's appearance in 2016. Most took offense at Vance's simplistic and condescending characterization of his own family in eastern Kentucky (deeply rooted in Breathitt County) and, by extension, not only southern highlanders as a whole but even much of the Rust Belt's white working class, which he labeled "Greater Appalachia." According to Vance, the massive infiltration of mountain migrants throughout the Midwest meant that "the plight of backwoods hollers . . . has gone mainstream," as "hillbilly values spread widely along with hillbilly people." And while inherently linked by Scots Irish ancestry, Vance declares, a dilapidated culture of poverty, violence, alcohol, and drug addiction bound mountain residents with its outmigrants, including Vance himself, who was born and raised in Ohio. Their current hardships and hopelessness, he claims, are due to their own character flaws and moral weakness, which "increasingly encouraged social decay instead of counteracting it."[2]

Compounding Vance's offense is the self-congratulatory tone with which he takes credit for his own escape from that depraved world. Quoted in the *New York Times* in 2018, fellow eastern Kentucky writer Barbara Kingsolver joined the chorus when she declared, "I have no use for the 'barely got out of them hills alive' narrative. The region has been savaged by one extractive industry after another, and still its landscapes and people impress me every day. We're not one psyche, one color, one culture, J. D. Vance's cousins, and we're certainly not without hope."[3]

It is hard to know how fully the "pitiable monoculture" Vance portrayed in his book will make its way onto the screen.[4] Whether or not he intended it with some tinge of irony, the very title of his book (which the film will no doubt carry as well) serves as a red flag as to what we can expect. Much of the pessimism regarding Hollywood's approach to such a maligned portrait of the mountaineers in Vance's world lies in the film industry's long and continuing tradition of hillbilly movies that, as with other elements of popular culture, have depicted residents of Appalachia in a variety of demeaning ways.

The scholarly creation of Southern Appalachia as a distinct cultural and sociological entity began early in the twentieth century. Whereas most regional commentaries of previous decades consisted of local-color short fiction or travel narratives—that is, firsthand descriptions of scenic vistas and flora and fauna along with observations of the quaint customs and folk life of southern highlanders—by the turn of the century, such impressionistic, localized, and often anecdotal accounts began to give way to more serious and systematic ethnographic assessments of mountain people by missionaries, social workers, and academics. These in turn morphed into a more insidious "hillbilly" persona (most thoroughly chronicled by Anthony Harkins) as spokespeople for new mining and textile mill operations in the region embellished on an already "well-established vision of hopelessly isolated and irrationally violent" mountaineers by also calling them "a diseased, illiterate, undernourished, sexually promiscuous, and degenerate people."[5]

In explaining the mission impulse to the southern highlands in the 1910s and 1920s in his book *All That Is Native and Fine*, David Whisnant describes a somewhat more varied range by which residents were characterized or caricatured, noting that "popular understanding of the Appalachian South at the time reflected every shade of opinion. While for some, mountain people were backward, unhealthy, unchurched, ignorant, violent, and morally degenerate social misfits who were a national liability; for others they were pure, uncorrupted 100 per cent American, picturesque, and photogenic premoderns who were a great untapped national treasure."[6]

Thus began the so-called invention of Appalachia by outsiders with varied agendas regarding its populace, agendas reinforced over the twentieth century in no small part by the growing influence of film. For it was around the same time that the American motion picture industry began to emerge, and southern mountain movies much expanded public exposure to a particular version of "hillbilly" culture.[7] Over four hundred silent films—one- or two-reelers shown in nickelodeons—were produced between 1904 and 1920.[8] Most of these were action-packed melodramas, featuring violent encounters between moonshiners and revenuers, feuding clans, and romantic rivals, all the while perpetuating both comic and serious generalizations, distortions, and stereotypes. The industry, which by the 1920s had based itself in Hollywood, established a tradition that would extend well beyond the silent era; indeed, such tropes are very much alive and well today in the form of "hick flicks" and "hillbilly horror" movies.[9] It is in fact these current genres that have prompted early concerns as to how *Hillbilly Elegy* will be translated to screen.

Yet my contention here—and the theme of this book—is that Hollywood has done far more than perpetuate crude and demeaning stereotypes of mountain people. Much of the basis for that realization has come to me through classroom experience, specifically a first-year seminar called Appalachia on Film, which I taught for a number of years at the University of Georgia. Students viewed eight to ten feature-length films per semester—some iconic, others more obscure—followed by discussions through which we explored fundamental aspects of the southern highland experience and what it meant to be Appalachian. Drawing from those classroom experiences, I came to realize that when treating seriously both the content and the tone of these movies, they can serve as effective conduits into the region's history, some grounded firmly in historical realities, others only loosely so. In either case, I argue, these are films with more redeeming value than they've been given credit for in terms of creating sympathetic and often complex Appalachian characters who interact within households and communities amid a wide range of historical contingencies to create credible and meaningful narratives that respect (and at times romanticize) the particular times and places in which they're set.

Hollywood has never been known for its historical accuracy, and yet historians have found it far too easy to take a dismissive approach to cinematic treatments of historical subjects. In his book *Reel History: In Defense of Hollywood*, Robert Brent Toplin urges his fellow historians to take a more open-minded view of cinema as a teaching tool, arguing that movies can communicate to students of history important ideas about the past. The very nature of the medium prevents it from presenting factual realities in the same way one would expect from a published work of history or even a documentary film. Nevertheless, Toplin insists, "in many respects, the two-hour movie can arouse emotions, stir controversy, and prompt viewers to consider significant questions."[10] This is how I've approached both the films I've taught and those on which I focus in this study.

I should state up front that my study is not meant to replace, replicate, or even challenge Jerry Williamson's landmark 1995 work, *Hillbillyland*, which remains the most original, insightful, and wide-ranging treatment we're ever likely to have on "what Hollywood did to the mountains," and vice versa. In often free-wheeling style and broad geographical focus, Williamson explores the many facets of how "hillbillies" have been represented onscreen—from backwoods bumpkins to sinister, depraved monsters. They can be "clowns, children, free spirits, or wild people through whom we live vicariously," and it's our response to them—whether ridicule, fear, or even affection—that he explores so adeptly.[11]

My intent and method here are somewhat less original, and less sophisticated, than those of Williamson. Focusing primarily on how Hollywood has treated Appalachia's past, I build my argument on close readings of some two dozen films, all of them set squarely within the region. (There's very little overlap in the films on which Williamson and I focus; only two—*Tol'able David* and *Sergeant York*—are fully discussed by both of us.) My primary criteria for inclusion are the historical contexts within which these movies are set—those that their makers took seriously enough that many, if not most, of the central characters come across as admirable or identifiable to American audiences at least as often as they're diminished or demeaned by the stereotypes that Williamson deconstructs and complicates so brilliantly.

I admit that I originally conceived the course I taught as one that would, at least in part, examine these films in terms of how they perpetuate misconceptions, stereotypes, and clichés. Yet early on I came around to Robert Toplin's perspective. Although there is much that can be said about stereotypes and distortions in many of these films, more important, I think, is that most of these stories encompass human struggles brought to life through skilled writing and often great acting that grow out of actual historical situations or life stories. As such, I came to see these films as appealing and accessible means of drawing students into discussions of the realities conveyed—or merely suggested—onscreen. Students are certainly astute enough not to accept what they see onscreen as literal truth or documentary filmmaking, and thus not much of our class discussion focused on separating fact from fiction, as I had anticipated when designing the course.

After viewing each film, I asked students to write papers in which they responded to a set of questions centered on the tone taken by each film toward Appalachian life and culture (contemptuous? respectful? romanticized? satiric?); the virtues and vices of the characters, major and minor; the narrative techniques used to shape viewers' attitudes toward the region; what aspects of the film—music, speech patterns, location shooting—contributed to or detracted from its regional authenticity; and finally, what impact the movie likely had on how American filmgoers viewed the southern highlands. Over the course of the semester, class discussions grew richer and more rewarding in that each film built on those previously viewed, and students were able to assess them in increasingly collective and comparative terms. I came to appreciate more fully this cumulative effect: that the juxtaposition of particular films offered far more insight into both realities and perceptions of Appalachia and its history than one would have any right to expect from Southern California's "dream factory" or than any one or two of these films alone could offer.

In a 2010 essay titled "Claiming Appalachia . . . and the Questions That Go with It," Stephen Fisher, one of the region's most insightful scholars, expounds on the multiplicity of variables that go into shaping a culture and those who embody it:

> I'm convinced that the work to promote an empowering regional identity must be grounded at the personal level. We've got to come to understand and accept the reality of multiple Appalachian experiences, taking into account the specificity and the diversity of who we are. One way of doing that is by telling our stories. . . . I tell my story whenever I can; it makes me aware of the pain of fragmentation in my life and wary of making generalizations about what it means to be Appalachian. But it also reinforces my belief that only the willingness to share private experiences, to tell our stories, will enable us to create a collective description of the region that is truly ours.[12]

And so it is with these films that use storytelling to breathe life into the region's past by conveying its people and their "private experiences"—as individuals, as families, as communities—through a range of scenarios and settings, all of which contribute to our understanding of the broader whole we know as Appalachia. The fact that much, if not most, of the source material for these films came from voices native to, or close observers of, the region—through novels, short stories, memoirs, oral histories—also validates Fisher's sense as to who can and should lay claim to truths about the mountain South as they know it.

The chapter titles in my table of contents provide a fairly straightforward indication of the thematic and topical groupings of the movies assessed in each. Each of the six chapters consists of close readings of three to five films and the particular historical frameworks on which they build. I begin by exploring four films that center on the quest for farmland by individuals (women as often as men) who attempt either to acquire it or to hold on to what they or their families already own. Chapter 2 focuses on race, examining the few films that make the black experience integral to the stories told, from early slavery through emancipation and on to African American labor forces and the resistance they faced in the early twentieth century. That's followed by a chapter on the chaotic conditions that defined highland home fronts during the Civil War and a chapter that puts the infamous feuds of the late nineteenth century in family and community contexts. The fifth chapter offers a comparative perspective on three screen depictions of women mission workers—religious, educational, and cultural—who traveled to different parts of the highland South in the early twentieth century, and a final chapter juxtaposes film portrayals of coal mining communities on both sides of the Atlantic and the generational impulses to escape them . . . or not. Rather than further summarize the makeup of each chapter, I'd like to use the rest of this introduction to discuss other, more pervasive themes that transcend the specific focuses of each chapter and allow us to consider these films as a collective whole in terms of what they share and how they differ.

Perhaps the most obvious commonality that runs throughout is the interaction of southern highlanders with outsiders—through either the incursion of the latter into the region or the outgoing moves elsewhere by Appalachian natives. The intentions of strangers coming into the region vary greatly in these movies, as was the case historically. Academic fieldworkers, missionaries and educators, Union and Confederate troops, union organizers and company agents, strikebreakers, government officials, tourists (think canoers!), and the developers who cater to those tourists all serve as catalysts that set these films in motion and provide in many cases the contrasts—social, cultural, educational, moral—by which highlanders are defined or measured. In each case, it is the reaction of local residents to these individuals or groups and their various agendas that generates the tension, conflict, and emotional weight that propel the films' plots and dramatic resonance.

For those highlanders who move beyond the bounds of home and region, it is usually larger historical forces that draw them away; few leave willingly. Wars take some far from home and into alien environments, including Inman in *Cold Mountain*, Alvin York in his self-named saga, and Gertie Nevels in *The Dollmaker*. They each carry with them skills honed in the mountains—from shooting prowess to wood carving—which will contribute much to their survival in challenging circumstances elsewhere. And yet all are profoundly troubled by their displacement and long to return to the comfort and security of their highland families or communities—or, for Inman, merely the natural world (oh, and his sweetheart, Ada Monroe). The 1961 film adaptation (the most recent of several) of John Fox's classic novel *The Little Shepherd of Kingdom Come* focuses on Chad Buford and the impact of this young protagonist's move from the Kentucky mountains to the Bluegrass region, where he must wrestle with competing loyalties upon the outbreak of the Civil War.

Others were pushed out, or pulled out, of the region by coal—including adolescents Loretta Lynn and Homer Hickam, he far more willingly than she. Lynn was pulled cross country at age fifteen by a new husband who sought escape from a lifetime working underground; only by writing and singing about her life as a *Coal Miner's Daughter* did Lynn come to terms with her separation from home and family. As a high school student in Coalwood, West Virginia, Hickam used rocket science and a college scholarship as his escape hatch, and saw his memoir *Rocket Boys* almost immediately transferred to celluloid under an anagrammed title, *October Sky*. In two other coal communities, the central characters are young boys who also serve as narrators of their films. In *How Green Was My Valley* and *Matewan*, each seems destined by temperament and education to escape the mines as adults, but both choose to remain where they are, thus complicating the dynamics of family, community, and the staying power of home in both Wales and West Virginia.

A related theme in many of these films is Appalachians' attachment to land. The plots of films as varied as *Sergeant York*, *The Dollmaker*, and *The Journey of August King* center on the title character's quest to own his or her own land—or to expand their current holdings. As Alvin York's mother observes of her son's diligent quest to buy a piece of bottomland: "Queer how people that lives at the bottom looks down on the folks on the top." Others—from Charlie Anderson (James Stewart) in *Shenandoah* to Annie Nations (Jessica Tandy) in *Foxfire* to Ella Garth (Jo Van Fleet) in *Wild River*—are driven by a desperate struggle to hold on to land long owned when threatened by larger forces (the Union Army, real estate developers, and the Tennessee Valley Authority [TVA], respectively) that seek to separate them from it.

A somewhat more superficial, but equally pervasive, sense of loss is evident in *Deliverance.* As in *Wild River,* the damming of a river proves the impetus for the threats felt by its central characters, though the losses feared by four canoers from Atlanta couldn't be more different from those of Ella Garth. While she has far more at stake in defying the TVA, which is about to flood her island farm and destroy her home, the suburban adventurers on the Cahulawassee are merely interested in "doing the river" one last time before it is turned into a lake. Yet director John Boorman suggests that there's more than a wild river about to be destroyed. Perhaps borrowing from the earlier film, the final scene of *Deliverance* depicts graves being dug up prior to the cemetery's flooding, a ritual no doubt reenacted many times under the TVA's incursion throughout the region and a major point of concern to Ella Garth.

In the films on feuding, land—especially farmland—lends a sense of moral superiority to one combative family over the other. The Kinemons—the tenant farm family of the title character in the 1921 silent film *Tol'able David*—are warmhearted and close-knit and part of a pastoral valley community called Greenstream, no less. Almost without instigation, the Kinemons are egregiously set upon by the Hatburns, three hateful, bullying vagabonds who (not coincidentally) have no ties at all to land (or, for that matter, to wives or children). Audiences have no problem knowing whom to root for and against in this lopsided contest, with the farm family ultimately, and all too predictably, prevailing. Even the films dealing with the actual Hatfields and McCoys, while never attributing full culpability to one side or the other, make not-so-subtle hints that those cultivating the land have the upper moral hand. In the 1949 feature *Roseanna McCoy,* that advantage falls to the title character's family. Her father Ranel's opening words about the Hatfields establishes his contempt for them and the reason behind it. "Look at the land they settled on, and by their own choice," he rants. "Not fit to raise a field of corn. Hunting country, hunting people, idle, cutthroat drunken savages."

Hollywood almost always privileges farming over other livelihoods and does so consistently in the films considered here. In *Sommersby*—one of few Appalachian-based films focused on the Reconstruction era—a Civil War veteran earns the goodwill of those in the East Tennessee community to which he "returns" after the war by initiating a communal tobacco-growing operation that includes black as well as white participants. Though Jack Sommersby (Richard Gere) turns out to be a disreputable character, his agrarian pursuits allow him to retain much of the sympathy he'd earlier earned, including that of the audience.

The moral dilemmas that stem from such conflicts are often obvious in these films, with right and wrong, good and evil, defined in fairly simplistic form; yet closer examination often reveals subtle factors that defy such facile judgments. August King (Jason Patric) is obviously on the side of angels as he facilitates a young slave girl's escape through western North Carolina and makes ever-growing sacrifices to protect her (Thandie Newton) as she eludes her brutal master. Yet would he have risked as much for a male fugitive or for an elderly or unattractive woman? And while students recognize the strong antiwar messages of *Shenandoah*, *Cold Mountain*, and *Pharaoh's Army*—an intimate but intense Civil War drama of a Kentucky woman and her son held hostage on their wilderness farm by a group of Union soldiers—they must also confront the moral ambiguities inherent in a guerrilla war that blurred the line between home front and combat zone. All of these films—as different as they are in tone and scope—demonstrate the power of cinema to dramatize the very human scales at which the Civil War played out in much of Southern Appalachia and the added dilemmas faced by those who sought to forgo any loyalties to one side or the other.

Much of the effectiveness of Elia Kazan's *Wild River* lies in the moral ambivalence of TVA agent Chuck Glover, his protagonist. Glover fully recognizes the benefits of the TVA and the New Deal in improving the lives of East Tennesseans, and yet he also comes to exhibit increasing sensitivity to and admiration for Ella Garth, the elderly woman who refuses to abandon her island farm that will soon be covered by water. This delicately framed debate makes for very teachable moments, as it's an issue that resonates strongly in Appalachian history, as thousands of highlanders were forced off land claimed by the federal government for its creation of the Great Smoky Mountains National Park, the Blue Ridge Parkway, and Shenandoah National Park's Skyline Drive, in addition to those displaced by the TVA.

Students recognize the similar dilemma facing Annie Nations (Jessica Tandy) in *Foxfire*. This elderly widow still maintains her mountaintop farm in northern Georgia despite pressure from land-hungry developers to sell it so that they can make big profits from the scenic vistas and gated communities they can turn it into. Some of my students at the University of Georgia are familiar with the scenario behind Mrs. Nations' (only thinly fictionalized) story—the incursion of tourism and second-home development in the Georgia mountains—but they admit that their contact with natives of the area has been minimal and that they had never before thought in terms of the human and cultural costs of the easy access now provided them. Given how many of our students come from the metro Atlanta area, they react even more strongly to *Deliverance*, which, like *Foxfire*, was filmed in northern Georgia's Rabun County. But as Jerry Williamson has so astutely observed, "*Deliverance* is not about mountain people; it is rather a critique of city people."[13] By shifting discussion from the harassment by grotesque hillbillies and viewing the four Atlanta canoers as something other than simply the victims of mountain violence, we open a new frame of reference that informs several other films as well.

Both of these Georgia-based films reflect the assumptions of "whiteness" inherent in how Appalachia is so often perceived. Whiteness studies have emerged in recent years primarily as sociological and literary constructs for analyzing Appalachian culture and identity.[14] The premise that southern highlanders have long been (at least since Indian removal) a solidly white populace can, in itself, provide a racialized context for the region that perhaps most distinguishes it from the rest of the American South, where a biracial presence has long defined—indeed, driven—its history.

The sheer absence of African Americans in most of these films affirms not only the mountain South's presumed whiteness but often its ethnic purity as well. Claims of the region's solid British stock enhanced sentiments by other Americans who saw in Appalachia "our contemporary ancestors," which distanced them from the multiethnic immigration trends then fully underway elsewhere in the country.[15] From turn-of-the-century claims that "nowhere will be found purer Anglo-Saxon blood" and "this region is as free of negroes as northern Vermont" to J. D. Vance's recent assertion that the Appalachian character is in essence Scots Irish, such singular ethnic determinism, or "white-washing," has long been claimed for the region.[16] It plays out onscreen in several instances, including the English ballads sought after—and found—in *Songcatcher*, whose northern academic protagonist confirms the cultural roots of the western North Carolinians among whom she settles, as well as in much of the superstition and folk wisdom preserved and practiced by the elderly north Georgia widow in *Foxfire*.

In her recent book *Un-White* (one I wish I'd been able to assign to my students), Meredith McCarroll offers a provocative twist on the racialization of Southern Appalachians depicted onscreen. Applying theories of whiteness and other cultural constructs, McCarroll draws on a wide array of films to argue that the region's seemingly solid white populace has been subject to racial and ethnic "othering" by filmmakers, who subtly endow their characters with cinematic tropes ranging from Native American hunters to black mammies to Mexican migrants, while allowing them to maintain the badge of white privilege. Such depictions, she argues persuasively, allows movie audiences (largely white themselves) to identify with the mountaineers onscreen on some level while distancing them from their own self-perceived normality.[17]

My own approach is to examine these films in terms of a black presence—where it appears and where it is missing—and what this tells us about whiteness and how it shaped the attitudes and behavior of the white highlanders with whom the nonwhites must interact. One can count on one hand the number of mountain-based films in which Afro-Appalachian characters prove integral to the historical scenarios dramatized. Slavery is central to *August King*, although Annalees, the young woman on the run, is the only black character with a speaking part in the film (and is the only African American protagonist in any of these films); despite her tough, determined exterior, she remains a rather passive presence whose fate is fully in the hands of white men. *Sommersby* features an emancipated slave community in post–Civil War Tennessee, but makes them little more than pawns of the visionary title character, with white resistance directed more at him than at the freedmen themselves as he seeks to include them in his communal tobacco-growing scheme. Racial divisions among other labor forces are also evident in the strikebreakers (led by James Earl Jones, no less) who alter the dynamics of organizing efforts in *Matewan*, and in local white resentments over the New Deal policy of equal pay for black TVA workers in *Wild River*. As numerically insignificant as these nonwhite contingents were, their very presence threatened their poor white counterparts and, in each of these very different scenarios, resorted to violence not unlike that experienced throughout much of the rest of the South at one time or another.[18]

In several other films, the absence of African Americans where historically they should be—a function of what Edward Cabbell once labeled Appalachia's "black invisibility" problem—serves as an even more blatant layer of whitewashing imposed on the region by Hollywood.[19] Perhaps the most conspicuous example is the absence of any slaves in the highland-set scenes of *Cold Mountain*, despite the fact that its heroine, Ada Monroe, is a slaveholder and makes several references to her black "servants," who are apparently at her beck and call just off screen. Only two of the four other Civil War films set in the highlands feature even a token slave character—*Shenandoah* and *Pharaoh's Army*—and only the former acknowledges, even obliquely, that slavery played a causal role in bringing on the war. The white-only coal communities and labor forces depicted in both *Coal Miner's Daughter* and *October Sky* belie the significant presence of black miners in both Kentucky and West Virginia during those years. (It's ironic that black actor Paul Robeson's star turn onscreen as a coal miner takes place in Wales in *The Proud Valley*, which was produced in 1940 by Robeson himself, with a cast that's otherwise fully Welsh.)

These films also provide effective venues through which to explore gender issues. Strong women play such key roles in so many of these films (they're the title characters in six of the films, and the central characters in three or four others) and are so often accorded reverential treatment that students could easily conclude, based on Hollywood's version of southern mountain life, that Appalachia was a matriarchal society.[20] Jane Fonda, Jessica Tandy, Patricia Clarkson, Nicole Kidman, and Renée Zellweger made the most of formidable but vulnerable heroines in *The Dollmaker*, *Foxfire*, *Pharaoh's Army*, and *Cold Mountain*. They each face seemingly overwhelming odds that force them to fight for their families, their homes, or their own survivals, usually with little or no support from men. Fonda's performance, in particular, is an extraordinary blend of fortitude and tentativeness that embodies much of both the stereotypes and reality of Appalachian women. (She has said that Gertie Nevels is the role of which she is proudest.) Tandy plays an equally poignant character in *Foxfire*, whose fragility—due only to age—and stubborn attachment to her way of life, her land, and her memories suggest what Gertie Nevels might have been like thirty years later. Fully as notable are adolescent characters based on factual counterparts Christy Huddleston (Kellie Martin) and Loretta Lynn (Sissy Spacek), whose youth and inexperience make their transformations and growth onscreen endearing to viewers.

A rich array of secondary female characters populate nearly all of these films. They are often even more stalwart mountain women, played by accomplished character actresses: Jo Van Fleet as the stubborn island holdout in *Wild River*; Pat Carroll as Viney Butler, a curmudgeonly midwife who becomes the champion of *Songcatcher*'s title character, Lily Penleric (Janet McTeer), and the most authentic source of the music Penleric is collecting; Mary McDonnell as Elma Radnor, the boardinghouse operator in *Matewan* who stands her ground in supporting the local miners' strike and figures prominently—and triumphantly—in the film's climactic shoot-out; Eileen Atkins as the "goat woman" who rescues Inman and nurses him back to health in *Cold Mountain*; and perhaps the ultimate mountain matriarch, Ma York, played by British stage actress Margaret Wycherly, whose quiet dignity commands the respect and submission of her wayward son Alvin (Gary Cooper) and makes their relationship as much the emotional center of *Sergeant York* as the courtship of Alvin and his young sweetheart, Gracie (Joan Leslie).

Not all such women are admirable: Geraldine Page plays Gertie Nevels's overbearing and needy mother, who insists that Gertie join her husband in Detroit, which in effect forces her to give up the Kentucky farm she had scraped and saved so hard to acquire. In *Matewan*, Bridey Mae Tolliver (Nancy Mette), a rather empty-headed and man-hungry young widow, is easily manipulated into betraying the coal miners and their community, of which she herself had been a part. Otherwise, few of these women (other than Loretta Lynn and some—though not all—of the wives and mothers in the patriarchal-leaning feuding families) fully bow to the authority or power of men.

These films provide plenty of opportunity to scrutinize masculinity as well. It is the very essence of *Deliverance* that it, alone among the films discussed, depicts a mountain society devoid of women and thus a far bleaker and more threatening one. (Is it mere coincidence that Drew [Ronny Cox], the most sensitive of the four Atlantans and the only one to connect with a local resident—through their banjo duet—is the only one killed by those locals?)

There is no shortage of violence in these films, much of which is portrayed as endemic to mountain life: the decadent brutality in *Deliverance*; good-ol'-boy rowdiness and barroom brawls in several films, from *Sergeant York* to *Songcatcher*; an intense search party and gut-wrenching execution of a slave in *The Journey of August King*; the climactic, fact-based shoot-out in *Matewan*; and vigilante retribution rendered by local hoodlums on Montgomery Clift's TVA agent in *Wild River*. Shootings and sabotage in various forms are integral to the feud films, of course, though they make up more rampant and random elements of some movies than others. The Civil War imposed its own forms of violence on highland home fronts, whether by enemy incursions—which could be either Union or Confederate—or by local bands of guerrillas or "home guardsmen," who often proved to be even more serious tormenters of vulnerable residents. Unlike feuds, in which the embattled participants were almost always men, the wartime home front often made women equally subject to combatant status (as four of the five films centered on the war make evident).

The films focusing on feuds also take issues of manhood seriously, spinning their family rivals' seemingly relentless impulse to retaliate as a function of honor, either individually or, more frequently, as a band of brothers. It was also men (or boys) in love who, according to Hollywood, fueled feuds, so much so that all four of these films weave thwarted romances into their multistrand narratives. If one were to keep score, it quickly becomes apparent that mountain men have never been nearly as appreciated by filmmakers as have mountain women. Of male protagonists, only a few—August King, Inman, "Tol'able" David Kinemon, Alvin York, and Chad Buford in *The Little Shepherd of Kingdom Come*—qualify as heroes in terms of standing up for principles (and in nearly every case, much of their motivation in doing so is shaped by a woman). In *Matewan* and *Wild River*, it is outsiders, pacifist union organizer Joe Kenehan (Chris Cooper) and TVA agent Chuck Glover (Clift), respectively, who embody the moral compasses of their films when confronted with wrongs that need to be righted. More often than not, the native men in these particular movies come across as weak, irresponsible, rowdy, emasculated, malevolent, or intolerant. Women emerge as the guardians, even the repositories, of values, of culture, of tradition. This is particularly evident in films like *Songcatcher* and the television series *Christy*, both of which feature multiple major female characters. (It is probably no coincidence that the former, with six women in substantive roles, is also the only film under consideration here that was both written and directed by a woman, Maggie Greenwald.)

For a region often assumed to have been relatively "unchurched," religion factors—or sometimes merely seeps—into these Appalachian-based films more regularly than is true for most of Hollywood's output. It's usually cast as mainstream Protestant, and even that remains fairly generic in its spiritual context and how it's practiced. There are few indications of the specific sects so closely associated with the region—Primitive and Old Time Baptists, and the Pentecostal and Holiness movements—or of the practices associated with them, such as snake handling, speaking in tongues, or shaped-note singing (though in an extended scene in *Cold Mountain*, the congregation engages in what seems to be an authentic version of the latter).

The frequency with which church congregations are featured suggests a degree of both stability and civility in these highland communities and serves as an obvious means of linking the mountains with much of small-town and rural Americana. Preachers appear as influential members of the communities they serve, sometimes as social activists, sometimes as their moral consciences, and almost always as voices of reason and wisdom. The experiences of a Methodist circuit rider and his wife in Georgia's mountains dealing with the travails of their assigned congregations form the essence of *I'd Climb the Highest Mountain*, and *Christy* chronicles its title character's spiritual and social struggles as a Presbyterian teacher and mission worker, guided by an imposing Quaker supervisor, deep in the Tennessee Smokies at the turn of the century.

Several films feature at least one church service scene (and often more) that either reveals vital truths about local values or prejudices or serves as a crucial turning point in characters' lives. It's at a Sunday service that the rival patriarchs Anse Hatfield and Ranel McCoy first reconnect at the end of the Civil War in the miniseries bearing their names; *Sergeant York* opens with a hymn-singing congregational gathering, the major point of which is the rowdy Alvin's absence from it. Prodded by Pastor Pile (Walter Brennan), York's conversion experience and the pacifist convictions that accompany his newfound faith form the dramatic crux of the film's first half. Much of the tension and subterfuge of the labor strike at *Matewan* take place at nighttime church meetings, where the often inflammatory preaching comes from a pivotal character, fourteen-year-old Danny (Will Oldham), whose perspective provides the narrative thread through which the story of the massacre unfolds in hindsight.

It's while constructing a new church roof in *Cold Mountain* that Inman meets Ada Monroe, who's passing below (and whose father had brought her up from Charleston to minister to the mountaineers); during a service in the same church a few weeks later, news breaks of the first shots fired between the North and the South, and excited young men rush from the sanctuary to enlist. In *Shenandoah*'s final scene, Charlie Anderson and his grown sons are attending Sunday services when his youngest son, swept up by a passing army a year earlier and the subject of an intense but futile search by his elders, comes limping up the aisle to reunite with his joyous family, or at least those who aren't lying in recently dug graves in the church cemetery out front. For the most part, despite the drama played out in these small sanctuaries, such congregational gatherings are made generic—or bland—enough in terms of spiritual content and simple ritual in large part to make them easily relatable to American audiences.

The depiction of such gatherings also accentuates a strong sense of community among southern highlanders—a reality at odds with long-entrenched stereotypes of isolation and a lack of communal context in southern mountain life.[21] The bonds of community are more sharply defined in some films more than others. *Matewan* is the epitome of a fully realized community onscreen. I would argue, in fact, that no other film set in the region has conveyed as complete and complex a portrait of a single community as that re-created by John Sayles. Other films—such as *October*

Sky, *Sergeant York*, *The Journey of August King*, and *Cold Mountain*—make the collective values and agendas of particular communities central to the protagonists' own dilemmas and actions, as do several of the feud-centered sagas, particularly the two dealing with the Hatfields and the McCoys. In my classes, students often noted that while the Civil War brought out the best and worst of small mountain towns and rural settlements, such tensions are often conveyed only superficially (as in *Cold Mountain*), particularly when compared with those previously mentioned. All of these films, though, like *Matewan*, provide useful reference points for discussions of class differences, of shifts in power and powerlessness, of mob (or mere group or clan) mentalities, and of how outside forces serve to either unite or divide local residents.

Revealing too are those characters, such as the aforementioned Charlie Anderson, Gertie Nevels, Jack Sommersby, August King, Chad Buford, and Annie Nations, who, for reasons either forced upon them or self-imposed, are alienated or removed from the communities of which they were once a part or could have been a part. The resulting tensions between these individuals and those in whose midst they live can tell us much about the shifting dynamics within Appalachian society at various eras in its history.

Unlike the hillbilly images on which Jerry Williamson focused through mostly different films than those discussed here, there is a pervasive sense in these films of Appalachians fighting back. They are constantly under siege and regularly exploited, and yet there is no instance in which they become merely victims. These characters don't take their oppression lying down. Whether they're fighting for land, for family, for working conditions, for community, for tradition, for a way of life, or for their very lives, nearly all protagonists (other than some of the more ambivalent parties who are combating each other) take on heroic qualities that make us admire their willpower, courage, and determination, sometimes in the face of unbeatable odds. That this spirit is captured so effectively and through so many different stories and such a range of characters brought to life in often powerful performances is a point not often appreciated by those who have focused on the misrepresentations of Appalachia by outsiders—journalists, fiction writers, and playwrights as well as filmmakers.

Eliot Wigginton, the founder of the Foxfire project in Rabun County, Georgia, was among the many locals offended by the film version of *Deliverance* when it appeared in 1972 (and has since received far more attention—and condemnation—from Appalachian scholars than nearly all the rest of the films covered here combined).[22] In the first issue of *Foxfire* magazine published after the film's unveiling, Wigginton published an editorial titled "From the Land of Nine-Fingered People," in which he denounced the depiction of a region peopled almost totally by sinister and subhuman beings. "It powerfully reinforces a stereotype we have been fighting with *Foxfire* for eight years," he wrote, "that of the hick with his liquor still, ignorant, depraved, stupid—sometimes laughable."[23]

That statement does not apply to any of the films under discussion here. Of course, what these films do present are partial truths, often oversimplified, romanticized, or much embellished. Again, no one expects historical authenticity from Hollywood. And yet each of these films provides entrée into very real issues and aspects of the Appalachian experience, which allows viewers to recognize and examine them in concrete and tangible terms. In his book *The Invention of Appalachia,* Allen Batteau stresses the extent to which the region has often served far more national than regional agendas, and that in the American imagination, Appalachia has long represented far more than deprived and depraved hillbillies. As pervasive as those images are, Batteau argues that they have been offset by more positive images, which, he notes, "have become less symbols of Appalachian particularity than of shared American values—the dignity of labor, self-sufficiency, pioneering spirit, patriotism, and independence."[24] In essence, much of what he labels "Holy Appalachia" has been Hollywood's Appalachia. That's certainly the case with most of the works considered here.

According to his biographer, David Lee, Alvin York and the filmmakers reproducing his story onscreen bought into this notion that "Appalachia is somehow a special repository of 'fundamental Americanism,'" the one region in the country that has "preserved traditional American *values* in their purest form."[25] Like so many of the characters who people these films, York, his family, and his neighbors represented for white filmgoers their contemporary ancestors, whose spirit had made this nation great; no doubt much of his onscreen story's success lay in the timing of these patriotic sentiments on the eve of the United States' entry into another world war.

But Hollywood's sense of "Holy Appalachia" was neither unique to 1941 nor limited to periods of national crisis. In some sense, nearly all these films share to one degree or another ennobling depictions of the values of home, family, land, and tradition, and it is as important to recognize and discuss these themes as "inventions" as it is to debunk more denigrating stereotypes and distortions. Yet even if these positive images of the region may be no more historically accurate than the negative images are, these films humanize and complicate mountain people and their relationships with one another and with outsiders, which make them worthwhile as historical subject matter. The very fact that they confront real issues and events should allow us to approach them as glasses half full rather than dismiss them as glasses half empty.

This is the basis for Robert Brent Toplin's defense of Hollywood history. To grant him the last word, Toplin claims in *Reel History* that such screen depictions of the past are successful when "audiences receive a modicum of information about broad historical events but are, nevertheless, emotionally and conceptually rewarded. Memorable films address important questions about the past and attach viewers' emotions to the debates about them. Hollywood gives life and personality to individuals and groups that often appear rather sterilely in the pages of history books. Cinema helps transform stale, one-dimensional stories into lively, two-dimensional experiences to which audiences can readily relate."[26]

So it is, I would argue, for all the films discussed in the chapters that follow. Their redeeming value as teaching resources lies not in the literal truths that they convey but in the fact that they embrace real aspects of the Appalachian past and present in dramatic contexts that provide viewers now—as they have for much of the past century—with accessible, appealing, and multifaceted introductions to the region, its people, and the struggles they have undergone.

1 This Land Is My Land

Struggles over land, both acquiring it and holding on to it, have long been vital components of the Appalachian experience, and films set in the region have reflected that reality in a variety of ways. Several films set in the nineteenth century—such as *Shenandoah*, *Cold Mountain*, *The Journey of August King*, and *Sommersby*—highlight the centrality of landownership through a range of scenarios, characters, and historical contexts. Yet what most seems to distinguish these works as Appalachian in character is a fluid dynamic in which first-time claims on property remained viable long after that formative phase of frontier settlement had passed for most of the rest of the eastern seaboard. Even more striking is the extent to which that pioneer spirit and attachment to land remained prevalent for so many twentieth-century highlanders. As Cratis Williams once noted, a higher concentration of self-sufficient family farms remained in the mountain South than in any other part of the country in the 1920s and 1930s.[1] The characterization of the region—a major impetus for the labels of "contemporary ancestors" or "yesterday's people"—was based largely on southern highlanders' still visceral commitment to long-standing yeoman-based Jeffersonian ideals built on individualism and independence. For many in Appalachia, those ideals were manifested by strong emotional, psychological, and even spiritual bonds to the earth.[2] This chapter focuses on four films that dramatize those bonds and the challenges they posed to highland families and individuals over the course of the twentieth century, from the 1910s through the 1980s.

In his seminal *The Southern Highlander and His Homeland*, John C. Campbell characterized Appalachia as a region "where conditions found throughout the rural South were intensified."[3] While the situations dramatized in these films are indeed relevant to similar struggles, past and present, they have played out not merely in the South but elsewhere in the country and the world. Allen Batteau echoes many scholars of the region who have suggested that "Appalachia is somehow a special repository of 'fundamental Americanism' [in which] traditional American values in their purest form have been preserved."[4] The quest for land and the struggles to hold it are among the most fundamental of these values, thus giving these films resonance and relevance far beyond their highland settings. While never exclusive to the region, it is significant that filmmakers have so often chosen Appalachian settings and people through which to dramatize these issues so fully and so movingly. Even though these stories were built on sentimentalized and oversimplified notions of more complex realities, much of what makes these films such valuable resources and effective teaching tools is that they capture elemental truths about the emotional attachment to land through the particularities of place, time, and character.

Four of the movies putting these issues front and center are firmly grounded in historical moments of time—World Wars I and II and the Depression–New Deal era—which serve as catalysts for the landownership challenges faced by the protagonists of each. Two of them—*Sergeant York* (1941) and *The Dollmaker* (1984)—focus on the quest by individuals to acquire land; the other two—*Wild River* (1960) and *Foxfire* (1987)—chronicle ultimately futile attempts by longtime landowners to hold on to their property when challenged by powerful outside forces seeking to take it from them. Examined collectively, this foursome allows us to see in both tangible and intangible ways the moral, economic, and personal challenges that have long characterized southern highlanders' relationships to farmland and agriculture and, by extension, those of many other Americans as well.

• • • • • •

Sergeant York is, by most measures, the most successful Hollywood production set in Appalachia. Directed by one of the industry's most accomplished directors, Howard Hawks, the film earned more money at the box office than any other picture released in 1941. It was nominated for eleven Academy Awards, including Best Picture, and won two, including the Best Actor prize for Gary Cooper; it was also the most expensive film ever produced by Warner Bros. up to that point, and set a new record for the studio in the number of sets and speaking parts it incorporated. It also proved to be a timely—and effective—piece of propaganda, as American isolationists and interventionists in mid-1941 fiercely debated the merits of U.S. engagement in the World War II in Europe as it moved beyond its second year.[5]

For our purposes, it is equally significant as the first film produced during Hollywood's golden era to make a serious attempt to provide a full-bodied portrayal of Southern Appalachian society. Indeed, no film of that era was touted more vigorously or self-consciously by its makers for its authenticity—in no small part because its subject was still very much alive and involved in its production. It was Alvin York's actual heroics on the

French front during the World War I that drew filmmakers to his story; during the climactic Meuse–Argonne campaign in October 1918, his sharpshooting prowess enabled him to take out a German battalion of machine gunners, single-handedly killing 28 and capturing 132. That feat made him the war's greatest hero and a media-made celebrity upon his triumphant return to the United States and ultimately to his remote home community in Tennessee's Cumberland Mountains. York long resisted offers to translate his story onto film—or to cash in on his celebrity in any other way. It was two decades later that York finally gave in to the pressures of Hollywood, and he did so then with firm conditions. Most importantly, he insisted not only that the film be an accurate portrayal of him and his story but that it must be far more than a simple war story; he wanted it to provide equal coverage of his life before and after the war, thus making it an Appalachian story as well.[6]

Hollywood had no problem doing so; after all, much of York's appeal lay in the backwoods roots and pioneer lifestyle that so defined him. As York biographer David B. Lee has noted, millions of Americans, then living in an increasingly urban and ever more crassly commercialized nation, saw in this Tennessee sharpshooter "the incarnation of their romanticized understanding of the nation's past when men and women supposedly lived plainer, sterner, and more virtuous lives."[7] Or as a *New York Times* critic confirmed more patronizingly of the finished product: it "has all the flavor of true Americana, the blunt and homely humor of backwoodsmen and the raw integrity peculiar to simple folk."[8] Where else could one find a twentieth-century story that so fully captured the essence of early American values and lifestyles than one set in a remote corner of the southern highlands? York's celebrity also coincided with a crucial period of the nationwide "discovery" of his home region. Along with a new emphasis on the mountain region's cultural and socioeconomic "otherness" in which the best of America's pioneer past lived on, Appalachia also served as the epitome of pristine "whiteness" to a country more and more fraught by black migration northward and increasing ethnic diversity brought on by several decades of steady European immigration.[9]

Reinforcing such sentiments were a series of biographies and other treatments of York produced during the 1920s, most notably Sam K. Cowan's *Sergeant York and His People*, published in 1922, and Tom Skeyhill's faux autobiographical narrative, *Sergeant York: His Own Life Story and War Diary*, which appeared in 1928.[10] Both authors focused more on the mountain society and culture—past and present—within which Alvin York came of age than they did on the particulars of his own life story. Nearly two-thirds of Cowan's narrative focuses on York's highland roots rather than on his military experience; Cowan states in his preface that his "is not a war-story, but the tale of the making of a man. His ancestors were able to leave him but one legacy—an idea of American manhood." Skeyhill's coverage was equally prone to romanticized stereotypes, with chapter titles such as "Fighters," "Long Hunters," "Feudists," "Bushwhackers," "Moonshiners," and "Saddlebaggers," all related in a first-person narrative that presumed to be York's own words. When the narratives did zoom in on York himself, it was his sharpshooting skills that dominated their coverage. For Skeyhill, it took three other chapters—"Guns," "Shooting Matches," and "Hunting"—to capture the essence of that manly mountain culture, while Cowan devoted much of a chapter titled "The Molding of a Man" to the turkey shoots that provided York with his only claim to fame locally before his enlistment in 1917 and to the skill set that played most directly into his heroics in taking down German machine gunners a year later.[11] One critic's description of both authors' approach—"to render York's poverty picturesque, even character-building"—was fully embraced by the filmmakers as well.[12]

Indeed, Warner Bros. publicists stressed the fact that these books provided the basis for their film's "faithful" depiction of southern mountain life as it played out in the valley of the Three Forks of the Wolf River. Much was made of York's own involvement as active consultant in the development of the script, over which his contract gave him final approval, and of the local research and many interviews with York's friends and neighbors undertaken by the producer, Jesse Laske, and his team of screenwriters. York was purported to have had a direct hand in convincing Gary Cooper to portray him onscreen, despite the actor's reluctance to take on a living character, especially one so fully engaged in the film's production.[13] It took a trip by Cooper to Tennessee and a very congenial meeting with York to convince the actor that he could play him onscreen. (For all the emphasis on authenticity, the entire film was shot on a tremendous sound stage in Hollywood, complete with mountains, farms, training camps, battlefields, and trenches, not to mention numerous interiors—the largest number of separate sets yet assembled for a Warner Bros. film.)[14]

Just as Cowan's and Skeyhill's narratives were heavily skewed toward York's home life and environment, so too is the film, which waits until well past its midpoint before it moves York away from the mountains to undergo his brief but eventful wartime career.[15] It places its hero firmly within both a household—presided over by York's mother (played by stage actress Margaret Wycherly in her film debut) and including a much younger sister and brother (June Lockhart and Dickie Moore)—and a community.[16] A fully elaborated social network is re-created through a series of communal gatherings—at church services, at bars (or "drinking shacks"), at a country store, and at turkey shoots—with one or more of the York family intimately engaged in each. While certainly contentious and often competitive, local residents are depicted overall as a close-knit, relatively congenial group of neighbors standing together against the outside—and largely unknown—world.

For the most part, the script and the performances avoid cartoonish hillbilly stereotypes, allowing the characters a degree of dignity and genuine humanity not often seen in earlier depictions of Appalachians onscreen. This was intentional, given that if York was to serve as a "wake-up call for America," the audience had to identify with him and his world.[17] Even the violence that had by then become so endemic in regional stereotyping proves to be relatively tame. Ma's quiet authority and moral suasion over not only Alvin but her entire household of children render her a pivotal character despite what is a surprisingly small speaking part. Although her role was based heavily on the real Mary York (still alive when the film was made), one cannot help but wonder if another influence on screenwriters was the character of Ma Joad in *The Grapes of Wrath*, released the year before and earning an Academy Award for Jane Darwell. Her influence over her grown son Tom (Henry Fonda) and management of a large family much resemble Ma York's role; both films served as tribute to American motherhood as the backbone of the nation's pioneering spirit in an era of strong patriotic and historic sentiment. There are perhaps even stronger parallels between *The Grapes of Wrath* and *The Dollmaker* and between the two stalwart women (the latter played by Fonda's daughter) who attempt to hold their families together during the traumatic displacement forced upon each by the Great Depression or the onset of World War II.

Though based on fact and central to York's story, the film expedites the dual conversions he underwent in the months before and just after his military enlistment in two of its more melodramatic, though least credible, scenes. His mother; his newly acquired sweetheart, Gracie Williams (Joan Leslie); and his mentor, Pastor Pile (Walter Brennan), all wage a rather low-key campaign to bring the thirty-year-old rabble-rouser to religion—a transformation fully documented by his biographers and by York himself, who stated simply to his 1928 biographer: "I began to see that I was missing the finer things in life . . . so I decided to change. And I have done it. I give up smoking, drinking, gambling, cussing, and brawling. I give them up completely and forever . . . and have never backslided." Religion was at least part of the formula for change: "I would go and listen and pray and ask God to forgive me for my sins and help me to see the light. And he did."[18]

In the film, that light becomes an actual stroke of lightning that brings York to God, thus nullifying all the moral suasion applied by mother, sweetheart, and the good pastor. Literally knocked off his mule by a single bolt from above, which also mangled his rifle barrel, Alvin is converted on the spot and proceeds directly to the church, whose congregation seems to gather nightly. There, without a word spoken, all present recognize by his expression that he's been born again, and they surround and embrace him while belting out "Give Me That Old Time Religion" with great enthusiasm. (In addition to what's either divine or Mother Nature's intervention, this sequence is somewhat marred because Cooper, despite winning an Academy Award for his performance, comes across as too passive and well-meaning to be fully convincing either as the degenerate hellion those around him make him out to be or as the stalwart man of God he immediately turns into post–lightning strike.)

If finding religion resolved one crisis in York's life, it served to create yet another dilemma for him. Shortly after becoming reborn (in a period of time much compressed in the film), the United States enters the war in Europe, and Alvin must register for the draft. Though only vaguely familiar with any scriptural readings, he decides they are telling him that he mustn't take the lives of others, and Pastor Pile counsels him to apply for conscientious objector status. When the powers that be refuse his application for exemption from military service, he reports to Camp Gordon, Georgia, for basic training, where his exceptional marksmanship soon becomes evident. Aware of his conscientious objector status, a sympathetic commanding officer gives him an American history text, and lectures him on the values of freedom and patriotism that have long driven good men to fight for their country. He then sends Alvin home on furlough to contemplate his future role as a soldier, which leads to one of the film's most iconic scenes and one based largely on York's own account.[19] Alvin climbs a mountain with his hound and sits out on a rugged cliff overlooking the valley. With his Bible in hand and voice-over quotes from both it and the history text, accompanied by competing strains of "Give Me That Old Time Religion" and "My Country 'Tis of Thee," he wrestles with his allegiance to God versus that to country. As the music swells, a gust of wind whips the pages of his Bible open to a passage that Alvin picks up and reads aloud: "Render unto Caesar what is Caesar's, and to God what is God's," and his decision is made. He can go to war and can kill if called upon to do so.

These encounters with lightning and wind seem to diminish the role of serious theological or religious conviction, making it perfunctory and rather vague, but that mere lip service to his faith was a conscious decision on the part of the filmmakers (and typical of Hollywood's general light-handed approach to religion in film). Given the propagandistic purposes York's story was coming to serve, as the second war in Europe polarized American public opinion into isolationist versus interventionist camps in late 1940 and early 1941, the filmmakers, like York himself, fell firmly within the latter camp and felt it vital that audiences be able to identify with their central character if they were to make their case. Simply, his Appalachian roots did much to make the character of York appropriately palatable. As Jerry Williamson has so aptly pointed out, "Since the 1880s the mass-circulation middle-class American magazines had promoted endlessly the first belief that southern mountaineers were genetically *pure* Anglo-Saxon stock. In other words [they] were perfect and already well-formed symbols ready to march in the mass-media parade against degenerate Huns."[20]

Yet too devout a protagonist could be a turnoff for audiences, and York could have come across as a religious fanatic. Rather, the filmmakers relied not on his words but on music to convey the spiritual context of his thinking, with familiar hymn melodies on the soundtrack during such scenes and, where appropriate—as in his cliffside moment of truth—juxtaposed with patriotic tunes as well.[21] Yet it took more than minimizing York's religious convictions or acknowledging his Anglo-Saxon bloodline (which the film never does explicitly) to render him all-American enough for 1941 audiences.[22] Ultimately, the screenwriters resorted to a third, somewhat less fact-based narrative thread that spoke to a more relatable and universal American trait—the quest for land. While rarely acknowledged by commentators on the film, Alvin's struggle to acquire a piece of bottomland forms the most sustained narrative arc not only in the first half of the film but in its final, postwar resolution as well.

Curiously, landownership never seemed to have been a priority of the real York; neither his first-person "memoir" nor his diary entries make any mention of his aspirations to become a property holder. He acknowledged his family's long claim on the land but made clear that his own priorities were far more on hunting and sharpshooting, with only occasional—and always rather vague—references to farming.[23] Yet for the filmmakers it became

Gary Cooper as sharpshooting Alvin York in *Sergeant York*.

central; farmland, in terms of either its property value or its productivity, is referenced in almost every scene after Alvin meets Gracie.

The York family was hardly landless. It is revealed early in the film, and confirmed by factual accounts from the 1920s, that they owned seventy-five acres. But it was poor, rocky mountainside property that yielded little. As Ma notes to Pastor Pile in explaining Alvin's rowdy ways, "I'm right proud of Alvin. He works hard, Alvin does, patching and scratching that poor land. It's mighty hard work, digging corn out of rocks. . . . Who's to blame him if he busts loose now and then?" Yet it's only when he discovers his neighbor Gracie Williams and realizes he must compete for her hand that York aspires to take on more and better farmland.[24] Gracie has another suitor, Zeb Andrews, who brags that his farm yields sixty bushels of corn after Alvin has just told her that his yielded twenty. Gracie defends Alvin, stating, "There's a heap of difference 'twixt farming the bottomland and the top." Convinced that acquiring the former is what it will take to compete with Zeb, Alvin declares to Gracie that he'll get some bottomland and be back for her. When she scoffs at his assumption that mere property is what it will take to win her over, he walks away in a huff, then kneels in a nearby field, picks up a piece of dirt, and smells it.

The primacy of good fertile acreage as the ticket to upward mobility in this white mountain society (as it was historically for rural America writ large) is made even more apparent in the following scene, as Alvin walks into the York cabin, lays the clod of dirt on a plate, and hands it to his mother. She recognizes it as "bottomland soil" and immediately notes its implications in terms of class distinctions: "Queer how the folks that lives on the bottom looks down on the folks on the top," she muses. She goes on to tell Alvin that his pa once tried to get a piece of bottomland: "Like to kill hisself tryin'." "Well, I ain't a settin' myself up as a better man than Pa," Alvin responds. "But I'm a knowin' where there's a piece of bottomland to be had," and as the music swells, he declares, "and I'm a gonna git it." Ma states simply, "Well, maybe you will." As much as she provides the moral suasion for Alvin's behavioral betterment, she's also his biggest ally in his drive to do what her husband never could: to better his socioeconomic prospects.[25]

And so begins an extended sequence in which Alvin negotiates a price and payment plan by which he can purchase the land in question, then owned by Nate Tomkins, all laid out in very specific monetary terms. In an extended montage, York takes on a variety of jobs: he hires himself out to other farmers—plowing fields, carting off rocks and stumps, splitting rails—for 75 cents a day, and sells pelts to Pastor (and storeowner) Pile for three dollars. He drags himself home late every night and marks on a calendar his earnings for the day before dropping into bed, exhausted. Ma puts a blanket over him one night and whispers a prayer as she stands over him: "Lord, if you can, help him to be a gettin' his land. Amen."

The plot thickens—in fully fictional ways—when Alvin is forced to ask Nate for a four-day extension so that he can use his winnings from a turkey shoot, the full carcass of a steer, to raise the last of the $70 price tag. (Alvin sells the beef on the spot to the highest bidder, along with his gun.) But it's all for naught, as Nate informs him that he missed his deadline and that the land had just been bought and paid for by Zeb Andrews, his rival for Gracie's hand. York goes on a drinking binge and, vowing revenge on both Nate and Zeb, sets out to take them on when that fateful bolt of lightning brings him to God, to the church, and to expressions of full forgiveness to both of the men who'd foiled his plans. He even asks Zeb if he can work his newly acquired acreage for him, and Zeb, much taken with Alvin's new Christian spirit, tells him he can sharecrop it, with the option of ultimately buying it outright.

Again, all pure Hollywood plotting, but it keeps the issue of landownership front and center throughout these home-bound sequences. York's preoccupation with that goal is infused—none too subtly—in other scenarios as well. A scene of Alvin teaching Sunday school to a group of children, meant to establish how fully his conversion took, has him telling the story of Cain killing Abel, and stating that God's punishment of Cain was "that he wouldn't get no crops no more, and anyone who's a farmer knows what that means." Once he and Gracie are engaged, the two of them walk over the bottomland that he intends to make his own when he returns from the war, while he points out to her what he'll plant where, and where they'll build their house and dig their well. Even as he bids farewell to his family before reporting for military duty, his final words concern the land: "The corn's doing right good on the south hill; might need a little hoeing."

Most of the rest of the film takes York far from home, as he's moved from training camps in Georgia to trenches in France and on to the film's most extended sequence, which details his heroics in the Argonne on October 18, 1918. This is followed by several brief scenes in New York City, where he's feted as the hero he's become—from a ticker-tape parade to discussions with Tennessee senator Cordell Hull (who, by 1941, had been serving as the country's secretary of state for eight years) over the first wave of celebrity endorsements being thrown York's way. While he acknowledged that all that money would allow him to buy that bottomland he'd long had his eye on, he quite nobly told Hull that he'd have to turn it all down, explaining, "I ain't proud of what happened over there. . . . What we done in France we had to do; some fellers who done it aren't a comin' back. So the way I figure, things like that aren't for buying and selling."

The film's final scenes convey his emotional homecoming in Pall Mall, with Ma, Gracie, and his younger siblings all vying for his affection. Before heading back up to the York cabin, Alvin asks if he can see that piece of bottomland for which he had struggled so long and so futilely the year before. Gracie leads him to it, telling him to keep his eyes closed until she's ready to reveal to him not only the news that it is now his land—over two hundred acres of it—but also the house and barn already built on it. All of it, she gushes, was donated by the state of Tennessee. York, amazed at what he's seeing, utters the film's final words, "The Lord sure works in mysterious ways."

While it's true that the Rotary Club of Tennessee, based in Nashville, raised money to purchase a four-hundred-acre farm upon York's return, it was property with no house or other structures on it and for which the final payments were not covered by the funds raised; it fell to York himself to keep up those payments, making that gift of land a source of ongoing financial strain through the rest of the 1920s.[26] That more sobering reality was obviously unfit for the uplifting ending Hollywood demanded, and the filmmakers opted for the far more satisfying final scene, which also served as the perfect closure to a screen narrative that had centered on the quest for land throughout. At the time, no one dared mention the irony that York ultimately acquired the much sought-after farmland not because of any of those valiant pre-enlistment efforts he made to earn it but, as one commentator pointed out, "only because he'[d] gone to war, because he'[d] taken life, because he'[d] killed," the very things York had just pronounced onscreen that he had no intention of profiting from.[27]

• • • • • •

In 1984, ABC aired *The Dollmaker*, one of the more accomplished literary adaptations made for television. Like *Sergeant York*, it features an Appalachian protagonist whose quest to purchase land of her own is interrupted by the demands of a war that will force her from the region and into a very different sort of struggle in an equally alien setting. While its title character ultimately meets with a similar resolution in fulfilling that quest (at least in the film version), her achievement is the result of very different circumstances from those through which Alvin York reaped his rewards upon his return home. Based on the most popular and critically acclaimed of Harriette Arnow's six novels, *The Dollmaker* (1954) was the third of a loose trilogy set in Kentucky's Cumberland Mountains. It was hailed as her masterwork by critics at the time, one of whom called it "an unflinching and compassionate portrait of contemporary America"; much later, Joyce Carol Oates called it "our most unpretentious American masterpiece."[28] It was a runner-up for a National Book Award in 1955 (losing out to one of William Faulkner's lesser efforts, *A Fable*).

Arnow's protagonist is Gertie Nevels, the wife of a tenant farmer and the mother of five, who sees acquiring a farm of their own as their ticket out of the hardscrabble existence in which the family seems mired. Her plans are interrupted when her husband takes a job at a defense plant in Detroit late in World War II, and Gertie reluctantly follows with the children. There, confined to a crowded housing project for factory workers and their families, she struggles to adjust to urban and industrial life, hold her family together, and get ahead financially despite her spendthrift husband, whose priorities are very different from her own. At least in terms of place, Arnow draws on her own experience. She was born and raised on the western edge of Kentucky's Cumberland Mountains and later returned to the area as a teacher, where she stated long afterward that she came to know and much admire mountain women on whom she based the character of Gertie. She not only witnessed the out-migration of these women who followed their husbands to wartime industries in the North; she herself became one, moving in 1945 to a housing project in Detroit very much like the one in which the Nevels family found themselves during the war's final year.[29]

It was the film's star who set the project in motion. Jane Fonda read *The Dollmaker* in 1971 and immediately saw in it a potential vehicle for herself. She explained that much of its appeal early on had been that she saw in Gertie Nevels a feminine counterpart to Tom Joad in *The Grapes of Wrath*, portrayed onscreen by her father, Henry Fonda, in 1940. She was determined, she said, to play a woman "as gentle and as gallant as Joad—the female equivalent of a Prairie Galahad."[30] She later added, "I loved Gertie's courage in the face of bone-and-soul-crushing experiences. . . . I also loved her humility and her capacity for mothering."[31] (There are perhaps even stronger parallels between Gertie Nevels and Ma Joad—the role that earned an Academy Award for actress Jane Darwell; both are stalwart mothers who attempt to hold their families together during the traumatic displacements forced upon them.) It would be another decade before Fonda began to put the project together (perhaps realizing that by then, she would be in her mid-forties, a far more appropriate age for the part). In 1981, she hired the writing team of Hume Cronyn and Susan Cooper, who had just adapted *Foxfire* for the Broadway stage, to write a script, and signed a contract to produce it for ABC-TV.

Intrigued by the Appalachian setting and the strong, resourceful, but vulnerable women the region produced, Fonda asked Dolly Parton (with whom she'd just co-starred in *Nine to Five*) to take her into the mountains the Tennessee native knew so well and to introduce her to women like Gertie. Parton did just that, and they traveled together in her tour bus through Tennessee and the Ozarks, where she introduced Fonda to various relatives and other acquaintances. One elderly couple in Arkansas—Lucy and Waco Johnson—made such an impression on Fonda that she later returned and spent two weeks as a guest in their log cabin home. The seventy-four-year-old Lucy, a great storyteller who also made doll heads out of shriveled apples, proved to be just the inspiration that Fonda was seeking; she emerged from her stay with the Johnsons having mastered a mountain accent and gained some twenty extra pounds that she felt necessary to portray the "big-boned" Gertie.[32]

The Dollmaker's Appalachian scenes were filmed in Cades Cove and other parts of Sevier County, Tennessee, in the fall of 1983. (The Detroit segment, which makes up the latter two-thirds of the film, was filmed in

Chicago.) *The Dollmaker* first aired on Mother's Day in 1984 as the ABC Sunday Night Movie, where it enjoyed strong ratings and generally good reviews, especially for Fonda's performance, for which she earned an Emmy Award later that year.[33] Except for its conclusion, Cronyn and Cooper's script remained fairly faithful to Arnow's plot and characters, though by necessity, certain subplots and secondary themes from the sprawling novel were compressed or eliminated. One theme actually accentuated and sustained throughout the film perhaps more so than in the novel was that of landownership and Gertie's single-minded determination to buy a farm.

One critic noted that "structurally, Arnow gives Gertie a magnificent opening chapter," and the filmmakers wisely kept it intact as their own first scene and introduction to Gertie's physical prowess and fierce maternal instincts.[34] It's a harrowing scene in which Gertie on muleback, desperate to get her barely breathing three-year-old son, Amos, to a doctor, causes an army recruiter's car to swerve and run off a mountain road. With a rush of adrenaline, she nearly single-handedly pushes the car back onto the pavement and then performs an emergency tracheotomy on Amos; only then does the unsympathetic army officer allow mother and child into the car and drive them to the nearest hospital some twenty miles away. It is during that ride that Gertie explains who she is both to her escorts and to the audience. When asked if she farms, she answers, "Some," explaining that "we rent a place, give back half of what we grow, keep the rest." But she's quick to add, "I'm saving real hard. We're going to have a place of our own someday."[35]

At the hospital, once young Amos is settled and stabilized, her husband, Clovis, briefly joins her, and we begin to see that this is not a goal she shares with him. After Clovis leaves, Gertie sits on the floor of the hospital room and pulls from various pockets rumpled bills and coins that we quickly learn are her entire savings, secretly stashed, and begins to count it. Like *Sergeant York*, *The Dollmaker* takes monetary amounts seriously. Again closely duplicating Arnow's narrative, Gertie speaks to her sleeping son as she lays her coins and wads of bills on the floor: "Amos, look. That's the money for our farm; ain't nobody seen it but you. You ain't goin' to work your life away hoeing another man's land." It totals $310, plus $40 more that the admiring army officer had quietly slipped into her pocket as he dropped her off. "As soon as your poor pa gets in the army," she confides to her youngest son, "we're going to buy us a place of our own."

Set in 1944, Clovis (played by Levon Helm, three years after he'd made his acting debut as Loretta Lynn's father in *Coal Miner's Daughter*) had received his induction notice that week, despite his age and the large family dependent on him; Gertie sees his absence as the opportunity to purchase a piece of land she's long had her eye on—the old Tipton farm. In a lengthy scene in which Gertie strolls across that abandoned homestead with her oldest son, Reuben, she most fully expresses her aspirations for ownership, control, and other, less tangible benefits of this particular piece of property, including childhood nostalgia for a home place once owned by her grandparents. As they stroll around the grounds, mother and son point out to each other the land's more obvious virtues, from a sturdy old farmhouse, good garden plot, and small orchard to a deep root cellar and good fishing in a mountain creek running alongside the property. Reuben tells his mother that even if she had the money to make the purchase, his father would never allow her to do so. Gertie simply says, "Well, we're fixing to surprise him."

Arnow ties much of Gertie's yearning for land of her own to her affinity for nature; her sensitivity to the natural world, from woodland flora and fauna to nighttime constellations to seasonal changes, led one commentator to label her "an unconscious Transcendentalist" and another to proclaim the novel "one of the best twentieth-century presentations of the ageless theme of person-nature relationships."[36] The filmmakers convey this less through dialogue than by establishing a strong visual sense of place and setting. For the Kentucky-based segment of the story, nearly three-fourths of its scenes were filmed outdoors, taking full advantage of the fall foliage of the Tennessee Smokies—whether in yards, on front porches, beside creeks, or along roads and footpaths. (Conversely, once the family moves to Detroit, most of the action plays out in claustrophobic interior spaces, primarily the cramped quarters of the makeshift housing project adjacent to the factory where Clovis is employed.)

Shortly thereafter, Gertie acquires the funds to purchase the Tipton place. Her younger brother, Henley, had recently been killed in combat in Europe, and Gertie's mother (identified simply as Mrs. Kendrick) passes on to her an undisclosed but substantial amount of cash, which she says was Henley's cattle money that he wanted his older sister to have. One of Arnow's most indelible characters (as is Geraldine Page's embodiment of her in only two scenes onscreen), Gertie's mother is a scripture-quoting fundamentalist full of doom and gloom regarding what she sees as her children's godless ways and poor prospects for salvation. Mrs. Kendrick has little sympathy for her daughter's aspirations to be a farm owner, though ironically, she has just furnished her with the means to do so.

Gertie is quick to make a deal with the current owner of the Tipton farm, John Ballew; when he agrees to sell it to her for $500, she says with confidence she can pay "purt near all of it." Then, in a somewhat strained plot twist, Clovis finds that his enlistment is deferred and he chooses to go straight from the recruitment center to Detroit, sending word back to Gertie that he's taken a job at a defense plant there (a scenario that actually fueled considerable out-migration by Appalachian residents during the war years). Clovis writes that she and the children are to join him there, and that he's sending money for the train trip. Gertie's initial response is to stand her ground; she states that she'll never go—especially now that she's about to take ownership of the Tipton place. But ultimately, she bends to the formidable force of her mother. Mrs. Kendrick confronts her in a highly fraught exchange between mother, daughter, and grandson. Her mother accuses Gertie of bringing disgrace on the family. "St. Paul said wives should be in subjugation to their husbands," she insists, and then turns toward Reuben: "And your poor daddy, all alone up there working so hard to put food in your mouths." When Reuben argues, "But she's bought us a place of our own," his grandmother is firm in her response: "Your daddy wants you all to be there with him, and your mama's going to do her duty and take you to Detroit." Gertie is crushed but succumbs to the inevitable.

And so the scene suddenly shifts to Detroit, and with it, Gertie's discomfort and vulnerability move to the forefront as she attempts to negotiate this alien environment devoid of trees or any other form of nature's bounty on which she'd always thrived. As mother and children stumble off the train in a blistering-cold snowstorm, the setting itself offers a stark contrast to the wooded highland community in Kentucky. The film's set designers took Arnow's own description to heart. "Through the twisting, whirling curtain of smoke," she wrote, Gertie arrives and is immediately confronted by "black heaps of rock-like stuff strewn over a gray wasteland of rusty iron and railroad tracks," an apt description of the grim industrial landscape that remains omnipresent throughout the rest of the film.[37]

Though much pared down from Arnow's multilayered and meticulous narrative of life in Detroit, subsequent scenes generally follow the book's lead by centering on the family's trials and tribulations in adjusting to this bleak new world and in coping with the prejudice directed at their "hillbilly" origins, for which most of the Yankee city dwellers hold nothing but contempt. Gertie and the children take a taxi from the train station to their housing project, ironically called Merry Hill. The driver (a cameo by Studs Terkel) immediately pegs them as Kentuckians, much to their dismay. "I've met you'se at the station from two world wars," he tells them, then mockingly adds, "And you're going back pretty soon; once you've saved money to buy a farm—one of them big bluegrass farms, huh?"

Though she finds a support network among her neighbors, especially women, Gertie remains tense, worried, and out of place. She finds some relief in her wood carving, especially her obsession with an unfinished Christ figure she's long sought to wrest out of a large block of cherrywood that she transported with her from Kentucky. Her major source of worry remains the family's finances, and her differences with Clovis on spending and saving become more pronounced. Despite his (relatively) good wages, Clovis is already deeply in debt by the time they arrive. She remains fully committed to returning home and taking over the Tipton farm as planned. But her good intentions go awry when Clovis and his fellow union workers go on strike (a major plot development for Arnow that's much minimized in the film). This forces Gertie to dip into her secret savings to keep food on the family table, savings she had counted on as the means by which they'd become Kentucky property owners at war's end. That goal is dealt a serious blow when Clovis reveals that he has no intention of leaving Detroit. "What do we have to go home to? . . . I've got a good job, and the young'uns is all in school. We never had that with me hauling coal and you scrabbling on that farm."

Gertie falls back on her wood-working skills to make up for Clovis's lost wages, carving small animals and jumping jack dolls to sell. But tragedy strikes in a gut-wrenching scene in which Cassie, the youngest daughter, is killed when a train severs her legs while she is playing by the nearby tracks. This not only throws Gertie into a deep depression but further depletes her savings, which go to what Clovis calls "that damn crooked funeral parlor." It also leads to a final showdown between husband and wife.

Once Gertie reveals her hidden savings to Clovis, he tells her, "If I'd a knowed you had all that, I'd a said buy a place and wait for me. When the war was over, I'd a come rolling in and we'd be all set." "But you always hated the farm," she responds, again reminding him of all the other things he'd spent money on instead, much of it frivolously. He assures her that he just wants her to be happy, and then tells her to quit wasting time whittling her dolls, as he could have them cut out on the jigsaw he just acquired. At that, Gertie explodes: "Don't tell me what to do! For sixteen years, I dreamed of us having our own farm. And I worked and saved up . . . and *you* said come to Detroit. You didn't care what I wanted; you never asked. . . . Well, these dolls, they're all that's feeding our young'uns now, and they're mine!"

With that declaration, Gertie reemerges as the spirited, driven woman she'd been in Kentucky; when Clovis is injured in a clash between union workers and police and forced to go into hiding outside town, she takes matters into her own hands. In the first major deviation from the novel, Reuben, who'd left Detroit and returned home to stay with his grandparents, writes to Gertie to say that her father has died and that her mother wants to move to town. He urges his mother to come back and claim the family farm before her mother can put it up for sale. This opportunity spurs Gertie into action. She quickly trades Clovis's car (which is about to be repossessed) for an older—and cheaper—truck. In response to a lucrative bulk order for her wood carvings, she takes up Clovis's new jigsaw to increase her output. Clovis himself (in yet another deviation from Arnow's novel) expresses his own willingness to return to Kentucky.

Finally, in an act more symbolic than practical, Gertie takes her cherrywood Christ figure, which she'd worked on and obsessed about for so long, and has it chopped into small pieces that she can use for the small carvings that promise ready-made income. In taking the first ax stroke herself—in slow motion and with music swelling—we're meant to see this as her ultimate act of liberation and self-fulfillment. That iconic action carried a different meaning in Arnow's novel, where it served as the narrative's conclusion and the culmination of a far more spiritual quest with which Gertie had long wrestled. Much of its symbolic meaning is lost in the film, which dispensed with much of the religious context that Arnow had so carefully woven throughout her novel.[38] In the film, chopping up the cherrywood Christ serves a more practical purpose—that of financing the family's trip home to Kentucky. Immediately following the block's destruction, the film jumps ahead and we see Gertie driving her children and fully loaded new truck out of the city to pick up Clovis. He happily hops in the cab, takes over the wheel, and moves onto a highway heading south and east, where we're to assume the Nevelses, once home, will become farm owners at long last.

As well as these alterations work to provide a more appropriate and satisfying sense of closure to Gertie's saga on film, neither Arnow nor some Arnow scholars were convinced by this all-too-pat Hollywood ending. In an interview in August 1983, at which point Arnow had seen the final script, she expressed her doubts as to whether the new conclusion was indeed a more satisfying one. Fonda had apparently pushed for what she called "a more rounded and fulfilling ending," to which the novel's author responded, "I won't quarrel with Jane Fonda or the film," and yet she was quick to state that "I can't help but wonder . . . what they would go back to in the hills." She reasoned that they didn't have land (the option of taking over her grandparents' farm was a plot device of the screenplay, not the book), that the children wouldn't have good schools like they had in Detroit, and that Clovis liked his job in the factory (a point the screenplay refutes).[39]

The very fact that Harriette herself, along with her husband, chose to remain in Detroit for five years after the war ended suggests that she was not nearly as averse to city life as her fictional protagonist and that she could see Gertie adjusting to this new environment, just as she herself had. Arnow, who had also spent a number of years in Cincinnati before the war, once said, "I like to live near a city. A city is, or was supposed to be, man's greatest achievement—a symbol of civilization."[40] By the same token, she drew on yet another personal experience—the one attempt she and her husband made to live off the land. In 1939, the couple moved to an abandoned 160-acre farm in rural Kentucky. In later years, she acknowledged how fully they failed to make it work. "When planning our move, I had no qualms about my ability to be a hill wife," she revealed in a 1970 interview. "I quickly learned that observation is one thing, experience another." While their neighbors seemed suspicious or contemptuous of their efforts, "the most common attitude was compassionate wonder as to how a couple so ignorant and inept would ever manage." Thus, they were much relieved when the war took them to Detroit.[41]

If it was her own, very personal experience that shaped Arnow's belief that the Nevels family was better off remaining in an urban environment rather than returning to the Kentucky hills to farm, certain literary critics saw her drawing from that experience far broader conclusions about Appalachia's agrarian future. In an essay titled "The Demise of Mountain Life: Harriette Arnow's Analysis," Martha Billips Turner argues convincingly that in *The Dollmaker*, "Arnow sets forth a complex, coherent, and largely unexamined vision of life in the hill country of southeastern Kentucky . . . that not only evokes the natural beauty of the region and the innate dignity of its inhabitants, but also carefully depicts the forces—internal and external—contributing to the ultimate demise of an agriculturally based and highly distinctive mountain existence." By the mid-twentieth century, Turner maintains, that there was little future for subsistence farmers, for whom an increasingly cash-based, wage-driven economy had rendered their way of life no longer sustainable in the post–World War II era.[42]

If this was indeed the case, as the subsequent history of the region has confirmed, this would have been a subtle shift that was fully apparent only in hindsight and one that mountain farmers themselves—including those aspiring to enter their ranks, such as Gertie Nevels—would have either not recognized or not admitted at the time. For that reason, we should perhaps not be so quick to condemn the filmmakers' instincts to alter the novel's more ambivalent and less satisfying ending in a way that not only fulfilled Gertie's quest for land of her own but also made her an active agent in achieving that long-sought goal. Unlike the novel, in which Gertie merely bows to the all-too-formidable forces that kept her from returning home, the film allows her—and her alone—to grasp this new opportunity for landownership that presents itself (even if it does so through a rather contrived plot twist). While it may indeed have resulted in a "Hollywood ending," as Arnow charged, the film reflects sound storytelling instincts and remained true to Gertie's indomitable spirit while extending all the way through the film's conclusion both its narrative arc and its thematic thrust: the sanctity of property and the pull of home.

• • • • • •

For two other films, plots are driven by the struggle of mountain matriarchs to hold on to farms owned and worked by multiple generations of their families. Each taps into one of two very real forces that displaced many Appalachian farmers over the course of the twentieth century: first, the federal government, through which the Tennessee Valley Authority, the National Park Service, and other agencies claimed large blocks of wilderness or riverside or parkway property in the name of the public good;[43] and second, real estate developers and other corporate powers, which fed new demands for property by retirees, second-home owners, residential tourists, and commercial interests who began to flock to highland settings in massive numbers in the 1970s, 1980s, and beyond. As Ronald Eller described the process, "Flatland exiles seeking to possess a piece of the mountains and to control the views from the ridgetops clashed with local families who resented fence lines and No Trespassing signs and who struggled to find work and adequate housing."[44] And, he could have added, struggled to hold on to their land.

The film *Wild River* takes on the Tennessee Valley Authority (TVA) and is the product of an unlikely filmmaker—Elia Kazan, a Brooklyn-born son of Greek immigrants and an acclaimed New York–based director of both plays and films. While Kazan demonstrated a surprising affinity for the American South in much of his work in the 1950s, only once, at decade's end, did he turn his focus to Appalachia.[45] In so doing, he provided perhaps his most sensitive and sympathetic portrayal of southerners and their attachment to land. In *Wild River*, produced in the fall of 1959 and released in 1960, Kazan tells the story of a stubborn eighty-year-old woman, Ella Garth, who refuses to leave her island home on the Tennessee River despite the fact that a TVA dam a mile downstream has just been completed and is about to create a vast lake that will cover the island. A federal agent from Washington is sent to East Tennessee to coax or force her—along with her family and a host of black tenants—off Garth's Island, in effect setting up a compelling battle of wills between these two characters, even as the resolution of that contest is never in doubt.

While some fifteen thousand families were ultimately displaced from their farms by the TVA, it was less their plight and more the challenges they posed to TVA officials that first attracted Kazan's attention.[46] His initial conception of the story was to be an homage to the New Deal and the spirit of Franklin D. Roosevelt. The TVA agent would be the film's hero, as he took on "the difficult task of convincing 'reactionary' country people that it was necessary in the name of the public good to move off their land and allow themselves to be relocated."[47] Later, he imagined a full reversal of that moral imperative, envisioning instead a cinematic scenario reminiscent of Appalachia's age of discovery by well-meaning outside forces; in this case, as he described it, "a Jewish intellectual-activist, heedlessly driven by an ideal of social betterment, enters a primitive, instinctual culture determined to change it, and carelessly willing to destroy it as he pursues his abstraction."[48] Yet for a variety of reasons, Kazan's thinking continued to shift as the project evolved, and these competing interpretations gave way to a far more subtle and sophisticated treatment of what one critic termed "the hidden ambiguity of idealistic enterprises."[49]

Curiously, this New Yorker had actually encountered southern mountain people on several previous occasions, particularly in East Tennessee. As a Communist Party member in the mid-1930s, Kazan came to know and admire a party operative in Chattanooga and visited him there several times. While there, he came to see the TVA in action and later claimed that the idea for a film dramatizing its impact was born.[50]

Probably more influential on Kazan's sense of the region was his first venture into filmmaking, when, in the summer of 1937, he served as an assistant director for a short documentary on Tennessee strip miners and their attempts to organize. Called *People of the Cumberland*, this was one of several left-wing films produced at the time that focused largely on the plight of the rural poor and on the exploitative forces that held them down.

The crew spent several weeks in and around Monteagle and LaFollette, Tennessee, filming the miners and their families at work and play, and documenting the role played by the recently established Highlander Folk School to recruit the United Mine Workers of America to represent their interests.[51] While it is hard to pinpoint Kazan's contribution to the film, he later stated, somewhat patronizingly, that from this experience, he gained "great confidence in [his] ability to go into an environment and get drama and color and entertainment out of the most ordinary people" and began what he called his "love affair with the people in the back parts of this country—how much I love and admire them."[52]

Ultimately, it was two novels that provided the bulk of the more ambivalent story that Kazan would come to tell onscreen and that in his words made him "feel more humanly, and think less ideologically."[53] Around 1955, Kazan discovered William Bradford Huie's *Mud on the Stars,* a semi-fictionalized account of his own coming of age in the Tennessee River valley in northern Alabama during the Depression era.[54] Huie's alter ego was a descendant of the extensive Garth clan, presided over by a formidable matriarch, his ninety-year-old grandmother, Ella Garth. For much of her life, she had overseen an agricultural empire known as Garth's Island, which Huie described as "the two thousand richest acres in the Tennessee Valley."[55] The island, along with equally rich bottomland on the river's shores, supported nearly sixty families of "croppers and hands," mostly black.[56]

The early Depression years took a heavy toll on the Garth family fortunes, and by 1933, word began to spread that "the Gover'mint is a-comin!"[57] In August it came, and with it, Huie wrote, came "the beginning of the end of the Garth world."[58] It also brought on Old Miss Ella's last stand, a futile attempt to hold on to her black workforce, as the New Deal began to offer them alternatives to the hard labor extracted by the bullwhip she cracked. In what Huie called "the second Yankee invasion of the South,"[59] the battle to remove them from their land was waged and ultimately lost through legal channels, and though it was the story of that battle that Kazan wanted to tell, he turned to another source for a more dramatic and emotional way of telling it.

After struggling with several experienced writers—including playwrights Paul Osborn and Clifford Odets, and screenwriter and novelist Calder Willingham—over unsatisfactory drafts of a screenplay, Kazan discovered a new novel, *Dunbar's Cove,* soon after it was published in 1957.[60] Author Borden Deal, another Alabamian, was inspired both by his own father's loss of the family farm in Mississippi during the early Depression years and by the removal forced upon Alabama families with the construction of the TVA's Guntersville Dam (only a few miles upriver from Huie's Garth's Island). Deal constructed an entire novel around a single TVA agent, Crawford Gates, sent from Washington to purchase yet another family enclave, Dunbar's Cove, also to be covered by a lake created by a nearly completed dam ten miles downstream. Deal's narrative basically chronicles the long and increasingly painful showdown between Gates and the family patriarch, Matthew Dunbar, two good men who ultimately come to understand and respect each other.[61]

Both novels suggest the ability by opposing factions to empathize with each other at some level. That sentiment captures the essence of what Kazan drew from the two works; together, they provided him with the moral ambivalence that his two antagonists embodied so effectively—and sympathetically. *Mud on the Stars* gave him Ella Garth and her island. "I discovered an astonishing thing," he explained after reading Huie's novel. "I'd switched sides. Now I found my sympathies were with the obdurate old lady. . . . I was all for her."[62] And *Dunbar's Cove* provided him with his TVA agent: Crawford Gates became Chuck Glover, a far more multidimensional and humane character than the cocky, self-assured agent Kazan had initially conceived.[63] He later confided, "I think Miss Ella's right to want to stay on her land. I think Glover is right, too. There's a need to do things for the good of the majority. . . . But when you do that, some individuals are just ruled out, and I think that's a real loss and should not be ignored."[64]

For Kazan, the essential forces at play were "city vs. country, intellectual vs. uneducated, bureaucrat vs. emotionally committed peasants."[65] The fact that Montgomery Clift, at that point in his career a fairly fragile, insecure soul, was cast as Glover rather than the far more assertive Marlon Brando—Kazan's first choice for the part—contributed significantly to this more diffident and sensitive characterization. By the same token, his casting of so formidable an actress as Jo Van Fleet as Ella Garth rendered her a far more potent adversary and the film's most compelling character. "Above all, keep the people tough," Kazan wrote in a note to himself. "Don't soften Ella down into an articulate conversational stereotype." He sought to do the same for her fellow Tennessee highlanders: "What will attract the audience is their unremitting, uncompromising toughness, their unrelenting meanness."[66]

All of this was worked out over the course of 1957 and 1958, with a final script in place by early 1959 (with Paul Osborn listed as the sole screenwriter). Soon thereafter, Kazan began scouting locations by flying some 650 miles over the Tennessee River valley from Paducah, Kentucky, to Muscle

Shoals, Alabama, looking for the setting he saw in his mind. He ultimately found it in Bradley County, Tennessee, on the western edge of the Smoky Mountains, and, more specifically, in the historic community of Charleston, a center of Cherokee Indian activity in the 1810s and 1820s and a major point of departure for the Trail of Tears in 1838. It was there, along the banks of the Hiwassee River, about ten miles east of where it flows into the Tennessee, that Kazan found what a later filmmaker called "the film's most charged setting—a bend of river with history on one side, 'progress' on the other, and a pole-operated ferry for drifting back and forth."[67] That summer, Kazan assembled his cast and crew there, and over four months, he made what became the first feature film ever produced wholly in Tennessee.

The finished film, which premiered in May 1960, opens with newsreel footage of raging floodwaters washing away homes and farms, a touch meant to lend historical authenticity to what follows and to establish the urgency of the TVA's mission in bringing the river system under control.[68] The story proper begins as Chuck Glover arrives in Garthville and reports to the TVA Purchasing Office, where he's handed a file labeled "Ella Garth vs. Washington" and told that he'll be the third agent to attempt to get her off her island. Pleading, begging, and threatening by his predecessors have all failed to move her. Glover's response signals his qualified admiration for her spunk, at least. "That's the American way of life," he comments. "Rugged individualism is our heritage. Three thousand people settle, but Ella Garth won't sell. We admire her spirit, we applaud it, but we've got to get her the hell out of there."

In pulling himself over to Garth Island on that self-propelled ferry, Glover is confronted with a large hand-lettered sign, "TVA Keep Away," and notices two menacing farmers glaring at him from behind dried corn stalks. He walks across the island to the large rambling farmhouse where the eighty-year-old Ella Garth is rocking on her porch; she gets up and goes inside as soon as Glover approaches. (Even without a word, actress Jo Van Fleet, only forty-five years old at the time, makes an indelible first impression in a riveting performance that dominates the film despite her relatively few scenes in it.) In returning to the ferry, he faces the same farmers again, who he learns are Ella's three middle-aged sons. Glover asks them what they have against the very fair offer the TVA has made for the island and the promise of a new place to live onshore. One son announces simply, "My ma owns this property, and she ain't going to sell it." Glover sneers, "I've never seen so many grown men afraid of one woman," at which point one of the sons picks him up and throws him in the river.

TVA agent Chuck Glover (Montgomery Clift) confronts Ella Garth (Jo Van Fleet) over her island farm in *Wild River*.

What follows is a remarkable scene—perhaps the film's most pivotal—in which the full force of Mrs. Garth's resentment, her resolve, and the clout she wields over her tenant workforce is revealed through a lengthy speech. A day after Glover's failed attempt at a visit, the elderly matriarch gathers her black workers together and stands before them to explain "some kind of new government" that FDR has put together: "Mr. Roosevelt is going to flood this island. Yes, sir, he's going to take the best piece of land in these parts, and put it smack under the Tennessee River. . . . So the president, you see, he sits up there in that big white house and says, 'This country is just goin' to the dogs.' And the only way he can figure to do anything to stop it is to put my island under water."

At least one of her workers has already snuck off the island with his family, and she tells the rest that she doesn't blame him "because nobody wants to be put under water permanent." But she admonishes them for sneaking off in the middle of the night and insists that they can take the ferry and leave at any time. "There ain't nobody keeping you here," she says. "You go off and join the government. As I understand, they're going to put you all on relief; well, you just go on and get yourselves relieved . . . anytime you wanna. Me, I ain't goin'."

Mrs. Garth sees Glover approaching from the side and shifts her focus back to the issue of property rights. She singles out one of her black workers, Sam, and tells him she's going to buy his old hunting dog, Old Blue, who's lying at his feet. Sam (played by Robert Earl Jones, the father of James Earl Jones) responds that he's worth nothing and he won't sell him, to which she says, “Well you gotta sell him, Sam, because I’m gonna buy him.” Exasperated, he finally declares that the dog is not for sale and she has no right to make him sell, and she calmly responds, “Well, that’s true, Sam. Come to think of it, I don’t have the right, do I?” Turning to Glover, she states, “You see, young man, me and Sam, we don’t sell. Sam don’t sell his dog, and I don’t sell my land that I poured my heart’s blood into.” The point is made all too clearly, though it’s a bit ironic that she’s preaching about property rights to her tenants and can only muster up a dog owned by one of them to illustrate his right to resist pressure to sell property he doesn’t want to part with. One senses that her earlier harangue to the black families on their right to leave the island is perhaps the first time she’s actually acknowledged that they are not Garth property themselves.

That Socratic demonstration merely lays the groundwork for the more central exchange that ensues between Ella Garth and Chuck Glover, who enters the fray almost apologetically, stating, “Mrs. Garth, sometimes it happens that we can’t stay true to our beliefs without hurting a great many people. And I’m afraid this is one of those times. You’re the only person in the valley who hasn’t sold.” What follows is a sharply wrought debate over both the tangible and the intangible realities that define all that’s at stake here:

EG: Young man, do you know anything at all about land?

CG: Yes, ma’am, I believe so, that’s why I was sent down here.

EG: Oh. Well, when you go back down to that ferry, you just pick up a handful of that soil. That’s real bottom.

CG: And thousands of tons of it are being washed away every year. Mrs. Garth, you don’t love the land. You love your land. You know the Tennessee River has been a killer for years. Year after year, it’s taken God knows how many lives. Isn’t it just plain common sense to want to harness it? And you know what that will mean? Today, 98 percent of people in this valley have no electricity. The dam will bring them electricity.

EG: I guess that’s what you call progress, isn’t it?

CG: And you don’t?

EG: No, I don’t! Taking away people’s souls and putting electricity in place of them ain’t progress, not the way I see it.

CG: We’re not taking away people’s souls. Just the opposite. We’re giving them a chance to have a soul. And it isn’t just this dam. It’s dam after dam after dam. We aim to tame this whole river.

EG: Do you? Well, I like things running wild, like nature meant. There's already enough dams locking things up, taming them, making them go against their natural wants and needs. I'm agin dams of any kind.

When Glover asks what will become of her, she leads him up to the cemetery on the island's highest rise, points to two headstones, and tells him to read them out: "Woodbridge Garth, born 1839, died 1889," and the other, "Ella Garth, born 1853, died ___." "I'll stay right here," she declares. "On this land. The water'd never come up this far, would it?" She goes on to tell Glover that her husband had come down the river on a flat boat as a boy and settled on the island as its first inhabitant. "He cleared the trees, drained the fields, cleared the brush. He worked his health to death just to make these fields, and he told me never to get off. And I ain't. I ain't."

That said, she returns to her house, leaving Glover speechless, though her granddaughter Carol (Lee Remick) remains behind. He asks her why she's made no effort to get her off the island, knowing full well what's coming. Carol replies, somewhat prophetically, "Don't look to me, mister. I was born on this place. I know what she's talking about. You better believe it, if she has to leave this island, it will kill her." Nevertheless, she is a realist and tries to convince her grandmother that she must bow to the inevitable and abandon her home. As she becomes Glover's somewhat reluctant ally in that effort, a tentative romance develops between the two, which she sees as her best chance to get out and make a real future for herself and her children. In so doing, she emerges as the third pivotal character and another example of Kazan's admiration for these "back country" people that he portrays so sympathetically.[69]

Battered but not beaten, Glover must finally act on pressures from officials in Washington, who are by then insisting that he get Mrs. Garth off her island "any way you can." Glover comments, "But I thought you wanted to avoid the publicity," leading one bureaucrat to counter, "It'll be a lot worse publicity if she gets wet." It finally takes a warrant issued by a U.S. marshal to instigate her removal, and she offers no resistance when Glover makes one last visit to inform her that the eviction will take place the next day. It's obviously a painful task, and he admits to Carol that at one point he'd "been looking forward to it. Imagine. And now, I have to make sure I get her off alive." Carol, a bit bemused by his confession, responds, "You're getting awfully human, aren't you, Chuck?" thus articulating how Kazan's conception of both the characters and their moral agendas had evolved since the project's inception.

And get her off they do. The lack of confrontation or even high drama in doing so doesn't deprive the moment of real poignancy. Miss Ella, with hat and coat on, is sweeping her porch as Chuck, Carol, the marshal, and one or two others approach the house. With only a small bound box in one hand, she walks off the porch, speaking only to Glover: "Well, what are you waiting for?" As they move toward a waiting rowboat, her former black workers—now TVA employees—begin cutting the large trees in the yard; she looks back from the boat as the first ones fall. The following scene shows her settled on the front porch of a small house on the edge of town. Her cow—which in one of the film's most striking images is seen standing calmly in another boat as it's being rowed over—is grazing in her new front yard. The next day, while Chuck oversees the burning of her house and the massive pile of felled trees, Carol arrives and tells him that her grandmother has died.

The film ends with on aerial shot of Ella's burial in the grave she'd shown Glover a few days earlier; the camera pulls back to show the family cemetery on what is now a tiny island in the midst of a vast lake, and then it pans downstream just enough to reveal the big new dam behind all that's happened, as viewed from a plane by Glover and Carol as they fly to Washington.

An interviewer once asked Kazan about his attraction to the South and southern subject matter, to which he responded, "I spent a lot of time down there, and when I thought about it, I realized that the social conflicts in this country were often most visible in the South." Nowhere did he demonstrate that truth more fully than he did in *Wild River,* in which he took on issues of class, race, labor, property rights, and how the incursion of the federal government could wreak havoc with them all, even as its intent and even the results of its efforts served the greater good of those affected.

But Kazan also made it clear that he had a real affection for these people and much admired their resistance to such efforts to improve their lives. He once admitted, "I think I romanticize country people a bit but I do like them," and went on to say, "I believe in land and people caring for land." Of Ella Garth, he was even more explicit about his affinity for this creation of his. "I wanted to take the most reactionary person I could think of and show that there's a lot of good in her. . . . She loves her home and doesn't want to lose it. She is against all progress. She considers blacks chattel." And yet, he insisted, "I really love that character. I'll always be grateful to Jo Van Fleet for creating her the way she did."[70]

In these instances and others, Kazan did far more than romanticize his country people. He fully acknowledged that highlanders could be just as racist and as "redneck" as other southerners when put to the test, especially when such tests were imposed by outside bureaucrats.[71] Yet he also offered a much more nuanced, ambivalent, and realistic portrait of a significant segment of the highland South and the multiple ways in which its inhabitants responded to the upheaval in their lives brought on by "progress" and a striking parallel, little acknowledged at the time, to the civil rights movement underway when the film was released.[72] He used the New Deal and East Tennessee to dramatize that conviction and cast it as a conundrum all too familiar to the people of Appalachia both long before and long after the TVA moved into their midst. Perhaps it's no wonder that Kazan thought of *Wild River*, among his vast oeuvre, as one of his greatest achievements on film and one for which he always had a particular fondness and pride.[73]

• • • • • •

A television movie produced nearly three decades later took a very different approach to similar dilemmas in a different part of Southern Appalachia. *Foxfire*, which first aired as a CBS Hallmark Hall of Fame production in December 1987, featured Jessica Tandy as an Ella Garth–like character—an elderly widow living alone on a mountaintop farm in Rabun County, Georgia. Even as the burdens of single-handedly working the farm in her advancing years take their toll, she strongly resists a local developer's offers to buy her property so that he can turn it into a gated community of second-home owners and retirees.

The story had its roots in a more singular source than *Wild River*. Tandy's character, Annie Nations, was based on interviews with an actual woman who was featured prominently in the first volume of Eliot Wigginton's *Foxfire* book series. A sampling of the best interviews and essays that had appeared in the *Foxfire* magazine that Wigginton, an English teacher, had produced with his high school students at the Rabun Gap–Nacoochee School since 1967, the book, published by Doubleday in 1972, became a national best seller and spawned a twelve-book series to date. (The term *foxfire* is derived from a phosphorescent blue-green light that's emitted by fungi and decaying wood in the forests of Southern Appalachia.) Coinciding with the film version of James Dickey's *Deliverance*, filmed on location in Rabun County and released only two months after *The Foxfire Book* appeared, this corner of northeast Georgia suddenly became the epicenter of Southern Appalachia in the national consciousness, for both better and worse.[74]

Of several elderly residents of the area featured in interviews with the Foxfire students, perhaps the most memorable was Aunt Arie Carpenter, who makes her appearance in the book's opening pages and is introduced as follows: "Far back in the neighboring mountains, alone in a log cabin with no running water and only a single fireplace for heat, lives an elderly lady. She draws her water from a well; she raises her own vegetables in the spring. Even though her husband died several years ago, and one side of her body was later paralyzed by a stroke, Aunt Arie refuses to leave. With her husband's clothes still hanging inside, washed and ready to wear, her home has become a sacred place over which she alone must now keep watch."[75] What follows is a lively interview in which Mrs. Carpenter, with both humor and insight, explains a variety of local skills and traditions, from making souse meat to bottoming chair seats, from weaving baskets to making corn pone, from sharpening knives to planting by the phases of the moon, all the while offering commentary on her eighty-year life on the same farm. She, more than any other individual, embodies the essence of what the Foxfire project sought to capture in terms of the mountain culture and folkways still practiced by longtime residents of the region.

Hume Cronyn—Tandy's husband as well as an established character actor and writer—recognized the potential in Aunt Arie as a dramatic vehicle for his wife. He and his writing partner, Susan Cooper, composed a stage play in 1980 centered on a recent widow renamed Annie Nations. From Aunt Arie's commentary and that of others in *The Foxfire Book*, they devised a plotline involving the challenges posed by her continuing to work the land on her own as she aged and the pressures posed not only by a land developer but also by her grown son, visiting from Florida, and the "ghost" of her husband, Hector Nations, picking up on his lingering presence as suggested in the text (and thus providing a meaty role for Cronyn himself). (Coincidentally, Cronyn and Tandy would later play another Georgia-based couple in which one spouse was deceased, that one a 1993 TV adaptation of Terry Kay's novel *To Dance with the White Dog*, in which Tandy plays the dearly departed. Both projects were part of a Georgia spree late in her career, which also included her Oscar-winning performance in 1989's *Driving Miss Daisy* and Oscar-nominated role in 1991's *Fried Green Tomatoes*.)[76]

Foxfire debuted on Broadway in 1982 and was well received, running for six months and earning Tandy a Tony Award. That success led to a CBS contract, under which Susan Cooper took charge of adapting it for television, and Tandy and Cronyn re-created their stage roles. (In the interim, Cooper and Cronyn adapted *The Dollmaker* for television as well, as previously noted.) Filmed on location in Rabun County (only a few miles from where *Deliverance* had been made fifteen years earlier) and in nearby Highlands, North Carolina, *Foxfire* first aired in December 1987 to strong reviews and good ratings and went on to earn yet another acting accolade for Tandy—this time an Emmy.[77]

The film opens with a sweeping aerial overview of the north Georgia mountains as Cronyn's voice, as the disembodied Hector Nations, states, "The Blue Ridge. The Cherokee were here first, and then the likes of us—mountain people. It's tough land, but we's folks to match—my granddaddy, my daddy." As the camera zooms down on a modest expanse of rocky mountainside fields and fences, surrounding a rambling old farmhouse and a few outbuildings, Hector continues: "My daddy cleared this place, taught me to drag a living out of rough ground. Yes, sir, the Nations place. My land." Thus from the outset, it is clear what defines and drives these characters and how pervasive Hector's postmortem presence and value system will remain.

We then see his widow, Annie, standing over Hector's grave in a small family cemetery high up on the hill above the farm and quickly recognize the film's conceit—that not only does she talk to him (as she has done over the five years since his death), but he appears to her and talks back. She tells him that their son Dillard (John Denver), who lives in Florida, will be visiting later that day. He's a country singer who'll be performing at Hiawassee (site of the Georgia Mountain Fair), about thirty miles west of Rabun Gap. "He traipses around the country with a guitar," Annie confides to Hector and then reveals her own affinity for her husband's priorities in life, values seemingly lost on the next generation. "What kind of work is that," she asks, "when there's land that needs to be cared for?"

Soon the forces conspiring to remove her from that land make themselves felt. While not quite as formidable a force as Ella Garth faced with the TVA in *Wild River*, those pressuring Annie Nations to give up her farm are as fully determined and persistent as was Chuck Glover, and they consist of not one but two very different interest groups. One is her son Dillard, who simply worries that his seventy-nine-year-old mother is neither physically nor mentally (given that she talks to his long-deceased father) equipped to live alone on the farm, much less maintain it.

The other is a far more sinister force, embodied by a "city slicker," Prince Carpenter from the Mountain Peak Development Corporation of Greenville, South Carolina. As he huffs his way up the mountain to see Mrs. Nations, he exclaims to himself, "Look at that view—money in the bank." By this, he means his intent to turn the one-hundred-acre Nations farm into a posh gated community of retirees and second-home owners, like so many others that dot the coves and hillsides of Rabun County, the majority of whom hail from Atlanta or, worse yet, from Florida. "I've got a nice surprise for you, Aunt Annie—I'm here to buy your land," Carpenter announces after she's greeted him and enlisted him in helping her cut up a hog's head. He can barely contain his revulsion as she carves out its eyes and ears and scrapes the cavities within for the succulent "souse meat" she so craves, in a scene taken almost verbatim—as are others throughout the film—from the original *Foxfire* interview with Aunt Arie.[78]

Annie, far more affable than Ella Garth but fully as tough, enjoys Carpenter's company but graciously deflects any discussion of selling her land, leading him to speak more frankly: "Aunt Annie, you're a senior citizen; if you don't sell, your children will." Prophetic words, which are followed shortly by Dillard Nations' arrival. He too tries to convince his mother to move back to Florida with him and his two children. (He's divorced and a single father, though he insists it's not the child care she could provide that's behind his offer.) He even tells her they don't have to sell the farm. When she resists, Dillard asks her if it's "Pa who's keeping you here?" which inspires her fullest statement yet on her attachment to both place and the people on it (or under it).

Echoing Ella Garth's most poignant speech as to what she'd be leaving behind if forced off her island home, Annie tells her son, "You're talking about your Pa resting, and he is. He's right up there in the orchard with his Ma and Pa and your little sister and brothers. Now when my time comes, I'm going to be right there beside him, and nothing's going to change that—not you, not Florida, not nothing!" When Dillard responds, "Well, I'd sure sleep a lot better if you were off this mountain," she counters, "Maybe you would, but I'm not. I ain't slept in another bed since I was married, and I ain't about to." While for both Mrs. Garth and Mrs. Nations, sheer longevity has much to do with what ties them to their home places, there's something spiritual about those ties as well. What was said of Aunt Arie in *The Foxfire Book* is applicable to both of these cinematic counterparts: "Her home has become a sacred place over which she alone must now keep watch."

The next day, Dillard encounters Carpenter when he returns to try to coax Annie to part with her farm. The younger Nations is put off by the developer's tactics and seeks to dismiss his pitch by saying it's her decision to make, not his. Carpenter responds with a bit of wisdom that forms a meaningful subtext of the film: "It's your mother. Face it, Dillard. Things have changed since we were growing up in these mountains. All those kids with get up and go have got up and went. The old ones are just hanging on, like foxfire on rotten wood." This was—and remains—a hard demographic truth in north Georgia and many other parts of the mountain South. The Nations' children—the three who lived to adulthood—have all left the region, including Dillard. His mother reminds him that the farm will become his one day, given that his sister and brother are never coming back, and she apparently holds out hope that he will, forcing him to admit, "I do love this place, but I can't live here." "No, you never could once you were grown," Annie concedes.

This was a timely issue for much of Southern Appalachia when Cooper and Cronyn wrote both their play and screenplay, and *Foxfire* remains the only film I know to confront it so explicitly. The boom in retirement and second-home construction accelerated throughout north Georgia in the 1970s and 1980s. In 1980, these structures made up a fourth of all housing units in Rabun County; by 1990, they accounted for more than half. And while a variety of factors—most notably the demise of farming and the lack of alternative employment opportunities—explain the generational exodus, the most relevant explanation here, though only hinted at in the film, is this real estate boom and the resentment of the local populace to its impact on their communities, their lifestyles, and their economic well-being. One Rabun Gap resident spoke for many of his fellow highlanders in the early 1990s when he expressed his frustration at the vastly inflated property values and accompanying taxes that have either forced many to sell out or greatly diminished their chances of purchasing local properties. "The dang realtors are a terrible plague," he declared. "They've got land so dang high a native boy can't buy it at all"; or worse, according to another local, "It's got to where a man can't afford to keep his own place." The source of the problem, as he put it, all too succinctly: "Too much goddam Atlanta!"[79]

Cooper and Cronyn added another key character to hammer this point home. Holly, a young woman who teaches at the local high school, is an old friend of Annie's and fully supportive of her refusal to sell her farm. When Dillard asks her what she knows about Prince Carpenter, Holly is quick to tell him not to listen to him. She goes on to explain: "Him and his Ruby Ridge [a nearby development, already complete]. I was born over there. Four generations, we farmed that land. Prince Carpenter talked my daddy into selling out. Fancy homes for summer people, all over our mountain. Barbed wire to keep the hillbillies out. Those kids I teach. I want them to be smart enough to keep their own land, 'cause once it's gone they can never get it back. Don't let Annie sell, Dillard. Don't let Prince shove her out." "Oh, she don't shove easily," Dillard replies. "She knows what she wants. Always did. So did Pa. Two people and a piece of ground. That's all it took."

A series of flashbacks make up much of the middle section of the film. (Somewhat daringly, Cronyn and Tandy continue to play Hector and Annie at each stage of life depicted.) Triggered by reminiscing with her phantom mate, we see, along with Annie, their teenage courtship and the promise of a new and fulfilling married life on the farm they're inheriting from his parents; we see them as parents coping with Dillard's restless adolescence and her sadness as he follows his older siblings in leaving mountain life behind—"I'm weary of watching my children march down that hill," Annie says. In one of the film's most moving scenes, we see Hector's death and the mountain rituals to which Annie adheres in preparing his body for burial and the bell ringing by which the rest of the community is notified of his death (both taken directly from *The Foxfire Book*).

While all these episodes seem to reinforce her ties to the land and all it has meant to her and her family over the past half century or more, these trips down memory lane also serve as a release of sorts, and with it the realization that Dillard's offer for her to come live with him and her grandchildren in Florida is not only reasonable but an appealing prospect. In what proves to be the final exchange between Annie and Hector, she weighs her options and says to him, "Place or family—is that the choice?" Hector reflects on this and on Dillard's divorce and suggests, "Maybe we was lucky. We had no choices then. You got married, you stayed married. I'm still here."

Annie: No, Hector, you're not. You're up in the old orchard.
Hector: Well, you was the one who brung me down. You want to change that?
Annie: Things change. Whatever he [Dillard] is doing, there's two young'uns to be taken care of.
Hector: They're growing somewhere else; you and me, we're planted here.
Annie: To everything there is a season; a time to be born, a time to die. A time to plant and a time to pick up that what was planted. . . . Go away, Hector. I have to figure this out by myself. You ain't still here; it's the kids that's still here.

So we get a final scene similar to that in *Wild River* in which Annie Nations, somewhat more affirmatively than Ella Garth (perhaps because unlike Ella, the decision has been hers to make), leaves her house for the last time. She puts flowers on Hector's grave, and though he continues to speak to her, she no longer hears him. Carpenter stands nearby, eagerly looking over his prize acquisition, and says, "There's going to be some fine homes up here," to which Dillard responds, "Always was." Annie gets the last word in making Carpenter confirm that the cemetery will remain untouched and that she can come back and be buried in it; he assures her that that's the law. Dillard asks her if she wants to take one last look around before they move down the hill. "Honey," she tells him, "there ain't a rock, a tree, or a piece of grass here that I don't know better than my own hand. So let's just get along."

This, then, is *Foxfire*'s bottom line and where it differs the most from *Wild River*: that place matters only because of the people on it, and when all those people are gone (or in Annie's case, once she's willing to admit that Hector is among them), it's time to reconnect with family, even if it means leaving the land. In this respect, the plight of Annie Nations resonates even more than that of Ella Garth simply because for Annie, living people come to matter more than dead ones. Human connections must prevail over a mere attachment to place, as bound up in sentiment, memory, and nostalgia as such attachments may be. That realization, made by Annie Nations, represents an even stronger testament to the fortitude and resilience of these mountain women. Ella Garth may have been the more formidable adversary from the perspective of those trying to move her off her island, but there's never any sense that Annie Nations is going to die the next day simply because she's left her home of sixty-some years.

• • • • • •

In Wendell Berry's *The Unsettling of America*—his eloquent and often profound critique of modern agriculture—Berry muses over the connections or responsibilities we maintain between our bodies and the earth. While acknowledging that the answers derive from religious questions first and foremost, he insists that agricultural questions play a part as well, "for no matter how urban our life, our bodies live by farming; we come from the earth and return to it, and so we live in agriculture as we live in flesh."[80] This metaphysical sense of individuals' ties to farms and farming is evident to varying degrees in all four of the protagonists here, though it's especially strong in the three films that put women front and center. Despite its inherent hardships, which are fully delineated onscreen, working the land provides each of them with their most elemental form of purpose and emotional stability, an affinity with the natural world, and a more satisfying and well-adjusted life.

As no-nonsense and practical as Ella Garth seems to be, she frames the struggle she's waging with the TVA as one in which "people must give up their souls" in exchange for electricity, and it's too high a price to ask. Damming the river goes against her affinity for "things running wild, like nature meant." For her to move is to "go agin nature," which she won't do willingly. While her island never exudes the same sensual or spiritual allure for her as the others' land does for them, her response to being forced from it is the most extreme, given that she dies—indeed wills herself to die—the following day. (This is a bit ironic in that she's the only one of the three not pushed out of the region itself—she's merely moved from one shore of the river to another—making her demise feel more symbolic than real.)

For the Nations in north Georgia, it's a sentiment shared equally by husband and wife. "What kind of work is that," Annie asks in reference to her son's singing career, "when there's land that needs to be cared for?" It's obvious she relishes the various tasks she sets for herself—nearly all of which are performed outdoors—and that Hector, from beyond the grave, takes comfort in watching her work the soil and reap its bounty, as they did side by side for so many years. One critic's observation of Appalachian life in Georgia as conveyed in the stage version of *Foxfire*—"These vignettes evoke a gentle feeling of a magical time when crops did indeed respond to the phases of the moon, and herbal remedies did cure, because the natural, the human, and the cosmic worlds were one"—is fully applicable to *Foxfire* onscreen as well.[81]

In contrast, it's the very different—indeed competing—priorities of Clovis and Gertie Nevels that drive their story. To demonstrate that disconnect, Clovis confides to his oldest son early in the film how much he's regretted "wearing your ma out, breaking her back in some field," saying that "all her life she's had her hands in the dirt," and in Detroit "she could just watch the house." Her son responds simply: "But she likes her hands in that dirt," thus encapsulating both her tangible and her spiritual connection to the earth and revealing how much better he understands his mother than her own husband does.

It is also family history that binds our protagonists to the land on which they live or yearn to live. As Ronald Eller once noted, most simply: "Two factors—land and family—were interwoven as the basic threads sustaining the fabric of mountain life."[82] All four of these films make reference to earlier generations—especially fathers and grandfathers—who cleared the farms they still work or those on which they've set their sights. For Ella Garth and Annie Nations, family cemeteries serve as focal points on their properties, and both verbally express what those multiple plots represent in terms of the long-standing family ties to their land, including those of their own spouses. Even as they're forced off that land, both want assurances that those sacred spots will remain intact; Mrs. Garth takes comfort in the fact that it will be above the waterline once the rest of her island is submerged, and Mrs. Nations exacts a promise from the developer that the cemetery will not be built over and that she'll be allowed to visit it anytime. (One wonders if *Foxfire*'s screenwriters may have taken their cues from *Wild River* in this respect; Arie Carpenter, the real-life inspiration for Annie Nations, never makes reference to a family burial ground.)

Only for our one male protagonist, Alvin York, would acquiring a better farm be a first for the family, and his motive for doing so was far more practical and materialistic than the more sentimentalized yearnings of the mountain matriarchs in the other films. York's obsessive quest for a particular tract of good bottomland comes only when he begins courting a young woman for whom he feels he can compete only by having that more substantial property in hand. Social class is far more pronounced in *Sergeant York*; in order to win his girl, he must make a better living, which can happen only by acquiring better land. As his very wise mother observes, in these mountains, upward mobility is achieved by moving down in elevation.

Thus, despite a range of scenarios, relationships, and historical contexts around which these films are structured, attachment to land proved to be the common denominator and most defining trait of these four lead characters. Indeed, by so effectively focusing on those particular struggles to attain, retain, and actually work small family farms, filmmakers not only made their mountain subjects strong, sympathetic, and admirable characters but also made their plights resonate with audiences nationwide, portraying Appalachia as that "special repository of fundamental Americanism" in which "traditional American values in their purest form have been preserved."[83]

2 Afro-Appalachians

In Focus and Out

In Jerry Williamson's book *Hillbillyland*—the most comprehensive study of Hollywood's depiction of the mountain South—there is no mention of black people. In Thomas Cripps's *Slow Fade to Black*—the most thorough treatment of African Americans on film—there is no mention of Appalachia. Neither exclusion is at all surprising, given that the two subjects—race relations and Southern Appalachia—have only occasionally intersected to any significant degree in popular culture, literature, or film.[1] And yet there are at least four films set in the southern highlands that have taken the region's black presence seriously. These include one of the most sensitive and sophisticated treatments of slavery and antislavery sentiment ever conveyed in a feature film; another that tackles race relations in a more idealized form during the Civil War's immediate aftermath in East Tennessee; and two others that embrace fact-based subthemes in which black workers serve as crucial catalysts in very different labor struggles—one brought on by a West Virginia coal strike in 1920, and the other by TVA relocation efforts in the mid-1930s.

By the late nineteenth century and for much of the twentieth, the presence of African Americans in the southern highlands had received relatively little attention from either scholars or fiction writers. In fact, popular perception maintained that much of what distinguished the region from other parts of the South was its relative "whiteness" in terms of population and culture. In 1897, a journalist stated of the northern Georgia mountains: "Nowhere will be found purer Anglo-Saxon blood," while ethnogeographer Ellen Semple extolled the populace of eastern Kentucky on similar grounds in 1901, noting that they had not only kept foreign elements at bay but "still more effectively . . . excluded the negroes. This region is as free from them as northern Vermont."[2] Even in John C. Campbell's definitive (at the time) 1921 overview of Appalachia, *The Southern Highlander and His Homeland*, Campbell notes that "there were few Negroes in the Highlands. . . . They have never been a factor in rural mountain life."[3]

As late as 1985, Edward Cabbell—in one of the first major correctives to such assumptions, an essay collection called *Blacks in Appalachia*—labeled this the "black invisibility" factor and noted that Afro-Appalachians remained "a neglected minority within a neglected minority."[4] Cabbell and his coeditor, William H. Turner, bemoaned the fact that most chroniclers of the region conclude that "the number of Negroes in the [Appalachian] Region . . . is such a small proportion of the total population [that] . . . the social consequences [of their presence and migration] are not any great [significance]."[5] *Blacks in Appalachia* proved a seminal volume in terms of demanding that attention be paid to the biracial realities of the highland South—with most of its emphasis on African Americans' role in the coal mining industry and on their presence in broad demographic overviews. (Depending on how the region itself is delineated, its black presence consisted of up to 15 percent of its antebellum populace—the vast majority of them slaves—and averaged around 10 percent in the latter decades of the twentieth century.)[6]

Other scholars soon rallied to the cause, especially in their explorations of slaves and of coal miners, leading to a spate of studies on both that began in the late 1980s and continues today. More recently, "whiteness studies" have provided more theoretical underpinnings to the long-held assumptions that made whiteness a de facto reality in Appalachia's regional identity, indeed the essence of its otherness.[7]

Hollywood's treatment of the black experience in Appalachia has been only intermittent, with the vast majority of films set in the region full reflections of the "black invisibility" factor that evoked so much commentary earlier on. The presumed whiteness of highland society is in fact so pervasive onscreen that it makes especially exceptional the only four feature films that even acknowledge race or a black presence as integral to any part of the region or significant to its history.[8] These films alone make race relations substantive components of stories set within the region. Two are set in the nineteenth century, and two in the twentieth; they are discussed here in order of the historical eras in which they take place, rather than the order of their production.

• • • • • •

The Journey of August King (1995) is an exceptional film in several respects. First, it is easily among the most serious and historically accurate depictions of the antebellum mountain South ever put onscreen. At the same time, it is perhaps the only substantive treatment of southern slavery on film that does not play out within a stereotypical plantation setting and one of very few to put a fugitive slave front and center in its narrative. (A major addition came with *Harriet* in 2019, a well-received film treatment of the Maryland escape and subsequent exploits of Harriet Tubman.)

The credit for these distinctions, of course, lies not with Hollywood producers alone. First and foremost, it is John Ehle's 1971 novel that provides the basis for the film and Ehle himself who adapted the book to film.[9] An Asheville native, Ehle's literary career consisted in part of a vast fictional output (eleven novels), seven of which are deeply researched reflections on the historical experience of western North Carolina's settlement and subsequent development. His literary output, which ranges chronologically from the late eighteenth century through the post–World War II era, breaks through regional stereotypes in bold and substantive ways. According to his friend and one of the film's associate producers, Borden Mace, "John has revealed a greater truth and accuracy about Southern Appalachian life than many historians and sociologists," an assessment with which few critics would take issue.[10]

This is particularly true of Ehle's seventh novel, *The Journey of August King*, simply because he embraced the subject of slavery in a highland setting. The book, which Ehle translated to the screen with commendable fidelity, confronts in both subtle and not so subtle ways themes that historians have only far more recently tackled in regard to the mountain South.[11] The result is a film that not only explores the ways in which slaveholding, racism, abolitionist sentiment, and class distinctions played out in a highland setting but also conveys the realities of isolationism and connectedness, of subsistence and market economies, in this still formative society early in the nineteenth century. And all this is reflected through a deceptively simple escape story.

While returning home from a semiannual, week-long trip to a bustling market, identified in the book as Old Fort, North Carolina, August King, a recently widowed farmer, discovers in hiding an escaped teenage slave girl named Annalees. After fleeting encounters with her along his route through a sparsely settled wilderness, King reluctantly befriends the starving, footsore, and desperate young woman. Over the course of the next three days of trekking back to his farm in a remote cove community, he conceals her with great difficulty, shunning acquaintances and sacrificing his own newly acquired stock and supplies in order to protect her from her ruthless master and the fearsome search party her owner has hired to find her. In the process, King also falls in love.

Unlike more typical commercial Hollywood productions, the love story between King and Annalees remains, as it was in Ehle's novel, underplayed

Fugitive slave Annalees (Thandie Newton) attempts escape with the help of farmer August King (Jason Patric) in *The Journey of August King*.

and ultimately unconsummated. (In the novel, King was a somewhat older man, which lowered readers' expectations of romance between the two protagonists.) Yet it is obvious that the filmmakers sought to forefront the attraction between these two characters, simply by the casting of actors Jason Patric and Thandie Newton in those roles. (Newton had already scored onscreen in another strong role as a slave. As Thomas Jefferson's Sally Hemings, she created the most compelling character in the otherwise disappointing Merchant Ivory production *Jefferson in Paris* two years earlier.) The love story in *August King* amounts to a very tentative brief encounter that propels the story forward as this white man and this black woman climb higher toward home and freedom, respectively. It is also a tale of personal rejuvenation and even spiritual redemption for August King, though the terms of his psychological journey are not nearly as well developed in the film as they are in the book.

Particularly noteworthy is the specificity of time and place in both the novel and the film. The movie's opening credits appear as the camera sweeps from east to west over an early nineteenth-century map of North Carolina, from the Atlantic coast to the mountains, lingering only as we see the names of the last settlements, "Wilkes" and "Morgantown." Just to the west, the words "Appalachian Mountains" arc in much larger letters across multiple mountain ranges, sketchily delineated. The date is also revealed early on. As he makes a final mortgage payment on his small farm, August King's deed is marked paid and dated April 27, 1815.

The filmmakers are equally conscientious in their careful re-creation of a still remote but thriving frontier society. (The movie was filmed almost fully on location in scenic Transylvania County, North Carolina.) The Carolina highlanders depicted here are neither backwoods hillbillies nor "coonskin cap boys." They are hunters and farmers, most of them family men eking out modest livings on small landholdings. But they do not do so alone. Far from frontier loners enduring isolated existences amid an all-consuming wilderness, these early highlanders make up a thriving society driven by trade and commerce. There is a constant sense of movement throughout the film, as livestock and poultry crowd the roads as much as people and wagons do. The story is played out far more at trading posts; drover stands; and along roads, fords, and campsites than it is on farms or in cabins. Residents interact as close neighbors, as casual acquaintances, as merchant and customer, as debtor and creditor, as counselor and client, as employer and hired hand. This is one of Ehle's most adept achievements, in fact, and that of Australian director John Duigan, and yet they make equally compelling, through the character of widower August King in particular, the loneliness and isolation that was also integral to highland life during those formative years.[12]

Yet this sharply delineated sense of time, place, and socioeconomic development all serve as backdrop to a story that is at its heart a saga of slavery. Slavery in the mountains was well established by 1815, but few historians had acknowledged this basic fact at the time Ehle wrote his book.[13] Slaves played no part in the vast set of images, assumptions, and stereotypes on which popular—and even scholarly—understandings of Southern Appalachia were based. But bondsmen and women there were; according to census analysis, roughly 15 percent of the Appalachian populace in 1820 was enslaved, though only 10 percent of highland households held slave property.[14] By coincidence, possibly the first slave in western North Carolina was a young girl named Liza, brought into the area of Old Fort where August and Annalees first cross paths. According to a long oral tradition among her descendants in the Asheville area, Liza accompanied Samuel Davidson, generally regarded as the "first white settler west of the Blue Ridge."[15] But although slaves were certainly present in the mountains from an early time, they were a limited presence, and the film reflects this fact. Besides Annalees and Sims—a fellow fugitive from whom she has become separated—the only other African American characters are three or four servants who belong to the same owner, Olaf Singletary, and attend him as a silent and begrudging entourage.

From beginning to end, this is a story of escape and pursuit, and in that respect it is very appropriate that it is set in Appalachia. The idea of the southern highlands as a refuge for fugitives of various sorts has long been an integral part of the higher moral ground that many sought to bestow on the region. Abolitionist John Brown was by no means the first to acknowledge that the mountains of western Virginia, so integral to his Harpers Ferry scheme in 1859, "were intended by the Almighty for a refuge for the slave and a defense against the oppressor."[16] A recent scholar has echoed that theme, declaring that "the hills, in their exquisite isolation, became havens for the disenchanted black and white, who needed to escape burdensome drudgery and slavery."[17]

Yet Annalees is not a lowland fugitive who has lifted her eyes unto the hills. She is owned locally. Her master is well known to both August King and the others in the area, and she is simply moving deeper into the wilderness when she encounters King. Both novel and screenplay are vague in terms of where she is heading or *thinks* she is heading. On their first encounter, August King simply directs her to follow a stream headed north. At the film's end, he escorts her to a high ridge above his farm and points her to a "trail to the North." Whether or not the Underground Railroad ever moved through the southern highlands is open to debate. I have argued elsewhere that there is no real evidence of its presence in the region.[18] Even if some regularized escape route developed later, it is highly improbable that it would have been established as early as 1815. But that is obviously what Ehle had in mind as King sends his fugitive charge off with no reference at all to a destination, either short or long term. "The trail has been used for years. It's marked," he tells her vaguely in the film. "People will show you kindness on the way."[19] (The film's final and most striking, if unlikely, shot is an aerial view of the young slave girl, decked out in a bright red dress, marching northward on the Appalachian Trail as it follows the meadowed ridgeline of Roan Mountain, as if she no longer has any need to move undetected.)

The pursuers are as vital as the pursued in demonstrating the complexities and variables that characterized mountain attitudes toward slavery. Olaf Singletary is the story's sole slaveholder, referred to early in the film as "the wealthiest man in the mountains." In rallying a search party to seek out his two runaways, Singletary at first finds few willing volunteers, which forces him to offer rewards and payment for their services and those of their dogs. In the wariness of other characters toward both the man and his mission, Ehle depicts the uneasiness with slaveholding and slaveholders that fueled antislavery biases held by at least some white highlanders.

For some, the idea of the search itself is troublesome. One man states that it "hurts my conscience to set dogs on people," while another wonders about offering a horse as a reward for a human being. Such sentiments suggest a genuine sense of moral resentment at the dehumanization the "peculiar institution" imposed on its victims. For earlier chroniclers of the region, such qualms typified the views of freedom-loving southern highlanders. It fueled the image of "Holy Appalachia," where, according to one turn-of-the-century writer, those in the mountains "cherish liberty as a priceless heritage. They would never hold slaves and we may almost say they will never be enslaved." [20] Or as Harry Caudill noted much later, "These poorer mountaineers, fiercely independent as they were, found something abhorrent in the ownership of one person by another."[21]

Yet such idealized characterizations of antebellum Appalachian residents fail to acknowledge other, less noble factors that fueled their resentment toward slavery. Ehle lays them out as well. Alongside this indignation toward the debasement of slaves, he reveals the class-based contempt most feel toward the sole beneficiary of slavery in their midst. While his non-slaveholding neighbors fear Singletary and his power, they also see him as an object of derision and resentment. As such, they conform to what historian Carter Woodson once referred to as a "liberty-loving and tyrant-hating race," which exhibited "more prejudice against the slave holder than against the Negro."[22] For the first generations of southern highlanders, in particular, a common assumption was that they moved into the hills when slavery and the plantation economy it supported squeezed them out of the more desirable lowlands and fostered a resentment of the planter class that had driven them away. According to one version of this premise, "The aristocratic slaveholder from his river-bottom plantation looked with scorn on the slaveless dweller among the hills; while the highlander repaid his scorn with high disdain and even hate."[23]

Though hardly "aristocratic," Olaf Singletary provides a ready target for such resentment by his non-slaveholding neighbors. And yet in characterizing the film's single slaveholder, Ehle has stacked the deck. Certainly the least subtle aspect of the film is that Singletary emerges as a rather one-dimensional villain. As portrayed by Larry Drake, he is the least attractive character onscreen, fat and scowling, brutish and violent. His arrogant contempt for both his slaves and his poorer white neighbors is made abundantly clear.

From a dramatic standpoint, one can understand the need for a clear-cut villain, and who better than the man in pursuit of the film's heroine, the man who drives her—and her male lover—to flee in the first place. It is very clear that it is sharing his bed that the seventeen-year-old Annalees found most unbearable; further complications not fully explored lie in her revelation that Singletary is her father as well. When King asks her outright why she ran away, her response is simple but profound: "To keep him from taking my soul." Her master openly professes his love for her before the men he hires to retrieve her, but that does little to soften his portrayal or win him much sympathy from either the search party or movie viewers.

How much more interesting—and challenging—it would have been to make Singletary a character that scholars have suggested was more representative of the region's slaveholding class. More often than not, even in those formative years, mountain masters were merchants and professionals, doctors and lawyers. The commodities or services they provided the rest of the mountain populace made them integral and respected members of the community, which defused much of the resentment that their ownership of slaves might otherwise have generated.[24] None of those linkages are suggested here.

One must wonder, based on the film's depiction of such pervasive antislavery and anti-slaveholder sentiment in 1815, why these pioneers' descendants would so eagerly defend the institution two generations later and secede from the Union in order to do so. To have cast the upright, dignified, patrician Sam Waterston as Singletary, rather than the hulking Larry Drake, would have been both truer to history and more challenging for an audience who here finds much too comfortable a way out of the moral dilemma posed by the plot. In the late twentieth century, we wouldn't expect film depictions of our slave-owning ancestors to make them particularly attractive, high minded, or morally fastidious, yet with Larry Drake as Olaf, it's too easy for us to dismiss both him and the institution of slavery. A more respectable and benign man in the role of slave owner and captor would have provided even more subtle dimensions and moral shadings to this otherwise fairly sophisticated treatment of the multiple components of a slaveholding society. (Waterston all too predictably plays the dignified and impeccable Mooney Wright, who appears as the primary voice of antislavery in the film's closing scenes.)

Yet to both Ehle's and Duigan's credit, the despicable Singletary hardly carries the villainy of the film on his shoulders alone; his non-slaveholding neighbors can claim few moral exemptions, as they reveal their own shades of racial bias. Once recruited for the pursuit of Annalees and Sims, Singletary's henchmen are fully contemptuous of their prey, and though they are motivated by promises of material rewards, they are fully committed to seeing the system restored and those rebelling against it punished. The brutal execution of Sims, once he is caught, evokes no apparent protest or only slight squeamishness among the many who witness it. They merely speculate as to the fate of Annalees upon her capture, debating casually whether she too will be executed or simply forced to return to her master's bed, without indicating any disapproval of or discomfort over whichever option he might take.

Only in its final segment does the film present any sense of a communal abolitionist spirit within the region. King brings Annalees to his cabin in the remote cove settlement of Harristown, and after putting her up for a night, he sends her off, fortified with food and dressed in his dead wife's clothing. It is only after her departure that neighbors gather, and August must finally account for his actions. King had told Annalees earlier that "they don't allow slaves in the community I live in," and as its residents, led by Mooney Wright, confront him, it becomes apparent that they are sympathetic toward his actions but wary of the consequences he soon must face from Singletary. When, in an informal trial "of a sort" inside his own cabin, King stands firm in declaring the truth before the man whose property he helped escape, his neighbors can only watch as Singletary and his men inflict a costly retribution by burning King's house to the ground, thus completing his economic ruin. August himself seems fully complacent with that harsh judgment. His final words reflect his lack of remorse at what he's done for Annalees. As he watches his house burn, he states simply to himself, "I was right well-to-do. Only in a day or two, I lost everything. But I've never been so proud." So his journey is completed, and his conscience is clear.

The extent of that retribution is historically dubious. There is no evidence that I know of, in the mountains or elsewhere, of a slaveholder exercising such extreme extralegal vengeance on one who has abetted his slave's escape and the passive compliance in such a punishment by all who witness it. Yet by depicting this punishment as an almost ritualistic act, and one that is fully expected and ultimately accepted even by those supportive of King's good deed, Ehle suggests that it was a common and generally accepted occurrence. (Another oddity in this scene is that it's one of only two in which white women appear, even though they remain silent throughout. Their marginalization in the film seems to undercut, and even seriously distort, the gendered themes and tensions that derive from the relationship between August and Annalees.)

The antislavery sentiments that bound this community together, however, are somewhat more credible. There were indeed pockets of highland settlements in which a black presence was unknown and unwelcome, though it was often antiblack prejudices more than antislavery sentiments that motivated such bans. As Frederick Law Olmsted noted in moving through this very region several decades after the time of *The Journey of August King*, many highlanders found both the presence of blacks and the privileges that ownership of them bequeathed to other whites to be the worst features of a slaveholding society, and they fought to maintain their distance from both.[25]

Yet true antislavery activity spurred by humanitarian motives, such as those evident early in the film and embodied in Mooney Wright at its end, also found its place in Southern Appalachia. Sporadic efforts emerged and then faded out at Wheeling, Virginia; Berea, Kentucky; and Maryville, Tennessee, throughout the antebellum era. Yet it was in the area closest to the fictional Harristown settlement—both geographically and chronologically—in which Appalachian abolitionism most flourished. In the 1810s and 1820s, fledgling organizations in northeastern Tennessee, just across the state line from Harristown's probable location, took the form of manumission societies and abolitionist publications. They were usually based in towns and instigated by New Light Presbyterians and Quakers from Pennsylvania and Ohio.[26] While such circumstances would hardly have penetrated into remote cove settlements like August King's, it would not have been improbable for a collective resentment of both the system and its beneficiaries to have developed in such communities. Mooney Wright makes it clear that he is acting from a sense of decency that opposes anyone's enslavement and that he silently applauds Annalees's triumph over the system. But it is never clear if the same higher ground lies behind the other neighbors' willingness to stand by August King. The basis for their opposition to Singletary and sympathy for Annalees is, perhaps fittingly, left ambivalent.

Part of the power of both the film and the novel lies in the fact that Ehle sets his story so early in the nineteenth century and thus so early in the development of Appalachian society. These western Carolinians—and August King in particular—are forced to deal with a moral dilemma that has not been fully articulated as such up to that point. This is an escape story set well before the Underground Railroad was in place; its characters wrestle with the wrongs of slavery well before a full-fledged abolition movement has articulated those evils. It is a relatively spontaneous situation with two opponents—one fighting for her freedom, the other fighting for the recovery of his legally owned property—that forces this community of white highlanders to confront the legitimacy of the institution for the first time. They are well aware of the legalities of slavery. King's initial reaction to Annalees's request for help is, "You know I can't do that. It's against the law." When King's complicity in her escape is revealed and he must face Singletary's retribution, Mooney Wright—in typical Sam Waterston deadpan—states simply why such punishment must be accepted: "Laws have been broken, property rights violated."

August King seems to have had little reason to question that truth until he makes this fateful journey. As played by Jason Patric, he is a simple farmer, an everyman whose quiet strength and moral resolve audiences are meant to identify with. Neither he nor his neighbors own slaves, but neither have they taken a stand against a system that allowed "a horse in exchange for a man." Yet when the opportunity to fight that system presents itself in the form of this beautiful, vulnerable, and irresistible young woman, King rises to the moral challenge and in his small way helps to undermine the institution that had so victimized her.

Both Ehle and the movie's casting director have perhaps stacked the deck here as well. Given the obvious charms of Thandie Newton as Annalees, one wonders if King's moral courage has received a true test. August's explanation for his actions suggests his own ambivalence about his motives. "A spell came over me," he tells Mooney Wright and other neighbors. "I did a hundred things strange, nothing customary." Would he have driven as hard or risked as much if it were Sims he had first encountered or if Annalees were an old or even middle-aged woman? As is, his libido never seems far from his conscience. (This point is more obvious in the film than in the book, with the casting of a much younger actor in the title role.)

Yet the power of the story derives in no small part from the sexual tensions that drive it, and it seems unfair to suggest that those dynamics in some way compromise the strong moral fiber that grounds not only the film's title character but its overall tone as well. It is a film that works on a variety of levels, of which history lessons are only one. But to have so compelling, if relatively unexplored, a part of the Appalachian experience portrayed with as much talent, sensitivity, and integrity as is evident in *The Journey of August King* is commendable, particularly in light of how rarely feature films have sought to explore any aspect of race relations in the mountain South.

• • • • • •

Hollywood has rarely taken the Reconstruction era in the South seriously. The few exceptions most notably include D. W. Griffith's 1915 epic, *The Birth of a Nation*, and the latter segments of films more fully focused on the Civil War years, from *Gone with the Wind* (1939) to the recent *Free State of Jones* (2016). In all three of these films, the postwar era is characterized as one of racial tensions in the wake of emancipation, with the Ku Klux Klan or similar vigilante groups playing a pivotal role in repressing black aspirations and assertiveness.[27] One can add to these slim ranks the Appalachian-based film *Sommersby* (1993). While it too includes an obligatory appearance by a KKK-like group, it proves exceptional in other ways, most notably in its treatment of race.

Set in East Tennessee in the immediate postwar era, *Sommersby* is a loose adaptation of the French-made film *The Return of Martin Guerre* (1982), itself based on a true story of a sixteenth-century peasant who returned to his Basque village after nine years of fighting with the Spanish army, claiming to be Guerre. He reclaims his place with his wife, who accepts him as such for three years, before other family members publicly challenge his identity; those charges lead to two trials in which his true identity is revealed, resulting in his conviction for fraud and his hanging.[28]

Sommersby transposes that scenario to the post–Civil War South and follows only the basic plot points while imposing on that narrative frame an intriguing subplot of agricultural and racial reform efforts. These are undertaken by Jack Sommersby (the Martin Guerre counterpart) to compensate for the material losses, including slavery's end, suffered by the small, rural community in the placid Tennessee valley to which he's returned (or pretended to return). The film opens with a Confederate-clad Sommersby (Richard Gere) burying an unseen corpse and washing blood off his hands, then trudging—much like Inman in *Cold Mountain*—through a rugged wintry wilderness, passing by burned farms, makeshift graveyards, and devastated landscapes, all conveyed in a beautifully photographed montage. Presumably returning home from a war just concluded, he warily passes Union troops moving northward along the same wooded road and at one point hitches a wagon ride with a black family (with whom he seems to be on especially good terms—the first hint that we are not dealing with a typical white Confederate veteran).

By the time Jack Sommersby arrives home, it is early spring (presumably in 1866). He descends into a lush valley where he greets a farmer and his son. His first words are "good piece of land," to which the elder man responds, "It was," and Jack retorts, "Still is." He calls the two men by name, and after some hesitation, they recognize him, and soon he's warmly greeted by other neighbors who gather. It seems he's been gone six years, though no explanation is ever given for the extra time away (given that the war lasted only four years). A young black boy runs to tell Laurel Sommersby (Jody Foster), also working in a field, that her husband is back; her blank expression suggests that this may not be welcome news. She heads home to primp, entering a substantial two-story brick house, which makes apparent that the Sommersbys are the most affluent residents of this small mountain community, called Vine Hill. (The director, Jon Amiel, makes the most of the scenic beauty of the Blue Ridge foothills of Virginia, where the film was shot.) It soon becomes apparent that the Sommersbys had been Vine Hill's only substantial slaveholders.[29] An elderly black woman (Clarice Taylor) is among the first to greet Jack with a warm embrace, obviously exuding her affection for her former owner. She informs him of the war's impact on the community: "Everybody here is missing somebody . . . and everybody that ain't dead is leaving. This town's finished, Mr. Jack. Ain't nothing left here but hard ground and nobody to work it" (a strange statement given the size of the crowd of white and black residents in whose midst she pronounces this).

The central plot is driven by a delicate courtship between husband and wife (it seems there had been no love lost between the two when he left six years earlier) and by increasing suspicions among the local populace that the returnee is an impostor. Those doubts are driven in part by his kindness and generosity not only to his wife but to the community at large, and though no one states the obvious, his liberal agenda in creating a biracial communal farm is hardly that of a former slaveholder and Confederate veteran. That racial subtext is what provides the film's relevance in this chapter.

Jack's color-blind attitude becomes apparent in a scene set later on the evening of his return, when at a pig roasting and barn dance, a contingent of ten or twelve African Americans—men, women, and children—approach Jack while remaining at the edge of the enclosure. Sommersby has no such qualms about their presence and carries a plate full of hog meat over to them, which they decline. Their spokesperson, a large black man (Frankie Faison), whom Jack fails to recognize, introduces himself as Joseph, enough

Returning from the Civil War, former slaveholder Jack Sommersby (Richard Gere) confronts his wife, Laurel (Jodie Foster), in *Sommersby*.

of a prompt to jog Jack's memory, adding that "my daddy paid $100 for you," the only explicit reference to the Sommersbys' former ownership of them. He invites them all to join the party, but Joseph declines again, saying, "No, thank you; we just came by to say welcome home," thus seeming to confirm that he had been their master. His white neighbors observe this exchange and rib him about it. "Jack, you're still a rebel, ain't you?" one asks. "Best not to get too friendly with the niggers." Another informs him, "We had to chase some off." Nodding at Joseph, he says, "That one there has been living on your land. Next thing you'll know, they'll be moving into the big house."

The narrative then shifts to Jack's interest in revitalizing his own and the community's agricultural output. He brings local residents together to make a rather radical proposal for doing so in that postemancipation era in which slave labor was no longer an option. Burley tobacco, he tells them, is the wave of the future as the most promising cash crop for the region. He proposes to give a significant portion of his own vast acreage over to a tobacco crop, and to split the profits among everyone—white and black—who's willing to work a piece of that land, with the option of ultimately using their earnings to purchase what they've worked outright, a pitch that seems especially aimed at the freedmen and freedwomen in the group.

This raises the hackles of some whites; one woman is quick to declare, “I ain’t living next to no nigras!” to which Jack replies, “So where you going to live then, Mrs. Bundy? In the poor house?”

Given the high price of burley seed and the need to purchase tools and mules, Jack, with the strong support of his wife, Laurel, urges his still skeptical neighbors to pool what little they have and allow him to take the collected funds and goods to make the trade at a distant and unnamed market. Eventually most come around, as indicated in a scene in which people are lined up to donate jewelry, watches, china, silver sets, and other fine furnishings; black families contribute as well, with Joseph handing over a carved tusk (obviously African), which he says his grandmother’s daddy gave to her the day she was married. Jack asks how many acres he wants to work, to which Joseph responds, “About ten, sir,” before seeking reassurance from Jack that he’ll ultimately get to purchase it. Jack loads it all onto a wagon and heads out; even then, there’s some worry about whether he is who he says he is and whether they’ve just become the victims of a major scam.

Sommersby eventually returns, but after so long that there’s real suspense built up as to whether he actually intended to. By this time the land has been cleared and laid out in plots, and the community of investors is quick to get the precious tobacco seed into the ground, black and white working together in what amounts to more of a communal enterprise than the sharecropping model it was first pitched as. In another skillful montage, the full process is laid out onscreen, making this one of only a few modern films to take agricultural production and processes so seriously.[30] (The film crew actually planted, cultivated, and harvested thirty acres of tobacco on its filming location in Virginia.) Some critics, however, found all this a distraction from the central love story and the mystery of Sommersby’s identity. One groused that given the convoluted turns in the impostor story, viewers might leave the theater thinking they’ve seen a film “about worn out land, crop rotation, and fertilizer.”[31]

There were at least two examples of actual communal-like agricultural settlements established by former slaves in postwar Appalachia that could have served (though there’s no evidence that either did) as loose models for the fictional biracial experiment undertaken by Sommersby on film. The so-called Kingdom of Happy Land was built on the farm of a slaveholding widow, Serepta Davis, in Henderson County, North Carolina, when in the summer of 1865 she offered its use to a group of freedmen and freedwomen who moved into the area from Georgia and South Carolina. In the early

1870s, those settlers purchased some two hundred acres of land from the Davis family, who allowed for a forty-year existence of an all-black community that supported itself mainly by subsistence farming and as hired labor for nearby white residents.[32]

In Kentucky's Cumberland Mountains, near the Tennessee border, Coe Ridge emerged around the same time, though from somewhat less auspicious circumstances. In 1866, a white planter, Jesse Coe, bequeathed a remote forested ridge adjacent to his valley property to a former slave couple, Ezekiel (Zeke) and Patsy, who saw the property as an opportunity both to hold together the Coe slave community before they scattered in the wake of emancipation and to reunite their families, some of whom had already moved elsewhere. While ultimately successful, the Coe Ridge colony proved a far more contentious operation than did Happy Land, if only because it attracted outlaws and other disreputable elements, including white women, who targeted the community as a menace, and led to a series of violent confrontations with hostile whites in the 1870s and 1880s.[33]

Of course, there are differences in the two historic communities and the fictional Vine Hill created in the film. The most significant is that the tobacco-producing enterprise initiated by Sommersby is biracial in nature and a reflection of the black and white makeup of the community as he found it, unlike the fully African American populaces of Happy Land and Coe Ridge, whose residents moved to those sites from elsewhere. (One wonders if the assumption of more benign race relations in Appalachia than in other parts of the postwar South led the screenwriter to situate his story in East Tennessee.) The fact that the community's freedmen and freedwomen did not initiate the communal experiment that drives the film and were merely permitted to participate due to Sommersby's personal largesse also renders it a very different scenario. Finally, neither of those two communities saw tobacco or any other single cash crop as its economic mainstay (though it was one of several crops grown by Coe Ridge residents).[34]

Yet *Sommersby*'s case for burley tobacco as a profitable new force in southern highland agriculture is grounded in historical reality. In his recent study of Reconstruction across the state line in western North Carolina, Steven Nash makes the fullest case yet as to the dramatic surge of tobacco cultivation in the immediate aftermath of the war. Like Jack Sommersby, regional spokespeople touted it as "the great money staple of the Western part of the State" throughout the late 1860s and 1870s, noting soil and climate conditions as especially conducive to the quality of mountain-grown tobacco and thus especially profitable for the expanding manufacturing centers throughout the upper South.[35] (Just how this returning prisoner of war was privy to knowledge of this breaking development is one of several holes in the film's plot.)

Not surprisingly, even in Southern Appalachia, such an idyllic biracial enterprise soon becomes the target of opposition, in this case by the Ku Klux Klan—or, as it is labeled here, the Knights of the White Camellia, a more elitist and short-lived variant of the Klan that thrived primarily in the Deep South states of Louisiana and Texas. (It seems a little odd that the filmmakers made use of this group rather than the Klan itself, given the latter's origins in Tennessee, though its presence in East Tennessee was minimal.)[36] Just as the tobacco crop comes to term, a burning cross appears in front of Jack's house, and the so-called Knights inform him that they've beaten Joseph, noting, "You've broken the law, and he has paid for it." Jack asks what law he's broken and is told that "a nigger can't own land." As tempers flare and the confrontation escalates, shots are fired, which send the mob members fleeing into the dark. One shot hits Joseph, who, as he's helped to his feet to have his wound treated, is quick to ask Sommersby, "It's still my land?" with Jack responding, "You own what you pay for."

Little more is made of this confrontation, other than that several of the white cappers seem to recognize Jack as someone they know from a neighboring county. Those suspicions result in a plot contrivance in which Jack is arrested on a charge of having killed a man over a card game shortly before he returned home. The scene quickly shifts to a courtroom in Nashville, where the climax plays out. While dramatically effective, much about these courtroom scenes strains credibility. One of its boldest—if somewhat questionable—features is that a black judge (played by the formidable James Earl Jones) presides over the trial. There are gasps from the assembled white crowd when he enters and muffled smiles of approval by the black attendees relegated to the balcony. (Two Union soldiers stand guard in the courtroom, yet another reminder that we're fully in the federal occupation phase of Reconstruction.)

On the assumption that the actual Jack Sommersby was guilty as charged, Laurel attempts to save his life by testifying that he's not Sommersby. That he's an impostor is given further credence by another witness who testifies that he had a long history as a con man and scam artist from a neighboring county; worse, he was a coward and a Confederate deserter during the war (all of which raises the question of how he transformed himself into such a saintly if anachronistic do-gooder by the time he reached Vine Hill).[37]

Sommersby (who by this point viewers know is someone else) in turn tries to discredit this hostile witness by accusing him of being one of the Knights of the White Camellias who burned a cross in front of his house in Vine Hill and beat a black man who tried to farm a piece of land for himself. "The real reason you're here is to stop Jack Sommersby from selling a piece of land to a colored man," Jack's lawyer charges, "which would then make him a property owner like yourself and your equal in the eyes of the law." The witness calls the judge a "nappy-headed son of a bitch" and predicts that "as soon as the Yankees are gone, you'll be back in the field where you belong." The judge sentences him to sixty days in jail for contempt of court. And so one of the central issues of Reconstruction is thrust back into the middle of a narrative that otherwise doubles as romantic drama and suspenseful con game.

To have a black judge presiding over a Tennessee murder case two years after the war's end is a bold move on the part of the filmmakers and one that historically occurs much too soon. While Reconstruction was certainly marked by the election and appointment of African American officeholders throughout the South, judicial appointments such as the judge played by Jones would have been highly unlikely, especially as early as 1867, when this takes place. In fact, the first judicial appointments of blacks in southern states were to those with higher jurisdictions, such as federal courts or state supreme courts. Only in 1873 did Mifflin W. Gibbs of Little Rock, Arkansas, become the first black judge in American history to preside over a trial court with general jurisdiction.[38]

Nevertheless, Sommersby himself feels no slight at an African American judge presiding over his case, indeed determining his fate. And the judge shows no partiality toward a white plaintiff who's done so much to champion the interests of his former slaves and others of color. As Jack clings to his new identity in a rather contrived bid for honor and respect, he all but assures his death sentence, which the judge not only confirms but orders that it be carried out on a jail-yard gallows the next day. If the film's denouement rings false, it is the character of Jack Sommersby who nonetheless remains the most compelling yet puzzling element of the story. In his quest to redefine the lay of the land in terms of both shared ownership and marketable product, he demonstrates the social reform impulses and material ambition that embodied much of the carpetbag agenda of Radical Reconstruction, despite the fact that he claims to be a mere mountain farmer and former slaveholder no less—one ultimately willing to give his life to protect the honor of his name and the rights to land in which his black benefactors have invested so much.

As for its Appalachian setting, little or nothing is made of the divided wartime loyalties that characterized much of the region during this era; in fact, the only white sentiments expressed in the film are those of ex-Confederates, this despite the reality that East Tennessee contained the southern highlands' (indeed, the South's) highest concentration of Unionist sentiment. Rather, the most relevant—and credible—feature of the film lies in its racial demographics, conforming as it does to the reality of a relatively small concentration of blacks in the mountain South. This in turn drove the apparent goodwill engendered here between former slaves and their former master, and the more likely viability of a biracial accommodation to the new economic and agricultural order of the day than would have been tolerated in the lowland South, with its far larger, and often more threatening, presence of freedmen and freedwomen.[39]

This is not to say that there was no racist resistance to such reforms, but the opposition expressed within the Vine Hill community seems easily quelled, leaving the more violent demonstration of such objections to outsiders in the form of the Klan's incursion from another county. Most locals, at least tacitly, seem to buy into Sommersby's scheme and its promises of profits, however widely that wealth must be spread. Yet even in this highland setting, the level of cooperation and interaction in this biracial communal enterprise seems to reflect more a presentist idealism of the 1990s than it does historic realities of the time and place it portrays, even as it acknowledges through its setting that this is one of few southern venues where such a scenario might even be contemplated with any degree of credibility.

• • • • • •

African Americans serve more as collective catalysts in two twentieth-century-set films in which racial conflict is integral to the power dynamics documented, though black characters rarely move center stage. Their presence provides much of the historical context of West Virginia coal miners organizing in 1920 (*Matewan*) and the recruitment of TVA workers in the mid-1930s (*Wild River*). Yet in both cases, they're marginalized as mere backdrops—or pawns—to the central elements of those struggles, with only a single black spokesman receiving any significant screen time in each.

In *Matewan* (1987), John Sayles—as writer and director—re-created the struggle between coal mine owners and their striking workers as it played out in the small southern West Virginia town in "Bloody" Mingo County in the weeks leading up to the massacre of May 19, 1920, a shoot-out on the main street that left ten men dead. Juggling a large cast of characters and never shunning the intricate and shifting dynamics that played out among locals and outsiders, this low-budget independent production was much acclaimed at the time of its release and has earned a reputation since as being not only among Sayles's most notable achievements but also one of the most historically astute film treatments of twentieth-century American labor struggles.[40] (It will be more fully discussed in those terms in chapter 6.)

Equally significant was the means by which Sayles gave those African American strikebreakers a leader and a voice. As he began to construct his cast of characters, screenwriter Sayles looked for those with what he called "an archetypal outer appearance"—the stranger in town, the violent lawman, the company man—which he then expanded into more humanized, well-rounded personalities.[41] Among those was a spokesman for the black workforce, and for that role, he thought back to an actual historical figure whose name he had come across in the early reading on West Virginia's coal strikes. He was known as Few Clothes, "the John Henry of coal," a giant black miner who wore battle scars from both the Spanish-American War and the Brownsville, Texas, race riot of 1906.[42]

According to historian Ronald Lewis, the elusive Few Clothes was actually a miner named Dan Chain, who became a local hero among United Mine Workers of America (UMWA) members by putting himself on the front lines of violent frays in the Paint Creek–Cabin Creek strikes of 1912 and 1913, just north of Mingo County. Somewhat ironically (given his first scene in Sayles's film), Few Clothes most distinguished himself by combating strikebreakers brought in by train to the Camp Creek coal fields. "His size, nerve, and fighting ability," Lewis writes, "made him a favorite among strikers when it was time to confront the transportation men at the railroad depots."[43] He was arrested and convicted for just that in 1912 and sentenced to five years' imprisonment. Pardoned two months later on the condition that he not participate in any further obstruction of trains or the passengers they delivered, Few Clothes soon showed up at UMWA headquarters in Charleston still dressed in his prison uniform, which may have been the origin of his nickname. Incarcerated again for further strike activity, the "black hero of Camp Creek" faded from public notice even as he became a fixture in West Virginia folklore, from which Sayles brought him back to life on film.[44]

It was a somewhat daring move on Sayles's part to drop a known—though perhaps not well known—participant in earlier mine wars into his

Few Clothes (James Earl Jones) leads a group of black strikebreakers as labor tensions escalate among West Virginia coal workers in *Matewan*.

particular piece of that struggle, even though there is no reason to think Few Clothes was actually involved in the events that unfolded at Matewan in 1920. It proved to be an effective decision, especially because it lured to the production the most prominent actor in the cast: James Earl Jones. In 1987, Jones was the only full-fledged star in a cast of otherwise promising but relative newcomers to the screen.[45]

Early in the film, we see UMWA representative Joe Kenehan (Chris Cooper) traveling by train to rally striking Matewan miners, when the train stops in a forest clearing before it reaches town. The doors of a boxcar are opened by coal company guards, who order a group of ten or twelve young black men inside to step out, then welcome them to their new home. Few Clothes, an older man and obviously the leader of this group transported up from Alabama, looks out warily and dares to ask, "Why ain't we stopping in town?" At that point a mob of mine workers rushes out from the woods, pelting the black men and the company guards with rocks and striking them with bats and clubs, yelling, "Goddamn scabbin' sons of bitches!" The train pulls away as Kenehan, from his passenger car window, watches as Few Clothes and his comrades are left to fend for themselves against their attackers.

We next see the black strikebreakers several scenes later as the mine company supervisor is distributing equipment to them and lecturing them on the terms of their employment. As they pass picks and shovels to each other, they're told that payment for their equipment will be deducted from their first paychecks, as will other expenses, such as use of the wash house, access to the company's medical doctor, and the cost of their train ride there. Looking more and more troubled at the mounting costs and being paid in scrip, redeemable only at the company store, the men look to Few Clothes, who finally speaks up, asking, "What's to keep y'all from jacking up them prices in your store?" Other than asking and recording his name, the company rep ignores his question and continues to reel off various expenses for which they'll be charged as he begins escorting them to the camp where they'll be staying. Once there, he says, somewhat tongue in cheek, "There's some Italian gentlemen who are very eager to meet you."[46]

This scene serves as a vital preface to a showdown shortly thereafter that captures the complexity of the tensions at play among an ever more defiant workforce over which Joe Kenehan must preside. At a secret late night meeting of UMWA strikers at a local restaurant, one agitated worker speaks for many when he states, "The first thing we got to have is alla these niggers and alla these dagoes that come in here to take our jobs thrown outta the mines," to which another responds, "Mines, hell, They got 'em in our houses! They're sitting at our tables now an sleepin' in our beds while we're out living under a piece of canvas at the back of the holler!" (The very act of going on strike led the mine owners to evict union members from company housing, which became a central issue in the escalating unrest within the community and ultimately the impetus for the massacre several weeks later.)

A sudden knock on the door brings the discussion to a halt. It is Few Clothes, who tentatively enters the room of this all-white gathering and says simply, "I got bidness with the union." When hostile miners respond with "Go home, nigger!" and "Goddam scab," it's the latter that sets off Few Clothes. "Watch your mouth, peckerwood!" he retorts, as only Jones could likely do with any credibility in this situation. "I been called nigger and I can't help that, the way white folks is, but I ain't never been called no scab and I ain't startin' up now. I go ton for ton loadin' coal with any man here and when I do I 'spect the same dollar for the same work." The restaurant owner, a key union operative, is quick to tell this unwelcome intruder: "You get outta this holler alive, son, you'll be doin' pretty good for yourself."

At that point, Kenehan takes the floor and, in an impassioned harangue, seeks to reason with the men to avoid violence and unite. Pointing to Few Clothes, he says, "You think this man is your enemy? This is a worker! They got you fighting white against colored, native against foreign, hollow against hollow, when you know there ain't but two sides in this world—them that work and them that don't. That all you got to know about the enemy." Kenehan continues to lecture them on the power and sheer logic of solidarity, insisting that everyone who walks out of the mines on their own steam—whether hired as scabs or not—earns their place in the union. When one man attempts a final but feeble protest, "All the dagoes and all the colored?" Kenehan responds with the last word: "That's what a union is, fellas. Better get used to it."

Few Clothes makes the case for joining the union to his fellow Alabamians; though well aware that they are caught between a rock (the mine owners) and a hard place (the mine workers), they cast their lot with the latter. And so a biracial, multiethnic coalition is formed, indicated primarily by the merger of activities in a single encampment just outside of town, built by and for locals, Italians, and black strikers; as one of the white strikers states in voice-over commentary: "All we got in common is our misery . . . and the least we can do is share it." This new spirit of unity is symbolized most adeptly by a joint music-making effort around a late night campfire, in which an Italian mandolin player's soulful ballad is taken up by a country fiddle and guitar, and finally by a blues riff on it all from a black harmonica player.

That coalition proves to be fleeting, or at least the black presence is soon marginalized, perhaps because Sayles felt that at this point, he had to defer to the historical reality that African Americans had not participated in the Matewan showdown of May 19. He built in an out for them in a scene of the strike committee as it plans a showdown. The Italians declare themselves in, stating, "You make syndacato, you do what syndacato decide. I listen to Joe." When asked if the Alabamians are in as well, Few Clothes asks, "Gonna be shooting white folks, right?" When that's confirmed, he reasons, "People hear about black people shootin' white people, no matter what it's for, there gonna be hell to pay." The union spokesman concurs, saying, "You got a point. Well, then, if you gentlemen will excuse us . . ." Thus ends the black presence in the film, (though not to be deprived of Jones's star power, Few Clothes continues to appear as a bodyguard for Kenehan, who's been explicitly targeted by the mine owners' hit men).

In *Matewan*, then, we see one of the few instances in an Appalachian-based film in which black characters, both as individuals and as a group, assert themselves and interact—if only momentarily—with white counterparts on relatively equal turf. As Sayles's own research documented, this reflects realities in both earlier and later coal wars, including Few Clothes's own proactive participation in the strikes of 1913 and that of other African American strikers in 1920 and 1921, in the aftermath of Matewan.[47] And yet for all the promise of James Earl Jones's formidable presence in the film, he and his fellow strikebreakers (and ultimately strikers) are phased out of the story as it builds to its dramatic climax. Few Clothes's last appearance is a very brief one the night before the massacre, in which he tells a black companion sitting before a campfire, " Best to stay out of town tomorrow." "Something up?" his friend asks, to which Few Clothes says, "I got a feelin'. You know how white folks get when they get excited." It's disappointing to see these contrived evasions—rationalized by Few Clothes, no less—that blacks shooting whites could exacerbate further hostilities or, worse, that they simply want to avoid confrontation in what they had come to view as a white men's fight. As reasonable an assumption as at least the first of these seems, it all too conveniently serves to shut African Americans out of the picture in the film's final act, even if it's done in the cause of historical truth.

• • • • • •

Tensions involving a later and somewhat different sort of black labor force play out in Elia Kazan's 1960 film *Wild River.* This film involves TVA dam construction and river clearance in the mid-1930s rather than the mining wars of the previous decade, but like *Matewan*, the presence of black workers makes up no more than a subplot of the central story Kazan tells (which is covered more fully in chapter 1). He infuses into the film racial issues both historical and topical, given the accelerating momentum of the civil rights movement in 1959 and 1960.

As in *Matewan*, the conflict in *Wild River* is driven by the appearance of an outside agent into a community to resolve an ongoing struggle. A TVA agent, Chuck Glover (Montgomery Clift), is sent from Washington to convince a stubborn old mountain woman, Ella Garth (Jo Van Fleet), to move off her family's island farm in the middle of the Tennessee River before the Garth property and all on it are flooded, including a number of black tenants. One tactic for forcing Mrs. Garth to leave is to deprive her of her workforce by wooing them away with the offer of New Deal jobs. Here, Kazan draws directly from William Bradford Huie's 1942 novel *Mud on the Stars*, in which the Garths' tenants—mostly cotton pickers—are lured away by better-paying government-funded work (through other New Deal–generated programs that were in place before the TVA began its operations in the area).[48] In the film, Chuck Glover is up front in urging the men on the island to consider employment opportunities with the TVA. This comes just after they've informed him that much of their reluctance to leave lies in the fact that "Miss Ella. She looks after us good," to which Glover replies, “Wouldn’t you rather look after yourselves?” and urges them to report to the TVA office the next morning, which most of them do.

When Glover reports that he’ll soon have at least twelve good black men from Garth’s Island as additional manpower for clearing the shoreline, the mayor of the local shoreside community is dubious about putting African Americans to work alongside whites, and then objects completely when Glover insists that they be paid the same wages. The following day, local businessmen meet to express their qualms about Glover’s idea, insisting that the black men work in separate gangs from the white workers and be paid a mere $2 a day, rather than the $5 paid to whites. “It would ruin our whole economy down here,” insists one of the men, and another adds, “Why, I can get you any number of the biggest, strongest, best-looking bucks in this county for $2 a day.” Finally, they warn Glover that they’re the “responsibles” in town, but that there are plenty of others “who aren’t so responsible. We can control them only to a point.”

In one of his more decisive actions—and perhaps his only act of courage—the low-key Glover refuses to back down on the issue of wages, and by the following day, he has offered jobs to nearly all the black men on Garth’s Island. We last see them and their families loading their wagons and heading for the ferry. The African Americans remain little more than pawns in this struggle between federal authority and local tradition, with Sam (the only black character consigned a name or a speaking part, however brief, and played by Robert Earl Jones, the father of James Earl Jones) the sole worker who puts his loyalty to Mrs. Garth before his self-interest. In his insistence that he won’t leave her, she’s allowed one of her more generous moments, or at best, a fleeting glimpse at paternalism still in play. “Git up! Look at you,” she scolds. “Never did have no brains, did you? Don’t you know what’s coming? . . . Now, you go on, Sam. I want you to.”

Kazan drives home the economic implications of Glover’s actions through a far more menacing encounter between Glover and R. J. Bailey, a landowner and one of those rougher “less responsibles” he’d been warned about. In a tense scene, Glover learns just what he’s up against when he finds Bailey waiting in his hotel room with a story to tell. Bailey informs him that he works four hundred acres of cotton, and that picking started the day before. “One of my best boys, Ben, he took off and joined that new gang you started, $5 a day. When I heard about it, I went back to the house, and cut me a stick about so long, and so thick.” He then sought out Ben, ordered him back to his house, took him behind the barn, and beat him severely. Then Bailey comes to the point, which is, on the surface at least, mere financial recompense for Ben's brief absence from his cotton fields: "Oh, he's all right now, in his thinking that is. Of course, he couldn't work yesterday, and couldn't work today. So I figure you owe me what I had to pay someone to replace him. Two times $2 a day—that equals $4. . . . You see, Mr. Glover, if you go on stealing my field hands at $5 a day, you're going to be dealing with a lot of my friends too."

When Glover refuses to hand over the $4, Bailey slugs him, takes the cash from him, and passes it along to the hotel clerk as he departs, instructing him to use it to buy Glover the best bottle of wine he can with it. Glover will pay an even heavier price for his liberal principles when that symbolic gesture—taking $4—later escalates into far more serious action by a Klan-like mob led by Bailey. Surrounding Glover in his car, they turn it over, drag both him and Sam out, and beat them unconscious, all the while claiming they're giving him a farewell party and "kicking him all the way back to Washington." (It's also noteworthy that the community's only organized opposition to the Tennessee Valley Authority comes from its racial hiring policies and not from any sense of solidarity with, or even sympathy for, the plight of Ella Garth and her family.)

In light of the more multifaceted and complex issues that historian Nancy Grant chronicles in her book *TVA and Black Americans*, Glover's stance and the hostility he stirred up as a result come across as simplistic. Racial equity in employment opportunities and wages were only two of many factors with which federal authorities had to contend in dealing with the grassroots democracy in the Tennessee valley, and rarely if ever did field agents dictate such policy at the local level; nor is there any evidence of white mob action directed at either TVA officials or black employees. Yet it's to Kazan's great credit that he never shied away from dramatizing the racial dilemmas posed by the TVA or the challenges and limitations faced by those well-intentioned progressives based in Washington—and occasionally in Tennessee. It's also worth noting that in order to do so, Kazan had to relocate to the Tennessee mountains a racial reality that actually played out in the cotton-producing area of northern Alabama (as described by Huie), which had a far greater concentration of black residents. (Grant states that 90 percent of all African Americans hired by the TVA were employed at three dams in the Muscle Shoals area of northwest Alabama, where blacks made up 40 to 50 percent of the populace, as opposed to only 10 percent for most areas of the Tennessee valley; more specifically, fewer than 4 percent of Bradley County residents were African American at the time.)[49]

While Kazan can't—and doesn't try to—defend Mrs. Garth's racial attitudes and behavior, he boldly incorporates those elements into his story in ways that few other filmmakers were doing in the 1950s.[50] His black characters are crucial to the struggle over the island and its evacuation. Even though they are rarely more than pawns in his hands or those of his white characters, he treats them with dignity and takes seriously their welfare along with that of those who own the land they work. It's only when he stands up for their rights that Glover demonstrates any genuine courage or moral certainty in his handling of the situation he's come south to resolve, and it's only in Mrs. Garth's final encounter with Sam, in which she urges him to leave the island along with everyone else, that she demonstrates any real concern for her (now former) employees—or, for that matter, concern for anyone other than herself. And finally, it is only the matter of racial equity that evokes any collective opposition from the local white community to the full-scale transformation that the TVA is so rapidly imposing on their world.[51]

• • • • • •

Ultimately, one can make the case that all four of these films fit into Hollywood's "white savior" scenario or "mockingbird syndrome"—a reference to the classic *To Kill a Mockingbird* (1962), in which Gregory Peck as Atticus Finch serves as the white hero who fights for racial justice for black victims who can't fight such battles for themselves.[52] To varying degrees, August King, Jack Sommersby, Joe Kennehan, and Chuck Glover each serve an Atticus Finch–like function in the racial scenarios built around them, in that each serves as the most active agent in behalf of an African American constituency or cause in the face of considerable opposition from the local white populace.

Still, it's the passivity of the black workforces in *Sommersby* and *Wild River* that perhaps most differentiates them from the black strikebreakers in *Matewan* or the young slave girl on the run from an abusive master in *The Journey of August King*. In all four films, a sole spokesperson was delegated to represent the black agenda onscreen; indeed, they are virtually the only African American characters with speaking parts. In each case, they defer to the agenda set by some representative of the white establishment, even if it's not an agenda embraced by whites at large. The only full-bodied protagonist here is Annalees, given that it is her escape that drives the plot; but even she takes a back seat to the conscience-ridden title character, through whose shifting mindset the film unfolds. In the Reconstruction-set drama

Sommersby, in which one would have expected racial issues to be at the forefront, only Joseph makes fleeting appearances to speak for the freed black community, and he pays a heavy price for that assertiveness in that he alone is attacked by the local Klan-like mob.

In the two twentieth-century-set films, the black spokesmen are coincidentally played by the two Joneses, father and son. In *Wild River*, the former, Sam, embodies the complacency of his fellow tenants, though even they take more initiative in sneaking away from the island under cover of darkness, while Sam alone seems reluctant to abandon his employer, Mrs. Garth, and offers to stay as long as she does. Rather, it is a white man, Chuck Glover, who identifies their plight and fights for their interests in confrontations that show him perched firmly on his most courageous and morally high ground, even if he's using them primarily as bargaining chips in establishing a new labor source to carry out the TVA's agenda.

In contrast, the character of Few Clothes in *Matewan*, portrayed by James Earl Jones, is far more forceful and self-assured in articulating the interests of his fellow Alabamian strikebreakers. (For that matter, he's also the most forceful and self-assured character in his much smaller role as the judge in *Sommersby*.) Yet ultimately Few Clothes, like Joseph and Sam and those they represent, recedes into the background once the final showdown approaches and the focus tightens on the plight of the white superiors—Joe Kenehan, in this case, and Jack Sommersby and both Ella Garth and Chuck Glover for the others. Thus, the impact and agency of black characters remain limited; in the end, it's left to the white male protagonists to create and orchestrate the various opportunities in which African Americans are invited to be at least partial beneficiaries.

3 The Civil War

Highland Home Fronts as Holy Hells

Given the relative scarcity of Hollywood treatments of the Civil War home front—*Friendly Persuasion* (1956), *Raintree County* (1957), *The Free State of Jones* (2016), and the biggest of them all, *Gone with the Wind* (1939), are among the few major examples that come to mind—it is striking that at least five such films have been set in wartime Appalachia. Produced between 1961 and 2003, they make for a disparate sampler. Three are based on novels—*The Little Shepherd of Kingdom Come* (1961), *Menace on the Mountain* (1970), and *Cold Mountain* (2003)—the first and last of which were major best sellers when published in 1903 and 1997, respectively. The other two are based on original screenplays—*Shenandoah* (1965) and *Pharaoh's Army* (1995), though the latter was inspired by an actual incident. Three are mainstream studio productions, one an independent film, and one a made-for-television movie. Two are set in Kentucky, two in North Carolina, and one in Virginia.

Despite these variables, all five films embrace similar themes drawn from the experiences of highland families and communities caught in the throes of the region's brutal inner war, exacerbated by a wide range of factors, from divided loyalties and material hardships to guerrilla and other forms of irregular warfare. All five dramatize—for the most part, quite effectively—the blurring of lines between the home front and combat zones that typified so much of the conflict in the mountain South and that often made the struggles there such "holy hells." As such, all five films share a decidedly antiwar stance, with little attempt to privilege either the Union or the Confederate cause through plot or character.

Southern Appalachia's Civil War often meant simply the efforts of mountain residents—usually futile—to maintain their neutrality and keep the war at bay. Most such struggles played out on an intensely localized level and were usually far removed from the bigger, more momentous military campaigns waged elsewhere. As with other screen depictions of the southern mountain experience, there is considerable truth behind these cinematic renderings of the assorted perils and traumas with which so many men, women, and children had to cope and which in some cases (though by no means all) they triumphed over. Considered collectively, these films serve to remind us of just how many different forms the region's irregular conflict took, with guerrillas, bushwhackers, and other renegades representing only one manifestation of the unconventional warfare that made these home fronts so traumatizing for many Appalachian residents.[1]

• • • • • •

The Little Shepherd of Kingdom Come was based on John Fox's 1903 novel, a classic of Appalachian literature and one of the most widely read novels set in the mountain South. Released in 1961, this was the third screen adaptation of Fox's best seller; it followed two silent versions produced in 1920 and 1928 as part of a vast wave of mountain-based melodramas, or "hillbilly films"—more than four hundred over the course of the 1910s and 1920s.[2] The 1961 version was produced by 20th Century Fox in color and in the recently devised CinemaScope, which suggests that the studio saw it as more than a mere B movie, even though its casting, its screenplay, and other production values reflect a lower standard of quality. It was filmed in California's San Bernardino National Forest, just east of Los Angeles, which bears little resemblance to Appalachian Kentucky. This was an early film for director Andrew V. McLaglen, who went on to earn a reputation for a number of successful westerns throughout the 1960s and into the 1970s, many of which served as vehicles for aging stars John Wayne and James Stewart, including the latter's *Shenandoah* (which, unlike *Little Shepherd*, is generally recognized as one of McLaglen's best).

Probably no writer was more influential in conveying southern highland life to a national readership at the turn of the century than was John Fox Jr. Born in 1862 in the Bluegrass region of Kentucky, Fox was long fascinated by the contrast in that section of the state and its mountains to the east, which he came to know only as an adult. When he returned south in 1890, after a Harvard education and a stint as a journalist in New York City, he settled across the state line in Big Stone Gap, Virginia, where his father and brothers had relocated as part of a vast influx of outsiders taking advantage of the coal boom underway there. The mountain culture into which he was thrust and the tensions between locals and outsiders (some involving the Fox family) provided great fodder for John Jr., the writer, and inspired an outpouring of both fictional and nonfictional work. In 1901, he published a collection of essays and personal observations titled *Blue-Grass and Rhododendron*, contrasting the two regions.[3]

Fox was particularly intrigued by the divergent wartime loyalties evident in these two regions of his home state and soon opted for fiction as yet another means of dramatizing these differences at that most historically relevant juncture, which for many remained a source of intersectional tensions at the century's end.[4] That work became his first novel, *The Little Shepherd of Kingdom Come*. It's the coming-of-age story of Chad Buford, an orphan boy who, faced with the threat of a forced apprenticeship under a menacing neighbor, leaves the remote Black Mountain area of the Cumberlands and, with his dog Jack, finds shelter and sustenance with another family, the Turners, in the nearby valley community of Kingdom Come. After a year or so, during which he herded sheep for the Turners (hence the novel's title), Chad accompanies his new guardian and other local loggers on a rafting trip down to the Bluegrass region. What was meant to be a short visit turns into a long-term stint in Lexington when a well-to-do planter, Major Buford, takes Chad in, educates him, and provides him entrée into the city's elite social circle.

Over the years, Chad adjusts well to this new world and reaches manhood just as the sectional crisis comes to a head, and Kentucky, while remaining in the Union, finds itself internally divided along the lines that so intrigued Fox. "In no other State in the Union," he declares, "was the fratricidal character of the coming war to be so marked as in Kentucky, in no other State was the national drama to be so fully played to the bitter end." While enamored of Lexington society and much indebted to its Confederate-prone elite, Chad never forgot his mountain roots, and taking a stand proved a quandary. "If he lifted his hand against the South," wrote Fox, "he must strike at the heart of all he loved best, to which he owed most. If against the Union, at the heart of all that was the best in himself. In him the pure spirit that gave birth to the nation was fighting for life."[5] Ultimately, he makes the painful decision to back the Union cause and, in so doing, alienates himself from his Bluegrass benefactors, including his sweetheart. The latter half of the novel becomes a wartime melodrama in which these loyalties, old and new, play out on battlefields as well as on home fronts in both regions.

McLaglen's film adheres to the bare bones of the plot, at least for the first two-thirds of the narrative, but fails to capture the spirit of Fox's prose or the complexity of issues that he explored in considerably more depth through Chad Buford's saga. Perhaps the most serious departure from the novel is that onscreen Chad is an adult throughout and played by a decidedly B actor at best, Jimmie Rodgers, better known as a popular singer than as a movie star. Thus, the coming-of-age and loss-of-innocence themes so integral to the book and the basis for so much of its appeal to young readers are lost in the film, as is much of the logic in the film's first half, when a fully grown man (Rodgers was twenty-seven years old at the time) loses his foster family; is legally bound to yet another guardian, the brutish Nathan Dillon (George Kennedy); and is then adopted by Caleb Turner and his family in Kingdom Come. By compressing the novel's chronological span of eight years to a mere two (based on the 1859 date on the tombstone of his foster father in the opening scene), the arc of Chad's growth and maturation is short-circuited and not nearly as convincing or as moving as Fox's prose, which moves a ten-year-old into late adolescence by the time he must make the decision to become a soldier.

Once Chad makes the move to Lexington (where some scenes were actually filmed), the screenplay offers mere lip service to the adjustments required for a mountain boy—who states at one point, "I've always lived up high"—to settle in the flatlands of the Bluegrass region. Yet such distinctions, including the political sentiments embodied by each section—the Bluegrass region as solidly Confederate; the mountains as solidly Unionist—remain simplistic and relatively unexplored in the film. Curiously, the issue of whether or not Kentucky will secede from the Union is never raised. Chad's wrenching struggle as to where he should cast his allegiance—which plays out over three full chapters in the novel—is resolved more abruptly in the film. Just as Major Buford (Chill Wills), decked out in perhaps the most garish Confederate uniform ever depicted onscreen, presents his young charge with a slightly more modest one of his own, Chad tells him he's going to enlist in the Union army, and explains to his guardian only that "all my ancestors came from the North," to which the major responds with tears in his eyes, "For a while, it was like having a son. Good-bye, son. I pray to God we never meet again." The movie also makes clear that in turning against his benefactor, Chad is also alienating other Lexington friends, including the Dean family, whose daughter Margaret he had been courting.

Perhaps not surprisingly, slavery as an issue plays no part in their decisions, at least as articulated on either side. John Fox made much of Chad's racial innocence; a key scene in the novel is of his first encounter with blacks, which comes only after he moves to Kingdom Come. In a much quoted exchange, Chad asks his companion Tom, "Whut've them fellers got on their faces?" When Tom responds that "lots o' folks from yo' side of the mountains nuver have seed a nigger. Sometimes it skeers 'em." "Hit don't skeer me," Chad insists. In the film, slaves appear as marginal characters as soon as the scene shifts to Lexington (there are none in Kingdom

Come), though Chad never expresses any curiosity or apprehension about them. And just as the ownership of human property remains an unspoken factor in regard to the local elite's Confederate leanings in the film (though Fox made clear that their slaveholding status drove their decision), Chad's decision is also devoid of any racial sentiment. Even Fox noted that Chad's exposure to slavery had been so brief that "it never troubled his soul. . . . Unlike the North, the boy had no prejudice, no antagonism, no jealousy, no grievance to help him in his struggle."[6]

Chad heads for a Union recruiting station in Cincinnati, where he runs into Caleb Turner, who heads up a company there and makes Chad its dispatcher. He confides to Caleb how hard it was to turn on his Lexington friends, noting, in a direct quote from Fox's prose, "It's mighty hard for a man to find his belonging place." The last third of the film follows Chad's military exploits, though in much more compressed form than in the novel. While much of the actual fighting is presented through poorly done montages, the sheer focus on military action distinguishes *Little Shepherd* from the other Civil War–based films considered here, in which battlefield clashes are portrayed only fleetingly, if at all, and have little relevance to the plot.[7] Assigned to dispatch duty, Chad passes through Kingdom Come on one occasion and learns that the Turners and other families have been plagued by Nathan Dillon, Chad's early nemesis, who is the leader of a pro-Confederate band of guerrillas preying on Unionist families in the valley. Chad is on hand when they swoop onto the Turner farm and initiate a shoot-out; he fires the shot that kills Dillon's son, thus intensifying the vendetta Dillon already holds against Chad for evading his attempt to claim him as an apprentice.

These divided loyalties return to haunt Chad when he becomes part of an occupying force in Lexington (as happened in September 1861) and is charged with removing a Confederate flag from the Dean family home, which leads to a bitter showdown between Margaret and her former beau. When the Union forces make the Deans' home their headquarters, they discover son Richard (Margaret's brother), a captain with John Hunt Morgan's raiders, hiding in the attic. It's left to their former friend, the Union mountain boy, to make the case for sparing him execution as a guerrilla, given that he was captured at home, where he'd come to bury his dead father, and thus merited status as a mere prisoner of war. Ultimately Richard is spared, and for the first but not the last time we see Chad's capacity to empathize with those on both sides of the war's great divide, thanks to his bi-regional and bicultural experiences, as charted through the first half of the film.

The film's climax comes as Chad is ordered to guide a Union regiment into the Kentucky mountains to stop Morgan's Confederate force as it attempts to head east into Virginia. Almost immediately we are thrust into a full-scale but crudely staged battle on what looks like a vast and barren plain (that doesn't remotely resemble any southern highland terrain).[8] There, all the major male characters—Chad's friends and foes—converge and face off against each other. Chad finds himself in face-to-face combat with his nemesis, Nathan Dillon, and this time kills him. His two benefactors—the Confederate Major Buford, who had once vowed never to see his adopted son again, and his Union commander and guardian, Caleb Turner—are both mortally wounded and face agonizing death scenes in Chad's arms. Tearfully, Chad turns to prayer, vowing to God that he'll return and bury both men together in a single grave, reasoning that neither man was in the wrong, as each fought for a cause in which he genuinely believed. "If you let me live, Lord, when this war is over I'm coming back right here to this place," Chad prays in Jimmie Rodgers's most saintly, even sanctimonious, mode. "Maybe by then I'll know which of their two ways is my belonging place—the bluegrass or the mountains. Amen."

Perhaps the most radical departure from the novel is the film's conclusion. Fox ended his narrative with Chad returning to Lexington and reconciling with Margaret, who's forgiven him for his Union service. She encourages him to settle down and take over Major Buford's plantation. By the novel's end, it looks as if Margaret has won him over. In the film, Chad, recognizing that he's still a mountain man at heart, returns to Kingdom Come and reunites with Melissa Turner, stating in a voice-over, "I know my belonging place now." Beyond his dueling romantic options, Chad's highland acquaintances, most notably the Turners, are more consistently sympathetic characters than those in the Bluegrass region in both Fox's novel and McLaglen's film. Yet the film ultimately opted for a happy ending by sending Chad back to the Cumberlands. In so doing, it endorsed the values of the Appalachian culture as those of its hero, thus making that choice—a return to his roots—his most viable, and satisfactory, option. Fox, on the other hand, eschewed so simple and sentimental an ending by tipping his hat, and Chad's, to his own Bluegrass roots, which makes for a more nuanced and perhaps less sentimental resolution than does the screen version.[9]

. . . . . .

Andrew McLaglen returned to some of the same themes four years later when he brought *Shenandoah* to the screen.[10] This time he worked from an original screenplay, shaped specifically for James Stewart (in the first of four films the director and actor would make together). This 1965 feature, originally to be titled "Fields of Honor," proved to be one of the star's biggest successes of the decade, both critically and at the box office, and his performance has been widely acclaimed as one of the best of his later career.[11] While some critics at the time dismissed *Shenandoah* as what one termed "an imitation John Ford Civil War–lite family saga," film historians since have shown more appreciation for it.[12] With Vietnam looming on the horizon, one critic called it "the most powerful anti-war statement of the sixties."[13] In his study of Civil War films, Gary Gallagher noted that *Shenandoah* marked a turning point in "Hollywood's relationship with the Lost Cause."[14] Not only was it as blatant an antiwar film as had yet been produced about the Civil War; it was also the first such film set in the South to offer a strong antislavery stance, and perhaps most notably, it acknowledged more openly than any film up to that time that slavery was the primary impetus for the war.[15]

Set somewhere in the northern end of the Shenandoah valley (based only on a casual reference to Winchester in the vicinity), the movie tells the story of a prosperous widower, Charlie Anderson (Stewart), who works a large farm with the help of his six husky sons, all but one an adult—and, as he states proudly, with no slaves. If *Shenandoah* eschews an explicit mountain setting more than the other films under discussion here, the sentiments of the Andersons and the means by which they are ultimately pulled into the conflict accurately reflect the attitudes and actions of many southern highlanders. So too is their socioeconomic situation, which put them among the region's elite. Such affluent farmers often dominated the broad, fertile river valleys of Appalachia, though very few with holdings as large as the Andersons' five hundred acres—planted primarily in wheat and corn—would have operated without slave labor.[16] (Much to the chagrin of many Virginians, the film was shot near Eugene, Oregon, where the area's wheat and corn fields and surrounding wilderness passed, fairly credibly, for the title locale.)[17]

Yet opposition to slavery, such as that espoused by the Andersons, was not unknown in the Shenandoah valley; in fact, the mixed religious and ethnic makeup of the northern part of the valley, particularly that of nonconformist groups such as Mennonites, Methodists, and Anabaptists (or "Dunkers"), meant a significant streak of antislavery conviction in parts of the Shenandoah that generated considerable local tensions in some areas.[18] Yet there's no indication of any such denominational affiliation to account for so admirable a sentiment in Charlie Anderson and his offspring. Nor was the correlation between non-slaveholding status and antiwar attitudes conveyed in the film nearly as pronounced or as clear-cut in actuality as one might expect for the region. Nevertheless, the logic of such a stance is readily apparent—one might even say belabored—as articulated by the Anderson patriarch; no film, in fact, makes neutrality more central, or more virtuous, than does *Shenandoah*.[19]

The movie opens with a clash between Union and Confederate forces (one so generic that it and other battle scenes consist of recycled footage from 1957's *Raintree County*).[20] Hearing cannon fire, one of the Anderson sons comments, "They come closer every day, Pa." "Are they on our land?" Charlie asks, and when told that they're not, he retorts, "Then it doesn't concern us, does it?" What follows are three extended scenes that make up much of the film's first half, in which the elder Anderson pontificates on why this war being waged up and down the valley, often within earshot of his farm, has no meaning for him or his family.

At the family dinner table that night, he engages in a Socratic dialogue with his offspring when one dares to challenge his neutral stance on the grounds that "we're Virginians and I believe that anything that concerns Virginians concerns us." (The mere fact that such issues are being raised suggests that the film is set early in the war, though later references reveal the time frame to be late summer and early fall of 1864, which seems far too late for the airing of such sentiments.) After establishing that none of his boys own slaves or ever would, Anderson asks them, "Suppose you had a friend who owned slaves, and suppose somebody's gonna come and take 'em away from him, would you help him fight to keep 'em?" to which another son, presumably speaking for all, responds, "No, sir, I wouldn't. I don't see any reason to fight for something I don't believe is right, and I don't think a real friend would ask me to."

The next day, Anderson has to make the same case when a group of Confederate soldiers led by Colonel Johnson, an acquaintance of his, stops by for water. Johnson asks the old man, "When are you going to take the war seriously, Mr. Anderson?" and then proceeds to tell him that they're short of men and that it "seems strange to quite a few people around here that none of your sons is in the army." He then announces that the real reason they've come is to take the sons. (Again, the fact that it's been two years since the Confederacy's Conscription Act went into effect and that they never invoke the law to do so makes the story's timing suspect.) Anderson says that he'll let his sons answer for themselves. He calls the boys to gather

Charlie Anderson (James Stewart) is determined to keep the war at bay and his sons at home in *Shenandoah*.

around the visiting troops in the yard and tells Johnson to give them one good reason "why I should send my family, that took me a lifetime to raise, down that road like a bunch of fools to do somebody else's fighting?" Johnson replies simply, "Virginia needs all her sons." Anderson is quick to counter with one of the film's most quoted lines: "That may be so, Johnson, but these are my sons. They don't belong to the state. . . . We never asked anything of the state and never expected anything. We do our own living and thanks to no man for the right." (Here as elsewhere, the only basis for allegiance expressed is to Virginia; neither the term "Confederacy" nor "the South" is ever used in the film, which for this state rings true for many, if not most, of its residents, including its army's commander.)[21]

Anderson knows he speaks for his offspring as well and knows he's safe in letting them make their own choice. "But if any of my boys wants to join in," he states, "he's free to do it. If you wanna dress up like these fellas, go ahead. Here's your chance." The sons say nothing, and the troops head off, with no further challenge from Johnson or his soldiers. (To me, one of the film's more serious flaws is that not one of the sons, some of whom seem to be in their thirties, has a mind of his own. The script gives them little to say or do other than follow their father's orders and bow to his judgment, more often than not in monosyllabic responses, if they speak at all.) The troops ride away, only to be ambushed and killed by Union renegades a mile or so away. As the Andersons inspect the dead bodies, one son asks, "Does it concern us now?" to which his father gives no response.

Just as conscription was seen by southern highlanders, in particular, as one of the most oppressive of the Confederacy's overreaching policies, later legislation—impressment and tax-in-kind laws passed in the spring of 1863—were equally as resented. This is the next thing that the Andersons must confront, thus providing Charlie yet a third opportunity to tout his noninterventionist convictions. Curiously, it is a group of Federal purchasing agents—finely dressed civilians all—who approach the farm seeking to buy horses and mules, rather than Confederate officials, perhaps a means of making the point that for those attempting to claim neutral status, both sides could be equally threatening and abusive.[22]

When Anderson tells the agents that their animals are not for sale, they respond that they're authorized to confiscate what they can't buy. When the youngest son, a mere sixteen, asks what "confiscate" means, his pa replies simply, "Steal." One of the agents suggests that "he sort of figured that anybody too yellow to fight wouldn't mind making a couple of dollars off the war." Those prove to be fighting words to the honorable Andersons, and they launch into a full-scale brawl that's played as much for laughs as for rollicking action. Suddenly a gunshot brings the fracas to a halt, and the camera pans around to show Jennie, the single daughter in the Anderson clan, aiming a rifle at the intruders and declaring, "If you and these other animals don't get off this farm this minute, I'm gonna shoot you stone dead." She's as belligerent as her brothers and, as such, demonstrates another basic element of most of these films and a basic truth in Appalachia's Civil War: the proactive role of women as combatants in defending their homes and their families. Ironically, Jennie has far more personality—and backbone—than do any of her brothers and is a far more interesting character.

Shortly thereafter, the war does engage the Andersons when the youngest son, referred to by his father as simply Boy (though it's also obvious that he's his favorite), is approached by a detachment of Union troops while fishing with his black companion, Gabriel, who's owned by a neighboring farmer. Because Boy is wearing a Confederate cap he had retrieved from the stream, the troops take him prisoner. He tells Gabriel to go tell his pa, which leads a black soldier to speak up and tell him, "You don't have to tell him nothin'; you're free." In what must surely be the first integrated Civil War unit portrayed in a feature film, it is a blatant falsification and a nod no doubt to mid-1960s presentism, coinciding as it did with the climax of the civil rights movement.

Once Gabriel has delivered his message, Jennie asks him if his master might be looking for him. The slave boy responds that he's gone to Richmond and left a "field boss" in charge, then asks Jennie, "Man said I's free; don't that mean I don't gotta go back?" She assures him that he doesn't. "You mean I can go down that road as far as you like?" he asks. "You can even run if you like," she replies.[23] In short, an Anderson has condoned self-emancipation for local slaves, yet another indication of the family's racial enlightenment and disengagement from their slaveholding neighbors.

When Charlie Anderson learns that his youngest son has been abducted by Confederate forces, he finally makes the pronouncement regarding the war that he's so stubbornly held at arm's length: "Now it concerns us." He and his sons quickly mobilize to go in search of Boy; as they gather on horseback in front of the house, Jennie shows up, dressed in one of her brother's clothes and mounted as well.[24] Charlie tells her she's a woman and to go back, which prompts a nice little speech from her: "Yes, I'm a woman, but I don't see anybody here that I can't outrun, outride, and outshoot. I'll unstrap for you, Papa; and I'll unhook, and I'll even sit here and watch you ride out of sight." "And then what?" Charlie asks. "Then I'll follow," she answers, to which her father capitulates, "That's what I thought." So off they go, where perhaps for the first time in these films (but by no means the last) a woman is drawn into the conflict well beyond the home front and on her own terms as a fully engaged combatant (though she also seems to do all the cooking for her menfolk en route).[25]

The second half of the film consists largely of the Anderson family's quest to find Boy and the formidable obstacles—military and otherwise—they face in doing so. Their confrontations with enemy forces (and given that they view Confederate as well as Union troops as antagonists, that means almost all their encounters) could be characterized as forms of irregular warfare. They ambush a train, release all the captives it's carrying to northern prisons, then burn it; one son is killed by random sniper fire from an inexperienced adolescent sentry; and back home, the one married son and his wife, who have stayed behind with their newborn baby, are viciously slaughtered by a band of scavenging deserters.

Boy himself manages to escape independently of his family's efforts and, with several fellow fugitives, eventually stumbles upon an outpost of compatriots (not quite outliers or bushwhackers but hardly regular troops, either). The film's only military action is an extended battle scene between this group and a Yankee contingent complete with cannon, artillery, and a cavalry charge. Improbably Gabriel, now in blue and part of a biracial company, shows up just in time to save Boy, who's been shot in the leg.

Soon after dragging himself and his family home through a desolate, burned-out landscape, with one son now a corpse draped across his horse, no sign yet of Boy or his fate, and having learned the news of his murdered son and daughter-in-law, Charlie Anderson sums up the ultimate meaning of the war in the last of several soliloquys he delivers at his wife's grave. "There's nothing much I can tell you about this war," he muses, before ironically delivering as succinct yet moving an antiwar statement as has ever been captured on film. "It's like all wars, I suppose. The undertakers are winning. The politicians will talk a lot about the glory of it. And the old men will talk about the need of it. And the soldiers . . . they just want to go home." The camera then pans the site, which his wife once occupied alone but is now surrounded by three fresh mounds of dirt. "I guess you're not so lonely now, Martha," he concludes. One film scholar only slightly exaggerated when he suggested that *Shenandoah* is "as effective an indictment against both the futility of war and the toll of human suffering as is contained in *All Quiet on the Western Front*," the widely regarded 1930 film based on German veteran Erich Maria Remarque's classic antiwar novel.[26]

Things brighten up briefly in the film's final scene, a well-earned emotional payoff, as Boy comes limping down the aisle during a Sunday church service and falls into the arms of his much relieved father as the small congregation bursts into song—the Doxology.

• • • • • •

It would be nearly a quarter century after *Shenandoah* before Hollywood made its next major feature film focused squarely on the war, *Glory* (1989). But one of the more interesting cinematic treatments of the war as experienced in Southern Appalachia appeared just five years after *Shenandoah*—on television. In 1968, Walt Disney acquired the rights to a historical novel written for young adults before it was published and moved quickly to adapt it as a two-part movie for its long-running Sunday night television series, Disney's *Wonderful World of Color*. The movie aired in the spring of 1970 and was distributed as a theatrical film abroad two years later.[27] Titled *Menace on the Mountain*, the book was written by Mary Hancock, a midwesterner who wrote magazine features and historical nonfiction before she moved to western North Carolina, where she was inspired by the region's unconventional Civil War history. What began as a nonfiction work, based on considerable archival research, turned at some point into a book of what was then termed "juvenile fiction."[28]

Perhaps unusual for that genre, Hancock stressed the historical reality within which her story played out. In an "Author's Note" at the end of the novel, again directed at young readers, she stated that "many of the background events are based on fact. The bushwhacker raiders of the Civil War period played a significant, if little known, role in the history of the Southern mountains. . . . The local names for the outlaw deserters and draft dodgers varied from area to area, but the plunderers had one thing in common. Acknowledging no authority or loyalties, they banded together to prey on the helpless." She followed this with lengthy excerpts from the reminiscence of a "real-life counterpart" to her thirteen-year-old protagonist, describing his "bushwhacker-terrorized boyhood" and those of Confederate veterans confirming the same conditions that so destabilized highland home fronts as they witnessed them in moving through the region late in the war.[29]

To the credit of both Hancock and Walt Disney Studios, the film version remained unusually faithful to the novel. (The author stated that she was very pleased with the adaptation, noting that the only discernible change was that "the villain was even more villainous.")[30] What makes *Menace on the Mountain*—both the novel and the film—so notable is that while it is geared for young audiences, it never shirks from portraying many of the grim realities of Appalachia's inner war. In fact, it provides as full and reasonably accurate an account of this facet of that conflict—bushwhacker harassment of civilians and the localized tensions brought on by divided loyalties—as any of Hollywood's efforts to capture that experience on film.

Like the classic Disney film *Old Yeller* (1957), *Menace on the Mountain* focuses on the travails of a mother and her three children (the youngest of whom is played by an eight-year-old Jodie Foster) while the man of the house is away, and a beloved family pet who serves as the catalyst for at least some of the crises faced on the home front. In this case, it's a pig rather than a dog, and Hancock wisely refrained from naming her novel for the pet in question, Blossom. Blossom belongs to the McIver children, especially the oldest son, thirteen-year-old Jamie (Mitch Vogel), whose father has long been gone, fighting in the Confederate army—though there's never any indication as to whether he went voluntarily or was conscripted.[31]

Set in North Carolina's Blue Ridge Mountains (though obviously filmed elsewhere, much of it in California's Sierra Nevada), the film opens as Jamie walks from his family farm to the nearby crossroads store to sell some produce, eggs, and other farm goods. Along with *Cold Mountain*, it's one of the few films that addresses the near collapse of local economies in much of the wartime South, especially in the mountains, by 1864 (when the story begins). Profiteering merchants, a shortage of cash, and drastic inflation all contributed to financial devastation for many mountain families and communities. When Jamie tells a family friend, Mr. Eberhardt, that they're in desperate need of "cash money and salt," Eberhardt warns him about the storekeeper: "That may take you a while. Ole Ben Forrest is skimming the hides off of almost everyone." He also acknowledges that there are larger forces at play as well, adding, "Nothing he can do about it. Yankee blockades cut most major goods to a dribble." Both are oversimplifications, of course, but are nevertheless worthy bits of background for a Disney television movie.[32]

Frustrated at how little cash or salt he received from Forrest, Jamie sees a flyer announcing a bounty for anyone who can kill a panther that's been wreaking havoc on livestock in the neighborhood and decides to go after it. That puts him at odds with Poss Timmerlake, an outsized bully (the "more villainous" villain Hancock referred to) who insists on exclusive dibs on both the panther and the bounty. He even tries to force Jamie to use Blossom as bait to lure the panther into shooting range. (Panthers were still fairly common in the North Carolina mountains during the 1860s, perhaps even more so by 1864 given that wildlife in general proliferated during the years when so many of the region's hunters were off at war.)[33]

In his own quest for the panther, Jamie stumbles upon a Union soldier hiding in a cave nearby. The "Yank" is on the verge of attacking Jamie when he collapses from weakness; somehow Jamie drags him unconscious back to his cabin, intending nothing more than to turn him over to the local marshal, who's pro-Confederate, as the majority of the community seems to be. They learn that their northern charge, named Aaron Galt, had escaped from a prison in Salisbury and was heading across the mountains to Union-occupied territory in East Tennessee. Mrs. McIver (Patricia Crowley) shows far more sympathy toward him than Jamie does, reasoning that if her husband was a prisoner in the North, she would hope that someone would provide him the same sort of care she's willing to provide this Yank. Jamie wakes up in the middle of the night to discover Galt sneaking out of the cabin with a roasted chicken in hand. The boy aims his rifle at him and orders him to stop, but the now well-nourished prisoner is defiant enough to say go ahead and shoot, that he'd rather die than be forced to return to prison. Jamie can't bring himself to shoot, and the fugitive sets out on his trek toward more friendly turf.

This episode reflects a basic and widely chronicled reality of the war in western North Carolina: the proliferation of fugitive prisoners of war, who took much the same route westward from prison camps—especially those in Salisbury, North Carolina, and Columbia, South Carolina—to somewhat more security in Union-occupied Tennessee. Quite a few wrote accounts of their escapes—some of which Hancock consulted when researching her novel—in which they described the mixed receptions they received from Carolina highlanders, depending on their allegiances and how deeply they were held.[34]

Shortly thereafter, while in pursuit of a runaway Blossom, Jamie stumbles upon his far more lethal enemy, the panther, and shoots it just as its about to pounce on the hapless pig. When the news of his conquest spreads through the town, a much resentful Poss confronts the lad with a whip. (The film, like the novel, juxtaposes these scenes to indicate the parallels between the hostile threats Jamie—and, by extension, other highlanders—faced from the natural world and from his human neighbors.) In a rather stilted incident, a three-man posse walks into the town square at that point and declares that Poss is under arrest "for failing to conscript for army service." Though at least acknowledging conscription, which the two previous films ignore, little about this scene rings true, from the timing of the move—late in 1864 and directed at a man who's been a public presence and nuisance for much of the war and thus easily accessible well before this point—to the ineffectualness of the threesome authorized to take this big brute in. In effect, Poss laughs in their faces, punches them out, and then gallops out of town, contemptuous of everyone he leaves in his dust.

Sometime later, as Jamie and his family are being presented with the bounty money for the panther, a wounded man straggles into town and announces that a band of bushwhackers, led by Poss, is on the rampage and headed their way. When one of the panicked townspeople asks where the army is to protect them (an odd question given the absence of any army presence in the area up to then), the wounded man answers, "Ain't you heard? Lee's done surrendered; there ain't no army protection now." This comes as a surprise to the locals, as well as to viewers, given how vaguely the narrative's timeline has been established (a flaw shared by most of these films). Yet with that statement, the film addresses head-on a little acknowledged truth about the war in the mountains: that it didn't end with the surrender at Appomattox. Nearly half of General George Stoneman's monthlong raid through western North Carolina took place after that landmark event of April 9, and more relevant here, bushwhacker activity took on a new urgency in some pockets of the region later in the spring and on through the summer, just as it does in the film.[35]

The bushwhackers appear soon thereafter. They are portrayed as a malicious, drunken band of misfits and ne'er-do-wells; some wear Confederate gray and a few are in Union blue, though most sport no military garb at all. (There is no indication as to where they've been or what they've been doing until mid-April 1865, although many such gangs formed only in the war's latter weeks and months.) Poss, in his ever more vindictive stance toward the McIvers, forces them out of their cabin and takes possession of it, a tactic described in several firsthand accounts, including at least one that Hancock drew on.[36] A montage of his gang's devilment follows, with scenes of their rampages across the county, shooting up towns, burning barns and houses, and plundering produce and livestock, which make for boisterous and drunken feasts back at the McIvers' cabin. All this is crosscut with the increasingly desperate efforts by Jamie and his mother to forage anything remotely edible for themselves and the two smaller children, who grow noticeably weaker. Finally, their father comes limping home, having been imprisoned in Maryland for nearly two years.

With their father home and a few days of recuperation behind him, the McIvers, along with a neighbor or two, are determined to take on the renegades occupying their farm. Through a series of convoluted plot twists, Jamie and his father seek and ultimately accept help from a Union company stationed in the area. It's a unit from which Jamie had earlier sought to steal rifles and discovered that the commander in charge was his former recaptured prisoner—now Major Galt, who offers the use of his troops in launching an assault against the guerrillas both as a return favor for Mrs. McIver's kind treatment and in an effort to restore order to the area. (Hancock specifically identified these troops as the 2nd North Carolina Mounted Infantry, made up mainly of New Yorkers, which did indeed serve as peacekeeping forces in western North Carolina at the war's end.)[37] Ultimately, the two forces converge at the McIver farm in a poorly staged and far too brief shoot-out. A cannon employed by Galt's forces tips the scale in their favor and leads to a relatively anticlimactic resolution when the cabin dwellers surrender with a white flag and Poss, along with his comrades, is arrested and escorted away by Galt and his men, allowing the McIvers—and Blossom—to retake possession of their farm.

If the ending is a letdown, it may be that so civil a denouement was devised specifically for the youthful viewership that Disney saw as its core audience. Given the limitations imposed on a family film for a television audience, *Menace on the Mountain* does reasonably well in capturing—sometime explicitly, sometimes more implicitly—many of the basic realities of the irregular war as experienced on highland home fronts. That credibility was due in no small part to the unusually accomplished historical context of the film's literary source, Mary Hancock's novel, and the serious research she undertook in constructing it.

• • • • • •

It would be a quarter of a century before another filmmaker took on Appalachia's Civil War home front, this time with a small-scale independent production, *Pharaoh's Army*, released in 1995. Produced, directed, and written by Danville, Kentucky, native Robby Henson, this gem of a film was based on an actual incident that took place not far from Danville in 1864. In Harry Caudill's classic portrait of the region, *Night Comes to the Cumberlands* (1962), Henson had found an intriguing anecdote in a chapter Caudill devoted to the war. With his father, the nineteen-year-old Harry visited a ninety-year-old mountain farmer; the old man led his two visitors up to a sinkhole high on a wooded hillside above his family farm to point out where he, as an eleven-year-old, had helped his fifteen-year-old brother, Oliver, bury a Union soldier the latter had shot and killed during the Civil War.

As the elderly storyteller related it to the Caudills, a band of some fifty Union soldiers showed up at his family's remote homestead "foraging" for food. "They went through the country robbin' widders and orphans," he told them, "and payin' them with greenbacks if they was on the Union side and nothin' at all if they was Democrats." The Yankees set up camp beside the farm and proceeded to "eat up all our ham meat and about ten fat hens." When they moved on the next morning, they took the family's cows and work stock; "their captain said he didn't have to pay us a cent because pap was a traitor." Oliver grabbed his father's hog rifle and the boys went to a ridge running above the creek bed along which the troops were traveling. Lying in wait until they passed by below, Oliver took aim at the last man in the procession and "shot him right betwixt his galluses." The two boys scampered back home, cleaned the gun, and were hoeing corn by the time the Yankees showed up with the corpse of their fallen comrade. As angry as his men were, the captain insisted that the boys were innocent (in an area full of snipers, that was not an unreasonable assumption). He led his men up to the family graveyard and had them bury the body in it. He then returned the plow mule they'd originally taken and warned the boys to stay out of trouble, saying he had two "young 'uns about like us" back home. To conclude the story in the old man's own words: "When they got plumb gone ma tol' me and Ol to go dig up that Yankee and git him outen our graveyard. So we uncovered him and pulled him up the hill and buried him in a sinkhole where a big tree had turned up by their roots. We didn't git him very deep though, 'cause a hog rooted him up and carried off his head. Ma said that proved that hogs and other Yankees were the only things that could stomach a Yankee, dead or alive!"[38]

Henson took Caudill's twice-told tale and made it the core premise around which he constructed his screenplay for *Pharaoh's Army*. Or, as he put it, "It's a pretty barebones little legend that we spun into a story."[39] (In the film's final credits, he acknowledged Caudill's anecdote as its inspiration.) The result is a darker and more somber film than the three previously discussed, with a more sophisticated narrative and richer, more nuanced characterizations. And yet it remains a deceptively simple story. It centers on a mother, Sarah Anders, and her single son (about eleven, the same age as Caudill's informant). With the man of the house off in Confederate service, the two are struggling to eke out a living on their small mountain farm along Meshack Creek in Kentucky's Cumberlands (the only one of these five films actually filmed—to very good effect—at the location in which its story is set). Instead of fifty Union soldiers, it is a mere five men who arrive on a spring day in 1862 and set the plot in motion.[40] Henson's time frame is appropriate in that Union forces occupied much of this region of eastern Kentucky in January 1862, and demands by such patrols on the Confederate minority in the area were all-too-regular inconveniences for much of that winter and spring.[41]

The film's opening scene is a burial, as will be its last; Henson uses this as a running motif for the deeply rooted animosity in the region. In this case, it is a young girl, the Anders's daughter, who is laid to rest in a church cemetery. In voice-over narration, an elderly man (the unnamed son in his later years) states, "When sister died, weren't none but women and old men to bury her," and follows with, "That night, some Yankee bastards dug her up and tossed her out like a rag doll, 'count of Pap siding with the South." Understandably upset, the mother (Patricia Clarkson) refuses the preacher's offer to rebury her daughter and insists on taking her back home. The preacher (a mere cameo by Kris Kristofferson, who nevertheless received top billing) responds, "There'll be hell to pay." And so there will be.

Soon thereafter, the five-man patrol appears in the distance, and mother and son scramble to hide everything, from hams, livestock, and firearms, to a photograph of her husband in his Confederate uniform. As his men scatter gleefully across the property to take what they can—primarily chickens—their captain, John Abston (Chris Cooper), explains that "your husband is fighting against his country," which makes their farm a legitimate target from which to "resupply with contraband from the enemy" to feed Union troops stationed nearby at Cumberland Gap. (This too conforms to the actual military situation, as Federal forces amassed at Cumberland Gap in May and June 1864 in preparation for a planned push into East Tennessee.)[42] Abston is civil, even apologetic about their mission, but Sarah remains cold toward him, muttering, "Why didn't you stay there?" under her breath when he says he has a farm much like hers across the Ohio River.

Newt, the youngest of the patrol, is seriously wounded when he falls from a hayloft onto a pitchfork, and the captain decides that they'll have to remain where they are until his fever breaks and he's able to travel. Sarah shows no concern for Newt's well-being other than the fact that it turned transient marauders into a longer-term occupation force. When her son (who, like Charlie Anderson's youngest, remains nameless) asks if the young soldier, then occupying what seems to be their only bed, is going to die, she replies coldly, "If the skinny Yank gets well, he might well be the one shooting at your pap." Captain Abston panics when Sarah seems to have disappeared, though he soon discovers her sleeping on her daughter's grave, guarding it against an earlier attempt by his troops to dig it up, over her frantic objections, to see if it too might be merely another ploy to hide goods from them.

Over the course of several weeks, the captain warms up even more to his reluctant hostess, and in small but fleeting ways she softens toward him, and comes to accept his efforts to help out with spring plowing and other chores. To the filmmaker's credit, their relationship never blossoms into a romance. In response to Abston's most direct attempt to court Sarah, she resists any impulse to reciprocate, telling him, "We ain't gonna be friends. Let's just keep to being enemies," to which he replies simply, "Yes, ma'am. I forgot. You've got a better memory."

Perhaps more than any other Civil War film, *Pharaoh's Army* manages to make its Union and Confederate antagonists—Captain Abston and Sarah—equally sympathetic figures, no mean feat given the seemingly one-sided power struggle between his role as an intruding occupier and hers as an innocent target, even victim, of that occupation. But also striking about the two is his consistently conciliatory and humane treatment of her, and regret at the situation to which they've both been subjected. He admits to the boy, when asked, that since enlisting, he had not yet taken another life (a record an earlier generation of Hollywood scriptwriters would not likely have attributed to a soldier of his stature). At the same time, the four men under his command are relatively benign as an occupying force. Despite the glee they take in their initial confiscation of the Anders's chickens, they never display any real maliciousness toward mother and son, with the exception of a single incident, discussed later, by the one soldier whose bullying ways simply point up the gentler demeanor of his comrades, especially that of Captain Abston.

A revealing exchange between Abston and the Polish private referred to by the others as "Chicago" takes place late in the film and gets at their motivations for enlisting in Union service while deepening our appreciation for the captain's strength of character. When Abston asks Chicago (Robert Joy) how he got himself mixed up in all this, he replies in broken English, "I think I get to see new places; I get tired of chopping sausages." The captain calls that "a pretty thin reason to get shot at," to which the Pole retorts, "You got better one? I heard your big ones—to save the Union, to free the slaves. Nobody I know wants to get killed for a bunch of nigs." "It's a mess, ain't it?" the captain replies, and when asked why he signed on, he says, "A minister brought a runaway slave into our church, ripped off his shirt, and shows us a back covered in the ugliest damn strap scars. And then right there from the pulpit, he asked for volunteers, and here I am stealing chickens." Like Chad Buford and Charlie Anderson, slavery mattered, either as a reason to get into the war or as a rationale for staying out of it.

On the other hand, we never get any sense of why Sarah became—and remained—such a diehard Confederate, nor what motivated her husband to join its ranks. (Harry Caudill quoted his elderly source as having said, "Pap warn't no nigger lover and on t' other hand, he didn't hate 'em. But he thought hit was right to own 'em because they are skasely human accordin' to the Bible. So when the war started Pap got ready and went off to fight fer the South.")[43] Sarah never expresses anything that could be remotely taken for pro-South or proslavery sentiment; rather, she acts almost purely out of a vitriolic hatred for Union forces or anyone else expressing Unionist sentiment. Thus, she remains unforgiving of Captain Abston and unwilling to respond to the abundance of goodwill he offers.

Yet perhaps the most chilling display of her deep-seated animosity comes in her reaction to the tragedy that befell those who seem to be her closest neighbors. Gunshots in the distance send three of the soldiers up the creek to see what's happening. (This incident generates the only reference to guerrilla activity in the film.) They come upon the charred remains of a farmhouse, still smoldering; and with the buzzards circling above, they find its occupants, an elderly man and woman, slaughtered and stuffed down their well. When the men report back to the captain what they've seen, he asks Sarah if she knows whose place it is. "Yankees," is her one-word reply. "Ma'am, they weren't Yankees; just some ole farmer and his wife," one of the soldiers responds. "They sent two boys into the Union army," she states smugly, before spitting off the porch and walking away, not at all disturbed by the news of their destruction.

This may be the most compelling theme that runs through Henson's film—the unadulterated hatred carried by mountain women for not only the war but for those oppressors, whether Union or Confederate, whether local or from elsewhere, who brought the war to their doors. Sarah Anders fully embodies that resolve, as does Patricia Clarkson's understated but highly disciplined portrayal of her. From her initial reaction to the desecration of her daughter's grave, presumably the first instance of Union abuse she experienced personally, to her brewing resentment of the Union patrol's theft and then occupation of her farm, she rarely wavers in her contempt for the occupiers.

That stance reflects a reality that a number of postwar observers seemed to detect more acutely in mountain women than in Southerners elsewhere. A Federal soldier who served at a refugee camp for Unionist civilians near Chattanooga at war's end recalled the Appalachian women who had sought safe haven there. "I heard them repeat over and over to their children the names of men which they were never to forget, and whom they were to kill when they had sufficient strength to hold a rifle," he wrote. "These women, who have been driven from their homes by the most savage warfare our country has been cursed with . . . impressed me as living wholly to revenge their wrongs."[44] Robby Henson may well have shaped the character of Sarah from another anecdote in Harry Caudill's book—this one the story of his own grandmother. She was thirteen years old when her Confederate father came home on furlough, or "crop leave," in 1864. One day while working his field, six or so Union guerrillas swept down and riddled him with bullets. His daughter rushed out and "held his shattered head while his brains ran out onto her aproned lap." Caudill concludes, "To the day of her death she was an unreconstructed Rebel, and her eyes glinted and her lips tightened into a thin line at the merest mention of even the grandchildren of her father's killers."[45]

The mood in the film remains one fraught with tension, as the other men grow restless and resentful of the situation and of each other. Rody, the most brutish of the group, threatens to destroy the delicate truce finally established primarily due to the captain's leadership—and his growing affection for Sarah. After a physical altercation between Rody and Sarah over his abuse of her dog, she instructs her son to go report their predicament to the preacher (Kristofferson) and ask him to send help. An enigmatic figure, the preacher is quick to see a biblical analogy when informed of the situation. "Pharaoh sent his army to smite Israel and they drowned in the Red Sea," he declares. "It was wrong what they did to your sister. God's will is a powerful thing," thus implying that he'll send help to smite this latest army of oppressors, hence the film's title.

That help comes in the form of a sole sniper, who, sight unseen, kills Rody with a single shot and sends the other soldiers racing to seek shelter in Sarah's cabin. Only Captain Abston gives chase, and only after a prolonged shoot-out in which he ultimately prevails does he discover the sniper's identity—the corpse is that of the preacher's slave, Israel. One could thus say that Abston, like Pharaoh, smites Israel, but the more interesting irony is that it's a slave who has been assigned and taken on the role of Confederate martyr (a plot point Gary Gallagher calls "an odd and unexplained Lost Cause twist" in an otherwise far more neutrally pitched narrative).[46] Henson himself commented on this key irony he constructed—that "the captain had never killed a man, he joined the army to free the slaves, and yet the first man he kills is a slave."[47]

Disheartened at the turn of events, Abston decides it's finally time to clear out, and he loads the still wounded Newt onto the Anders's wagon, taking both Sarah's mule to pull it and her cow, all but a death sentence from her perspective. Before leaving, the captain buries Rody next to the grave of Sarah's daughter, over her vehement objections. Her anger over what she sees as yet another defilement of her daughter's grave is compounded by the captain's retort as they head out. "What do you expect us to eat?" she cries in a panic, to which he responds, "Ma'am, tell that husband of yours to come home; maybe your boy can shoot squirrels." She raises the rifle he's left her, aims it at his back, and pulls the trigger, only to find he's taken the powder. The boy, perhaps inspired by his mother's despair and murderous intent, follows the departing patrol at a distance and, like Harry Caudill's elderly informant's brother, shoots and kills the last of the procession—in this case, the wagon-bound Newt—then races unseen back home. Again, true to the Caudill scenario, Captain Abston shows up moments later, but alone with the wagon carrying Newt's unmoved corpse, and confronts the boy. "Did you kill Newt?" he asks. "Your mother might tell you it's all right to kill Yanks, but I just want you to know that that boy had a brother no older than you, and he had a family just like you and he never hurt a fly." Sarah is quick to counter, "And he wouldn't be dead if it weren't for you bringing him here to steal from us." As he departs, Abston offers his final words: "I just hope whoever killed Newt has the common decency to give him a Christian burial, at least."

As soon as he's out of hearing range, Sarah orders the boy to "get that damned Yankee out of our yard." The voice of the boy-as-old-man chimes in, saying, "The captain asked us to do the decent thing, but I don't guess the war was about being decent." Mother and son proceed to dig up Rody's body and float it down the creek, and then, in his voice-over narration, he finishes the story: "We drug the skinny yankee up the hill to a sinkhole and throwed him in, and throwed some dirt on him; Pap never made it back; that war was a widow-maker. Ma told me to never, never tell anyone what we done, and I don't guess I ever did, except maybe once, or twice."

In this seemingly simple story of an act of militarily authorized confiscation gone wrong, it is a far more potent and emotionally laden issue that resonates more deeply—in both the memory of a ninety-year-old Kentucky farmer in 1941 and a young Kentucky filmmaker in 1995. The desecration of a daughter's grave by Union troops turns into an obsession for a mother, who ultimately turns the tables on a despised enemy and has the last word in a bitter struggle with Union troops by refusing a proper burial for two of their number. Far more than a framing device, death and the treatment of the dead become compelling elements in terms of what this war in particular came to mean to so many Americans on both sides of the struggle, particularly women, as Drew Faust demonstrated so effectively in *This Republic of Suffering*.[48] Given that women were most concerned and offended by violations of proper, even sacrosanct burial rites, it's ironic that this woman should join forces with her child to make such violations her final and most blatant act of defiance against her persecutors. It is no wonder that Robby Henson admitted, well after production was complete, his continued attachment to the original title he'd conceived for the film, *Sinkhole*.

. . . . . .

Finally, in *Cold Mountain*, both Charles Frazier's 1997 novel and Anthony Minghella's 2003 screen adaptation of it, Appalachia's inner civil war reached its broadest audience yet. Minghella's film is unusually faithful to Frazier's novel in re-creating Inman's encounters with beleaguered widows, bushwhackers, Union renegades, fellow deserters, and the seemingly omnipresent home guardsmen, who collectively suggest the disorder, desperation, and corruption that characterized Southerners' struggles to survive in an ever more lawless and dysfunctional society imposed by nearly four years of war. One of the film's great strengths is that these struggles are presented in such graphic, unflinching form, more often than not with violent resolutions that genuinely shock. Rarely has the collective plight of a people at war been conveyed to movie audiences as effectively as in this film's series of disturbing and emotionally charged episodes.

The screen adaptation does almost as well with the home-front situation in and around the community of Cold Mountain, North Carolina, embodied most notably in the unlikely partnership between Ada Monroe, an overeducated but hapless South Carolina transplant to the mountains, and Ruby Thewes, a brash local woman whose knowledge of mountain ways and sheer common sense ultimately save Ada and her farm. As portrayed by Nicole Kidman and Renée Zellweger (who won an Oscar for her efforts), their teaming makes for the film's most appealing and satisfying relationship, with the cultural disconnect between them providing much needed comic relief.[49] (It is also refreshing to see a character as inept and vulnerable—at least initially—as Ada is, thus providing a nice contrast to those more stalwart and all-too-formidable mountain women featured in *Pharaoh's Army* and *Menace on the Mountain*.)

Yet as vividly as the impact of the war on southern highlanders is rendered, this is a war devoid of much meaning. There is almost no indication as to the issues behind the struggle or why those from the community of Cold Mountain choose to fight for the Confederacy. A scene in which a church service is interrupted with the news that the war has begun leads to much excitement on the part of the local men and boys eager to fight. It is very much like the scene at Twelve Oaks in *Gone with the Wind*, where the same news is met with equal enthusiasm; but in that film, an earlier scene of Rhett Butler debating with hotheaded young Georgians at least provides some context and meaning for their exuberant response. In *Cold Mountain*, there's no such rationale for these highlanders' almost mindless revelry, the most distinguishable dialogue in the scene being, "We got our war, man! We got our war." (It's not even clear what spurs this particular moment: Is it the attack on Fort Sumter? Lincoln's call for troops to put down the rebellion? North Carolina's secession vote a month later?)

Perhaps Minghella's most notable deviation from Frazier's book is the elimination of Inman's internalized thoughts and feelings as he heads home. The novel is infused with a palpable sense of place, especially in Inman's yearning for his Blue Ridge home, which, along with his beloved Ada, he counts on to restore his sanity, indeed his humanity. The beauty of North Carolina's highlands (which this native western Carolinian must grudgingly admit is fairly convincingly portrayed by the Romanian Alps) is apparent throughout the film, forming a striking visual contrast to the wretched Virginia battlefield as the two settings are juxtaposed in alternating opening scenes.[50] With this cerebral side of the character so diminished by the screenplay, Jude Law's Inman comes across as far more of an everyman than does his prose counterpart, whose intellect, sensitivity, and emotional depth make him far more than the average Confederate soldier or deserter and thus a far more compelling and complex character.

Cold Mountain's men and women respond in a variety of ways to the violence and hardships forced upon them as the war devastates their households and communities, yet the one thing the rich array of characters—major and minor—share is a pervasive sense of war weariness. By the war's final months, when the film takes place (except for a few flashbacks back to 1861), not a single character expresses any support for either the Confederacy or the war. No film provides a more visceral sense of just how debilitating this war was as it moved into its fourth and final year, not only in the material deprivation, economic devastation, and breakdown of law and order, but also in the psychological and emotional desolation it reeked upon so many members of this war-weary highland populace.

If the film captures the sheer messiness of this internalized Appalachian war, it vastly oversimplifies the forces of good and evil that wage war on each other in the region, as Hollywood is wont to do. Perhaps because the protagonist, Inman, is first and foremost a deserter, all other deserters become sympathetic characters and innocent victims who pose little threat to anyone else. It is those who seek them out—the home guard—who become the film's unequivocal villains. From the war's beginning, Captain Robert Teague (a historically based figure) and his self-appointed band of local vigilantes are portrayed as menacing, power-hungry thugs who become increasingly ruthless, cruel, and destructive in their harassment of the very civilian population they are charged with protecting. In actuality, it was often the deserters, along with those avoiding conscription, escaped prisoners of war, and other outliers, who made up the bushwhacking bands who hid out in the more remote Carolina highlands and wreaked havoc on nearby towns and farms (as demonstrated most fully in *Menace on the Mountain*).

If the home guard serves as *Cold Mountain*'s most ruthless and disruptive force, a small band of deserters appear strangely benign, relatively harmless, and far more sympathetic characters than was often true of their real-life counterparts. This is even more the case onscreen than it was on the page. In the novel, this trio of bumbling ne'er-do-wells—Stobrod, Ruby's father; the feeble-minded Pangle; and a clueless young lad who goes by the name of his home state, Georgia—take up residence in a cave with other outliers and conduct occasional raids on prosperous farm families in the area, living off their plunder, drinking their good liquor, and eating nothing but stolen jellies.[51] Stobrod and Pangle appear only late in the film, as homeless drifters with no connection to any cause or larger group. They continue to wander aimlessly even after they encounter Ada and Ruby, who provide them with food and other supplies once the latter reconciles with the father who had abused her as a child. Teague and his henchmen stumble upon the two, by then joined with Georgia, as they're camped deep in the snow-covered wilderness. With no sense of recognition or hostility, they instruct Stobrod and Pangle to stand up and face them; seemingly clueless as to what's about to happen, they do just that and allow themselves to be executed by this firing squad. (Georgia, vomiting at the time behind a nearby log, escapes detection and lives to report the atrocity.) Such was hardly a typical scenario in the southern highlands' guerrilla war, and it's unclear why both Frazier and Minghella made the one major encounter between these irregular belligerents so one-sided.

Ironically, women often proved more effective in combating such aggression than did men. Minghella moves their plight front and center in his film, so much so that Gary Gallagher has called it "a feminist antiwar film."[52] In fact, *Cold Mountain* does so not only by fleshing out incidents that appear far more fleetingly in Frazier's novel but also by turning its female characters into far more active agents in their own defense and in the care and protection they provide for Inman and other males in the film. The wartime breakdown of conventional gender roles, as women are often either left without male protection or forced to serve as the first and last line of defense of their households—and even of their husbands, sons, or other male relatives—plays out as fully here as in any Civil War–based film.[53] Michael Fellman's characterization of Missouri's guerrilla conflict—"disintegration, demoralization, and perverse adaptation," in which women became forced participants with "varying degrees of enthusiasm, rage, and fear"[54]—is fully applicable to Southern Appalachia's inner war and to the female characters of *Cold Mountain*. Two of the film's three central characters are women, but so are several of the more vivid supporting characters, and their roles tell us much about this mountain war and the women who, very much like their real-life counterparts, fell victim to the desperation and lawlessness so rampant throughout the region by 1864 and 1865.

In one of a series of encounters Inman experiences in the course of his arduous trek home through North Carolina, he is taken in by Sara, a teenage war widow and mother, played by Natalie Portman, who's struggling on her own in an isolated mountain cabin to keep herself and her sickly newborn alive. Soon after his arrival, three Union renegades approach her cabin, demanding whatever food she has (in a scenario reminiscent of those in both *Menace on the Mountain* and *Pharaoh's Army*). Inman, having escaped out the back, watches and schemes as to how to rescue his young hostess. Here Minghella provides an intriguing twist on Frazier's narrative. In one of the novel's most riveting passages, Inman stalks the men as they depart with Sara's hog and several chickens—in essence, her only means of support. He follows them to their camp, picks them off one by one, and returns to Sara with her meat supply. Onscreen, Minghella compresses this sequence considerably by having Inman ambush and kill two of the three Federals inside Sara's house. He allows the youngest and least malicious of the three to leave unharmed, but as the grateful boy scurries away from the scene, he is suddenly shot in the back—by Sara. This is a war that has made killers of women and girls, in this case a killing driven by more vengeance and hatred than that exhibited by Inman, that most sensitive and compassionate of Confederate soldiers.

Equally harrowing is an incident in which a woman is even more fully victimized and left without any recourse to fight back. Sally Swanger, a very minor character in the novel, emerges in Kathy Baker's moving portrayal as the most prominent female in the Cold Mountain community, the wife of one of its more prosperous farmers and a neighbor fully sympathetic to the plight of the hapless Ada. Like many mountain women, she is forced to hide her two sons, who have deserted the Confederate army and returned home. Suspecting this to be the case, the malevolent home-guard thugs—in an effort to either force her to reveal their hiding place or draw them out to rescue their mother—bind her to a rail fence with a noose around her neck, place her fingers between the top rails, and dance sadistically along the top of the rail, breaking her hands in the process.

Young widow Sara (Natalie Portman) is among several mountain women who prove more belligerent in protecting their homes than do the men, such as Inman (Jude Law), the protagonist of *Cold Mountain.*

The historical record includes numerous accounts of just this sort of torture being inflicted on Appalachian women, along with babies being exposed to the elements and pets shot. The very incidents involving Sara and Sally Swanger were likely based on the brutalities inflicted by Confederate forces on Unionist wives and mothers as prologue to the infamous Shelton Laurel massacre in early 1863, as well as the experience of another Madison County woman, whose story is related in Muriel Sheppard's *Cabins in the Laurel.*[55] Wilma Dykeman conveyed the rail fence torture in the opening pages of her novel *The Tall Woman*, in which the mother of her heroine falls victim to a sadistic group of "outliers" seeking the meat supply that she has carefully hidden.[56] Frazier made only fleeting reference to such abuses in his novel, but Minghella uses them as the basis for an extended scene in the film, made all the more powerful because he and actress Baker have turned Sally into a more fully developed character, who in addition to her physical torture must watch her husband and both sons gunned down in front of her.[57]

So do other women serve as protectors and caretakers for men at war, whether stranger or friend. One of the novel's most compelling chapters is that in which Inman encounters a "goat woman" setting traps in the woods around Grandfather Mountain, and when he asks for food, this elderly woman leads him to her remote encampment on the side of the mountain, where she allows him to stay with her and her small herd for a day or so before he moves on. The power of this episode in Frazier's prose is not only that the independence and eccentricity of this unnamed hermit/oracle make her such an intriguing character but also that she forces Inman to confront and articulate the meaningless of the war and his participation in it.[58] Yet in the film, this character, vividly brought to life by British character actress Eileen Atkins, offers much more, though in considerably condensed form. For Minghella, she becomes Inman's savior, in that she finds him unconscious but still chained to an otherwise dead band of prisoners, all victims of cross fire in a skirmish between their Confederate captors and a small Union force that stumbles upon them. With great effort, the goat woman manages to get Inman to her shelter, where she treats his wounds and nurses him back to health over several days. She thus becomes an even more integral determinant of Inman's ever questionable fate; more importantly, however, her role stands as yet another indication of the degree to which men at war depended on women—known or unknown—for their very survival.

In the spring of 1862, a wife and mother in Macon County, North Carolina, just west of the actual Cold Mountain, confided to her soldier husband in a letter: "I wish I could be both man and woman until the war ends."[59] Referring primarily to the sometimes overwhelming burdens she faced in managing her farm without her husband's help, her wish no doubt reflected the sentiments of many Southern women during the war. That would include *Cold Mountain*'s Ada Monroe, who faces seemingly insurmountable challenges to survive after her father's death, and her first attempts at taking charge of both her household and her farm reflect how totally helpless she is in assuming any such manly roles. It takes one of J. W. Williamson's "mannish misfits"—the irrepressible backwoods woman Ruby Thewes—to join forces with Ada and, in effect, save her by saving her farm.[60]

It is only later in the war, and primarily in this highland environment, that many women were forced to take on even more of a man's role by engaging in the horrific guerrilla conflict that engulfed them. And so it is for Ada and Ruby. Like Sally Swanger, they find themselves drawn into that struggle simply by attempting to retrieve the bodies of Ruby's father and his renegade companions. The two women give up the comforts of home and farm, where providing sustenance and protection to these men was relatively easy, and head into the thick of the mountain wilderness, where they learn that their male charges have been murdered. In undertaking this grim mission, Ada and Ruby arm themselves and dress as men, further blurring the gender roles forced on them by the war. While the rough and ready Ruby has no problem adapting to the "mannish ways" of the sterner sex, Kidman's Ada Monroe is perhaps most distinguished from anyone else in the film by her femininity and gentility. Even when she ultimately resorts to wearing men's clothing—a sign that she's about to enter the fray in a serious way—little else about her appearance or demeanor seems to change.

Following an all-too-brief reunion of Ada and Inman, who has finally straggled almost home, all three major characters find themselves caught up in an extended shoot-out with the dastardly Teague and his ruffian "deputies," which leads to the film's tragic denouement and the plot twist that no doubt contributed significantly to the popularity of both the book and the film.[61] For all of the problems from which the film suffers in terms of how historical reality is compromised—and there are several—Minghella deserves much credit for how effectively he portrays the gendered nature of this very messy war as it played out on the many home fronts of Southern Appalachia.

• • • • • •

When *Cold Mountain* was published, a colleague of mine, a distinguished Civil War historian and biographer of Robert E. Lee, read it and wryly pronounced it to be "a cross between Larry McMurtry and Cormac McCarthy," with most of its characters "trailer park trash before there were trailer parks." Perhaps so. Not only *Cold Mountain* but most of the films discussed here depict a war and a people that Lee would probably not have recognized (except perhaps the Anderson family in *Shenandoah*); neither gods nor generals play much of a role in the inner civil wars waged elsewhere in the hills.

Novelist Adam Goodheart, in a review of Frazier's second novel in 2005, began by stating, "There's a certain kind of history that's made in out-of-the-way places: the swamps, the borderlands, the barren mountain ranges that no one claims. No grand political gestures, or even any memorable battles, unfold here. It's the terrain, rather, of squalid little deals, nasty skirmishes and forgotten massacres—where the reverberations of great events wreak distant havoc on singular, unchronicled lives."[62] This, he goes on to suggest, "is territory where novelists, not historians, sometimes make the truest guides."[63] And so it is—or can be—for filmmakers as well, at least those represented here. The struggles forced upon these cinematic highlanders were indeed functions of great events that took place elsewhere, and these unflinching portrayals of the bleak and unsettling home-front realities capture a far less familiar version of the Civil War than Robert E. Lee (or my friend, his biographer) might recognize or acknowledge. Yet they are stories that would have been all too recognizable to the thousands of hardscrabble Southern men and women who lived through them.

4 Family Feuds

As the concept of Appalachian "otherness" began to take shape and solidify toward the end of the nineteenth and the beginning of the twentieth century, feuding quickly came to the fore as one of its most pronounced and press-worthy components. In earlier eras, these localized kin-based vendettas, or blood feuds, had played out among Cherokee Indians and Deep South plantation owners (as most notably parodied by Mark Twain's battling Grangerfords and Shepherdsons in *Huckleberry Finn*) and through lingering remnants of home-front rifts ignited by the Civil War, particularly in the border states and on the western frontier.[1] Only in the 1890s did feuds come to be closely associated with a single state—Kentucky—and then to its eastern mountain counties, as certain locales and families attracted widespread, often sensationalized journalistic coverage. Notable settings included Clay, Breathitt, and Harlan Counties; the best-known (and most documented) of all was the war waged sporadically between the Hatfields and the McCoys on both sides of the Tug River valley that divided Kentucky from West Virginia.[2]

These incidents inspired fictional treatments, sociological analyses, and a plethora of silent films, which transformed historical reality into stereotypical contempt for this "strange land and peculiar people," which soon came to embrace Southern Appalachia as a whole.[3] The very nature of these sporadic yet often multigenerational bouts of clannish violence—murder, arson, ambushes, shoot-outs, and raids—served to affirm the primitive nature of mountain people and testified to their ever-growing isolation and alienation from the nation at large at the dawn of a new century. In 1901, Kentucky author John Fox, whose writings probably did more than those of anyone to popularize interpretations of such social behavior as endemic of—and unique to—southern highlanders, stated that feuds were the product of "ignorance, shiftlessness, incredible lawlessness, a frightful estimate of the value of human life; the horrible custom of ambush, a class of cowardly assassins who can be hired to do murder for a gun, a mule, or a gallon of moonshine."[4]

Chroniclers of this relatively brief era of localized warfare—most prevalent during the 1880s and 1890s—have put forth multiple causal factors to explain it. These include the imported clannishness of the Scots Irish, the region's long-lingering frontier character, personal vendettas, lingering resentment over opposing Civil War loyalties and home-front atrocities, local political rivalries (feud incidents often played out at polling venues on election days), inadequate law enforcement and court systems, and new social and economic tensions imposed by the incursion of industrialization—railroads, mining, timber—into parts of the region.[5] Cratis D. Williams, in his magisterial 1961 study of literary depictions of southern mountaineers, summarized the nature of feuds as adeptly as anyone: "Local grudges spawned neighborhood wars, marked by bushwhackings, forays, and outrages . . . and continued for generations among people whose lands join, whose political loyalties conflict, whose suspicion requires little evidence and whose vengeance demands a full level of satisfaction."[6]

While much of this characterization is evident in Hollywood's dramatizations of the phenomena as well, screen depictions of feuds over the years have also offered more complex, emotionally charged, and even sympathetic versions of feudists. For all the irrationalities that drove these localized conflicts, their participants often exhibited redeeming qualities for the simple reason that at the core of each faction were family units—both nuclear and extended. As such, audiences saw these warring camps first and foremost as households, made up of parents and children, husbands and wives, often covering multiple generations. Thus, for all the violence that played out onscreen, much of it appeared as less rash and irrational because it was generated within a familial context or household framework that served to temper the worst of their belligerence with audiences at the time—and even since.

Soon after these clan-based conflicts began to subside at the turn of the century, the nascent film industry came to see Appalachian life and culture as prime fodder for the screen and produced nearly five hundred such "hillbilly films"—mostly shorts made for nickelodeon showings between 1904 and 1928, with the vast majority appearing in the 1910s. Fully cataloged and described (with the studios' own synopses) in his invaluable compendium on the subject, Jerry Williamson shows that nearly a hundred of these southern mountaineer movies built their melodramatic plots on feuds (with moonshining as the only other topic garnering as much attention from these early filmmakers). The second such film produced—*A Kentucky Feud* (1905) by none other than Kentucky native D. W. Griffith—explicitly made use of the Hatfield and McCoy names, though little about the plot resembles that actual feud, which had come to a close a mere decade and a half or so earlier.[7]

• • • • • •

Of the many silent films focusing on highland feuds, none was more critically or commercially successful upon its release or has better stood the test of time than *Tol'able David* (1921).[8] Williamson, who's provided the most incisive critical commentary on the film, makes the bold claim that it remains "one of the most influential of hillbilly pictures. It was the first of a handful of movies—*Sergeant York*, *Thunder Road*, *Deliverance*, *Coal Miner's Daughter*—that were seen by millions, movies, in short, that dictated for a time the meaning of the southern mountains."[9]

"Tol'able David," a short story by a popular fiction writer, Joseph Hergesheimer, first appeared in serial form in the *Saturday Evening Post* in 1917.[10] In 1920, director Henry King, then at the early stages of what would be a long, successful moviemaking career, was operating his own production company in New York City when he bought the rights to Hergesheimer's story from D. W. Griffith. Together with one of Griffith's preeminent actors, Richard Barthelmess, who saw David as a starring role for himself, the two set out to bring this "hillbilly" tale to the screen.

Tol'able David was one of few silent films to be staged and shot almost entirely on location—in and around the small town of Monterey, Virginia, situated at the northern end of the Shenandoah valley. King, a native of the region himself (he grew up eighty miles away in Christiansburg), recognized the value of getting "the real atmosphere of the Virginia mountains."[11] The pastoral setting not only added a layer of authenticity to the story but also served to link the setting and its inhabitants with an idyllic image of rural America that was becoming more valued in light of an increasingly urbanized and industrialized nation elsewhere.[12]

Given that *Tol'able David*—like the short story it's drawn from—is first and foremost an adolescent coming-of-age narrative, the major flaw in the film's credibility lies in the casting of the title character. Barthelmess was twenty-seven years old, and fully looked it, when he played the sixteen-year-old David Kinemon. He often comes across as slightly ridiculous as he moves through his boyish life of leisure in pants he's long outgrown, with his trusty sheepdog Rocket as his constant companion. To his credit, David yearns for more responsibility; he's particularly eager to serve as the hack driver for the mail delivery service that operates throughout the valley, but he is constantly rebuffed as being too young and inexperienced for such an assignment. Only with an ensuing feud will David ultimately have the opportunity to prove himself in a more manly capacity. While the narrative—as framed by author Hergesheimer—was meant to serve as a modern rendition of the David and Goliath story, with young Kinemon forced to become the underdog combatant who will avenge the violence inflicted on his family by a particularly villainous brute, Barthelmess's David lacks the youth and innocence that made his biblical counterpart's feat so extraordinary.

Although *Tol'able David* is generally categorized as a "feud film," the conflict between families plays out in a far more ad hoc fashion, without the trappings of a long-standing multigenerational enmity between rival clans that generally define a feud. Indeed, during the location filming (perhaps to keep from alienating the Virginians in whose midst they worked), director King insisted that the film "is not a story of a feud or moonshiners and we have to go down among these people, absorb their mannerisms and ideas."[13] The filmmakers' fondness for the local residents they came to know that summer is very much reflected in the sympathetic—indeed respectful—portrayal of those characters onscreen. This placid, pastoral community, named Greenstream no less, could be set almost anywhere in rural America. The scene shifts inside a sizable two-story cabin where a tenant farm family—the Kinemons—sit around the fire, reading. Yes, reading. From his father with his newspaper to David on the floor with a book of Bible stories, one senses that this is basically a literate community, a point further reiterated by the mail delivery service provided by David's older brother, Allen, which plays a critical role in the film's plot. These are not primitive, ignorant hillbillies but upstanding farm families, with aspirations, at least, to middle-class status.

Into this idyllic, peace-loving enclave comes trouble in the form of three scoundrels. Fugitives from the law in West Virginia, this gruff threesome cross the state line and force themselves upon "cousins" who are neighbors of the Kinemons. They're identified as the Hatburns from the Tug valley—a not-so-subtle means of linking them to the historic feud that had wreaked havoc and much publicity some two decades earlier. Led by Luke, the most threatening and malevolent of the trio, the West Virginia Hatburns push their way into the home of these distant kin, an elderly man and his adolescent granddaughter, Esther, with whom David is smitten. They demand food, ogle their pretty young cousin, and announce they'll hide out there until the "trouble at home blows over." They taunt David and order him off

Young David Kinemon (Richard Barthelmess) remains only briefly in the background (far left, standing) when he and his neighbors are first harassed by villainous brutes in *Tol'able David.*

the premises, thus sowing the seeds of the conflict that will soon erupt into a full-scale, if fleeting, feud.

Back at the more hospitable Kinemon household, Allen's wife has just delivered their first child, much to the delight of the local menfolk, who gather to drink and smoke cigars with the new father. Allen soon resumes his duties as the postal hack driver, and in passing by the Hatburn house, David's dog Rocket jumps off the wagon to chase their cat, and Luke beats the dog to death. (Ernest Torrence's performance as Luke was much acclaimed at the time—and since—as one of the screen's "most despicable villains.")[14] Allen, furious, vows vengeance after he's completed his deliveries, but Luke, unwilling to wait, throws a large rock at Allen's head and knocks him unconscious. Carried home and the doctor called, it soon becomes apparent that Allen has suffered irreparable physical damage; his mother mournfully moans, "[He] will be helpless for life."

With the tranquility of the Greenstream community now shattered, the upstanding Kinemons are inexorably drawn into this Hatburn-inflicted vendetta imported from West Virginia. David's father becomes its second victim when, in his agitation and anger in loading his rifle to take revenge, he suffers a fatal heart attack. David, now the only "man" in the family, grabs his father's rifle and heads for the door, shouting, "Damn and damn the Hatburns! I'll kill them all!" A title card interprets the sentiment in more detached form, labeling his outburst simply as David's "realization that death has shifted the burden of the Kinemon honor onto him." But his mother insists, "You're my little David; they'll kill you," then more sensibly appeals to that other side of his new role, pointing out that with Allen's wife, new baby, and herself, "You're the only man we have now." Slowly that message gets through to David; he relents and stays put to comfort his mother.[15]

The loss of so much of the Kinemon manpower forces the family off the land they'd farmed for so long, much to their sorrow, especially David's. As they leave for more cramped quarters in town, he turns his back to the family as a title card asks the viewer, "How could David let them see the grief that was choking him at the destruction of what he most loved?" His resentment carries over to Esther; he responds to her effort to comfort him by yelling, "I hate you and everything that's Hatburn," and he stomps away, seeming to forget that she's being victimized by this demonic trio as well.

The Kinemons' landlord, Mr. Gault, who's sympathetic to their plight, offers David a position in his general store, though he still insists that he's too young to take over Allen's role in delivering the mail, the job he craves. A group of idle men overhear this exchange, and one says, "If I was David Kinemon I'd have fed them Hatburns a dose of hot lead." That's followed by a title card describing his reaction: "To David's unhappy mind it seemed that all the Valley held him a coward." Thus, as peaceful a setting as Greenstream had once been, a new standard of manhood had now been imposed on the community—eye-for-an-eye justice, vendettas, restitution, feuds.

Once that die is cast, David's manhood makes another advance, as a drunken mail driver forces Mr. Gault to give his young employee his chance at the reins. This seems to give David the confidence—or fortitude—to finally stand up to the Hatburns, whose harassment of Esther and her grandfather has grown worse. (The latter's pleas for legal intervention have proven futile, the sheriff reasoning that the next court doesn't meet for three months and he can't hold them for that long, a telling commentary on how minimal a justice system was required for this piece of pastoral America up to this point.)

David approaches the Hatburn house, where he finds Luke harassing Esther. This leads to a sustained climax that showcases King's filmmaking skills at their best: well-staged and well-paced action combined with expert cross-cut editing. David's confrontation with the "cousins" allows Esther to escape, though Luke follows her. By the time Luke returns, David has already shot and killed his brother and father, and an unusually prolonged brawl ensues between David and Luke, ultimately ending in the latter's death. Intercut with this drama are scenes of Mrs. Kinemon, waiting in front of the store for David to return with the mail hack, where she reminisces none too subtly: "It seems like only yesterday he was a child on my knee while I read him his favorite story of David and Goliath, and now, he's a man and driving the government mail."

Esther staggers up to the store, where a crowd has gathered, and declares that "they've killed David" before swooning in her grandfather's arms in what looks like her demise as well. (The body count seems to fast approach that of the final scene of *Hamlet*.) Meanwhile, young David, exhausted and aching, manages to finish his mail delivery and get the horses and mail wagon back home intact, then collapses in his mother's lap as Esther comes back to life. She sees him and exclaims, "David, you're wonderful!" to which he responds, tongue in cheek: "Ma's right, I'm tol'able, . . . just tol'able." Early 1920s audiences must have thrilled at all that was packed so consummately into the film's final fifteen minutes, which probably had much to do with the strong word-of-mouth and box-office success the film enjoyed. (It was the top-grossing film of 1922.) Such a simple, short-lived feud is fully resolved with the total elimination of all members of one side of it (three) by a teenage boy who's merely trying to grow up and win his mama's approval.

• • • • • •

The earliest notable fictional rendering of Appalachian feuding appeared in 1908. John Fox Jr.'s novel *The Trail of the Lonesome Pine* was a major best seller over the next several years, adapted as a Broadway play in 1912 and again in 1922, and served as the basis of no less than four motion pictures—three silent films (1914, 1916, and 1923) and one sound production in 1936 (which is the focus of the discussion here). An outdoor musical dramatization of the book has been staged in Big Stone Gap, Virginia—Fox's final residence—every summer since 1963.[16]

Fox, a native of the Bluegrass region of Kentucky, became one of the most prolific Appalachian chroniclers after his move to Big Stone Gap in 1890. He gave up a wide-ranging journalistic career in New York and abroad to join his father and brothers in a series of real estate and coal-mining ventures in the midst of a boom just getting underway in southwestern Virginia at the time.[17] That move, into the heart of coal country and just across the state line from Harlan County, Kentucky, where Fox had also spent time, spurred in him a new fascination with Appalachia, which became the focus of his subsequent writings, both fictional and nonfictional.[18]

In his first major literary success, *The Little Shepherd of Kingdom Come* (1903), Fox explored regional variations in Civil War loyalties. Its popularity and later adaptability to film (it too was adapted for the screen three times, one of which is discussed in chapter 3) led Fox to tackle more recent issues that were drawing attention to the mountains: the incursion of the coal industry and family feuds. (He first explored feuds in his 1898 novella, *A Cumberland Vendetta*, and in a 1901 collection of personal observations of Appalachian life called *Blue-Grass and Rhododendron*.)[19] In *The Trail of the Lonesome Pine*, vaguely situated in Kentucky's Cumberlands and based loosely on the recent Turner-Howard feud in Harlan County, Fox shaped these themes around a romantic triangle involving a mountain girl, her cousin, and a mining engineer from the Bluegrass region. Published five years after *Little Shepherd* in 1908, *Lonesome Pine* became Fox's most successful and enduring novel, best known now for the outdoor drama that so identifies it with Big Stone Gap.[20]

Not surprisingly, there were considerable variations in the silent film treatments of *The Trail of the Lonesome Pine*. The 1916 version (directed by a young Cecil B. DeMille) supplants feuding with moonshiners and revenuers as the central point of conflict, while the 1923 rendition downplays the third wheel of the love triangle and moves the feud back into the forefront.[21] The 1936 film, longer and somewhat more complex, restores other elements of Fox's plot but still takes considerable liberties with the source material and remains, like the others, a much compressed treatment of the novel. Filmed in the San Bernardino Mountains east of Los Angeles and directed by Henry Hathaway, it holds a place in film history as the first outdoor-set film shot in full Technicolor.[22]

It is clear from the film's beginning that the feud will hold center place in this version of Fox's tale. Following the opening credits, text scrolls across the screen pronouncing the indigenous nature of such home-grown conflict in the southern highlands: "Among the American mountains there are forgotten valleys where people dwell shut out. Old words, old ways, old codes have lived unchanged. Each family is at war with the other over deadly feuds whose beginnings they cannot remember." This senseless "reality" is then enacted in a prologue of sorts, in which a shoot-out takes place between the men and boys of the Tolliver family on their farm and those of the Falins, who fire down on the Tolliver homestead from rocky crags above. A baby is born in the Tollivers' crude mountain cabin in the midst of the gunfire, and the camera zooms in on the mother, Melissa (Beulah Bondi), holding her newborn daughter and praying to God: "Give her the strength to be good, and to never be hateful and never fight. And don't let her carry the burden of fear watching her loved ones and seeing them die; and always asking out of her heart, 'Why has it got to be? Why has it got to be?'" This serves as an ominous foretaste of the tragedy both mother and daughter will suffer over the course of the film.

The narrative jumps forward in time with a simple statement flashed onto the screen: "Today another generation has grown to accept the code of the Lonesome Pine," which presumably means the Tolliver-Falin feud, while giving the titular tree what little relevance it seems to have to the story at hand. The newborn baby, June Tolliver, who has grown into a "fetching" young woman (Sylvia Sidney), is wandering near the towering pine when a young man (Fred MacMurray) approaches on horseback and introduces himself as Jack Hale, an agent for a railroad company that's interested in building a line through local properties in anticipation of purchasing the rights to what's under that property—coal. As with many of these Appalachian-based melodramas, the forces of modernization—industrialization, law and order, exposure to an outside world—impose themselves on this primitive mountain culture, represented first and foremost here by feuding, in which both families and thus most of the mountain characters onscreen are fully engaged. (Moonshine serves much the same purpose in many other similar films.)

This meeting slowly leads to a relationship—as much mentorship as it is romance—between Jack and June, which serves as a source of tension, given that June's cousin, Dave Tolliver (Henry Fonda), who lives with June's family, is also smitten with her. (As another character coyly notes, "Cousins are always thicker than thieves in the mountains.") Such romantic triangles or star-crossed-lover scenarios had long been integral components or formulaic clichés in silent film narratives of feuding mountaineers, just as they had been in the sensationalistic journalistic coverage of such actual conflicts in the 1880s and 1890s.[23] Curiously, because this particular triangle does not involve a Falin but rather an outsider, Jack Hale, who comes between the two Tolliver cousins, it has little direct bearing on the feud per se. For Hale, the disruptions caused by the fighting families threaten the progress of the railroad and mine construction, and make him determined to impose some law and order on this violent community, on whose property and labor he's now so dependent. Several scholars have suggested that Fox modeled Jack Hale on himself or on his engineer brother James, or at least on the role they played as outsiders with entrepreneurial aspirations when the family first moved to Big Stone Gap.[24]

Hale wins over the Tollivers by surgically removing a bullet lodged by a Falin rifle in Dave's arm, perhaps symbolically marking the first step toward undoing the effects of the feud. The family patriarch, "Devil" Judd Tolliver, sells the rights to his land to the coal company and, shortly afterward, receives official papers regarding the deal, including a check for $5,000, none of which the Tollivers can read. With construction crews soon clearing land and setting up labor camps, June is delegated for a privileged role in the new enterprise. Jack Hale, who's infatuated with her, suggests that she can do much more than any other Tolliver women, whose main function seems to be bemoaning the destructiveness and senselessness of their men folks' fighting. Hale convinces June that an education—one that could only be obtained well beyond the mountains—would allow her to become the one literate family member who can oversee the new financial rewards they'll soon be reaping. Despite the opposition of her father, Judd—who reasons that there's nothing in her duties at home that she can do better by knowing how to read and write—June takes Hale up on his offer and prepares to leave home for schooling he's arranged for her in Louisville.

The rampant illiteracy displayed by both families, and even more so the men's objection to an educational opportunity for a female family member (even one that would much enhance the management of their newfound "fortune"), is one more example of the Appalachian backwardness that so characterized perceptions of the region's "otherness" as conveyed by John Fox to turn-of-the-century readers. And yet the equally damning male chauvinism on display within the Tolliver household would most likely not have troubled many of the 1930s audiences who saw these attempts to repress June's aspirations played out onscreen.

Dave Tolliver also disapproves of his cousin's "book larnin'" and resents Hale's role as her benefactor. In chasing after June and Hale as the latter escorts her to the train in Gaptown, Dave skirts Falin property, which is all it takes to signal a renewal of armed combat. One Falin shoots and wounds Dave, thus throwing the feud back into full fighting mode, which drives much of the subsequent plot, as Falins face off against Tollivers. After putting June on the train to Louisville, Hale returns to find his construction site in flames and vows to himself, "I'll put this railroad through if I have to use your dirty, rotten bodies for ties, and have to hire every man in Gap-town to finish the job."

Tensions remain high, but with the passage of time, progress on the coal operation continues. Jack has taken June's eight-year-old brother, Buddy, under his tutelage, much to Dave's resentment. In the Tolliver cabin, Buddy (Spanky McFarland) is learning the alphabet from a book that Hale has given him. As he asks a sulking Dave what certain words mean, Dave snatches the book from him and flings it into the fireplace. "I'll tell you what it means," he shouts. "Civilization!" Judd, his uncle, tries to calm him down, but Dave turns on him, accusing him of taking satisfaction in the "newfangled" machines that are tearing up their fields. "Them machines don't care who's been plowing here for fifty years. The Tollivers don't mean nothing to them!" After a heated exchange in which Judd points to the growing pile of company checks in a bowl and insists that "if that's what you call civilization, then I'm all for it," Dave walks out, stating that he's returning to where his own pappy raised him. "I belong to the earth; the plowed-up soil."

Soon thereafter, the Falins, observing the ongoing work on the mine and rail line from the cliffs above, take a shot at a dynamite pile near where young Buddy is playing; it explodes, and Buddy is killed. In one of the more far-fetched plot twists, June happens to be on the "newfangled" telephone with Hale when the tragedy occurs. She had just been telling him about her classes, saying that "just this morning, I learned all about the Revolution. It was just like a feud. In 1775—" when she hears through the phone line the explosion that killed her little brother.

Outraged and heartbroken over Buddy's death, Hale, who up to this point had maintained a neutral stance regarding the two families in whose coal-rich land he was so heavily invested, turns on the Falins. He resorts to legal means to bring this warfare to an end, urging the local justice of the peace to bring murder charges against them. The justice responds with a lecture on the futility of such a solution: "I can bring the Falins to court; maybe hang them. But that don't stop feuds; it makes them. There'd be killings like we never seen before. Mountain people don't seem to like the law, Mr. Hale. Down here, peace has to come from within. . . . It all seems kind of brutal and primitive, while it's boiling, but I was born here and I know."

June has arrived on the scene by then, and she unleashes her grief and fury on Hale in an exchange that becomes the emotional high point of the film. "Why aren't you with Buddy and the family," she asks, "rather than being down here with the law? You said you love Buddy, but you ain't done a thing about it. You ain't fightin'; you ain't killing!" In short, her education and social polish are easily dispelled when faced with the realities of the violent culture in which she'd been raised and show her still to be the "young savage" Hale had once called her.

June repeats her cry for vengeance just after Buddy's burial the next day, this time challenging Dave to take up his rifle "and act like a Tolliver." As he does just that and heads for the door, his Aunt Melissa, Buddy's mother, begs him not to go. "I ain't hating the Falins. I ain't hating nobody." Hale too speaks up, urging him not to go. When Dave tells him, "You ain't a Tolliver," Hale counters that "none of you could have loved little Buddy like I did. And he was killed because I taught him to love the things I did. And this matter of getting even is going to be my business until I've cleaned out every Falin that had anything to do with it." And out he walks.

The film quickly builds to its climax as Dave—at June's insistence—stops Hale from taking on the Falin clan by knocking him out. Dave himself then approaches the Falins' cabin, where he overhears the father berating his three grown sons for Buddy's death, sarcastically repeating, "We're all brave men. We kill children," and bemoaning the fact that people in town would look at him and call him King Herod, a man who killed babies. Dave knocks and is allowed to come in, clearly in a gesture of peace. "If I tell you I'm licked," Dave asks, "will you quit fighting?" The father accepts his offer and offers an apology for what's transpired. As Dave turns and walks away from the house, one of the Falin sons grabs his gun, breaks a window, and shoots Dave in the back. The elder Falin quickly grabs his own gun and shoots his son. "I thought you meant it," says the dying son. "I did, I did," replies his father.

In the film's final scene, Buck Falin carries Dave's wounded body back home, and before he can confess that it was his son who shot him, Dave himself makes a noble gesture by saying he tripped and shot himself, an explanation the Falin men are all quick to corroborate. The wounded Tolliver is surrounded by his family, all of them aware that he's dying, even as he and June discuss their upcoming nuptials in the spring. The fact that father Falin is among those gathered at his bedside suggests that the long-running feud may have just taken its final victim.

The novel's ending is much different and more convoluted than that of the film, yet the latter's more compressed, if more maudlin, conclusion seems typical of 1930s melodrama. It also reinforces the anti-feud message within which it's wrapped—demonstrating far more forcefully than does Fox's book just how destructive and meaningless interfamily warfare could be. But it also suggests that the three deaths (all of which came from shots fired by Falins, including that of the father who shot his own son) were sobering enough to end the senseless cycle of vengeance and retribution that had driven this family feud for so long. More subtly, the end of the feud denotes yet another form of progress on the part of Appalachian people, if only because the settling of interfamilial differences provided one less hindrance to the incursion of modernity in the form of coal mines and railroads, an assumption as inherent in this 1930s film as it was in Fox's novel produced thirty years earlier.

• • • • • •

The multigenerational feud that played out sporadically between the Hatfields and the McCoys over the course of two decades in the late nineteenth century remains the most familiar—indeed, the epitome—of Appalachian feuds and how Americans came to perceive them. Certain episodes generated sensationalistic journalistic coverage that reached a national readership, and these stories have remained the basis of the legacy that's expanded in both popular culture and historical scholarship. One of the first productions of the silent film industry was *A Kentucky Feud* in 1905, which explicitly referenced the Hatfield-McCoy clash as its subject. Both clans "are now about exterminated by years of duels and assassinations," touted a studio-generated synopsis of the D. W. Griffith–directed film, reflecting on how recently it had waned.[25] "Nowhere in the world, except possibly Corsica," the studio publicist continued, "has warfare between two families been carried out to such bitter extremes, and it is well known that no process of law has been able to prevent the ever-recurring bloody battles."[26] The Romeo and Juliet scenario—lovers from opposing families who meet tragic ends—was also introduced in *A Kentucky Feud* and played out in numerous other films through much of the silent era. In his topical categorization of Appalachian-based silent movies made between 1904 and 1929, Jerry Williamson lists nearly a hundred such productions with feud-centered plots. He subdivides those into two types—"Romeo and Juliet love stories" and "Others," with slightly more than half falling into the first grouping.[27]

Those trends waned by the mid-1920s and disappeared almost entirely with the onset of the sound era in 1929. It would be two decades later, in 1949, before Hollywood directly confronted the Hatfields and McCoys again. Interestingly, that film is named for a female member of one of the rival clans, *Roseanna McCoy*, and makes her its protagonist. Samuel Goldwyn, one of the leading producers of the era, had come upon a 1947 novel of that title by a prolific West Virginia author, Alberta Hannum, and commissioned another novelist, John Collier, to adapt it as a screenplay.[28] The title signals that it is to be a love story—and, given that the title character is a McCoy, that her affair with a Hatfield will be the central focus.

Historical accounts of that particular star-crossed romance provide only the bare bones of their story, which has been fleshed out considerably through myth and lore. According to scholarly sources, Roseanna, the twenty-one-year-old daughter of Old Randall (or Ranel) McCoy, and eighteen-year-old Johnse Hatfield, the son of Devil Anse Hatfield, met at a local election gathering in the spring of 1880. Though the feud between the two families was already underway, Johnse took Roseanna home to meet the notorious Hatfield patriarch. Predictably, Anse disapproved of marriage for the budding young lovers but tolerated Roseanna's presence and allowed the young couple to extend their courtship over the next six months, at the end of which Roseanna was pregnant and the relationship was broken off—at whose instigation it's hard to determine. Soon thereafter (and perhaps earlier), Johnse courted Roseanna's sixteen-year-old cousin, Nancy McCoy; they married in the spring of 1881. There's no indication of opposition to this match from the Hatfield and McCoy fathers, which suggests that the feud may not have been as central a factor in breaking up Roseanna and Johnse's affair as was previously assumed. The most authoritative historian of the subject, Altina Waller, assesses the romance's significance as "not a cause of the feud, nor was it especially relevant to later developments."[29] Yet "to middle-class America, with its rigid moral values and its obsession with sentimental love and illicit sexuality, the 'mountain Romeo and Juliet' story became the single most intriguing part of the feud."[30]

That description likely held true for 1940s movie-goers as well, thus providing the focus—hardly original—of the story Goldwyn and company chose to tell on screen. Goldwyn also sought to broaden the movie's audience by watering down the prestige adaptation for more mass appeal. According to lead actor Farley Granger, Collier's first screenplay captured much of "the mysticism of the mountains," but that proved too literary for the producer, who brought in other writers who "whittled it down to hokey melodrama and hillbilly clichés."[31] The casting itself reflected the less-than-prestigious project Goldwyn had settled for. The title role went to an unknown sixteen-year-old in her first screen appearance; renamed Joan

Evans, she co-starred with Granger as Johnse Hatfield. Only in the role of their parents do we get distinguished character actors giving more accomplished performances—Raymond Massey and Charles Bickford as the McCoy and Hatfield patriarchs, respectively, with Hope Emerson and Aline MacMahan each holding their own as their wives. True to its title, Roseanna is very much the focal point of the story, but, like Hannum's novel, the film also allows other female characters to play integral roles in establishing the relationships both between and within their families.

The film opens with two McCoy brothers (including a twelve-year-old called Young Randall or Rand) and their hunting dogs chasing a bear across a river. The older boy calls the dogs back, reminding Rand, "We have to stay on our side of the river; you know why." Though the river is never named in the film, it's obviously the Tug Fork of the Big Sandy River, which separates Kentucky from West Virginia and McCoys from Hatfields. (It was filmed in the mountains of California's Sierra Madre.) When the boys arrive home—a fairly spacious farm, with a comfortable house, a vast field of crops, and several sizable outbuildings—and report that they've been hunting, their father, Old Randall (the imposing Massey), launches into a tirade against the Hatfields, thus establishing the only discernible point of contention between the two families—their class distinctions. Calling the Hatfields "a tribe of savages," he says, "Look at the land they settled on, and by their own choice. Not fit to raise a field of corn. Hunting country, hunting people, idle, cutthroat drunken savages. I want these boys raised as good farmers—I don't want them to slip back to 'cabin folk' again."

McCoy is concerned about his eighteen-year-old daughter as well (the film knocks three years off her actual age at the time), and as she prepares to go to a local fair, his last words to her are, "Remember who you are, Roseanna; stay with your own kind." Inevitably, the Hatfield men, a distinctly rougher breed than the McCoys or most other attendees, march onto the scene, and the youngest son, a cocky Johnse, sets his sights on Roseanna, who's both repelled and attracted by his ever-more-aggressive attention. She gradually capitulates to his courting, despite her full awareness of the enmity between their families. She even accuses him and his cousin Mounts of having shot and injured her mother years before, bringing women into yet another role in the feud—as literal victims of its cross fire.[32] (That incident is dramatized in full in the next film discussed, *Hatfields & McCoys*.)

Roseanna returns home, and not long after makes a promise to Johnse that she'll cross the river with him the following night, and he'll introduce her to his parents and other relatives. The house to which he takes her is a cruder cabin perched on a mountaintop cliff, illustrating, not so subtly, the Hatfields' less comfortable and more isolated circumstances. Roseanna notes how "wild it is," with "no place for a garden, or flowers." (Factually, the opposite was true. As Altina Waller makes clear, Devil Anse Hatfield's socioeconomic status was far more stable and on the rise than was that of Ranel McCoy or any of his family.)[33] Only Johnse's mother, Levicy, and the younger children are at home when the couple arrive, and there's obviously tension over Roseanna's presence, especially as they anticipate Devil Anse's appearance on the scene.

When Anse does appear, he is indeed displeased with the news and with the presence of a McCoy under his roof. So begins a heated discussion of what's to come. He tells his son outright, "You're a Hatfield, ain't you? There'll be no talk around here of marriage into storekeepers, clodhopper farmers, and such trash." Levicy asks her son what he thinks the McCoys will do when they find out that Roseanna has become a Hatfield. "You're right," Anse replies somewhat sarcastically. "We haven't had any fighting around here for a long time and I've missed it. Keep her around. She'll draw trouble sure as honey draws flies. We'll see if McCoy's money can wipe that out."

Soon thereafter, Anse rallies his sons and tells them to round up all the men of the clan, and all the ammunition they can, in anticipation of McCoy retaliation or a rescue attempt, thus signaling a re-escalation of violence and a new phase of the feud. Roseanna is spunky enough to berate the old man, angrily telling him, "You want to go kill my folks just because Johnse and I love each other. You don't want him to be happy. You don't want to make him kind and good to folks, but to be hard, and wicked and cruel and miserable as you."

In one of the film's tensest moments, Roseanna is left alone at the Hatfield cabin (when Johnse has gone off to find a preacher to marry them) and is surprised by the sudden appearance of Mounts at the door. In a chilling portrayal by Richard Baseheart, Mounts simultaneously taunts and threatens her at knifepoint; she realizes that he's the man who shot her mother years earlier, which he acknowledges. She runs from the cabin just as Anse arrives home; he takes Mounts's knife from him and orders him to stay away from Roseanna. Like his wife before him, Devil Anse has softened in his attitude toward this outspoken yet vulnerable young girl, who had earlier accused him of cruelty, wickedness, and misery.

In order to avoid the open warfare that's looming, Roseanna agrees to return home (though Johnse has plans to elope with her the following night).

She begs her father's forgiveness, though she confides to her mother her frustration at his continued hostility to Johnse and his family due to "what other people did years and years ago." "It ain't that," her mother responds. "They're a rough, wild, no-good sort of people," once again reducing the enmity between the families to the simplistic contempt of farmers for hunters, and vice versa.

On his way to the McCoy farm the next night to speak with Old Randall, Johnse and two other Hatfields stop by a nearby general store, where they're confronted by several McCoys. The face-off quickly turns from a brawl into a shoot-out in and around the store, in which one of the McCoy boys is seriously wounded. As Old Randall retrieves and carries home what is by then his son's lifeless body, he declares all-out warfare: "All these years, I've hated the name and sight of those murdering savages. Now we'll speak that hate with guns. We'll ride the hills and rouse every McCoy from his bed."

What follows is just that: an extended final sequence (fully fictionalized) in which men on both sides are roused into action and a full-scale battle is fought over the cliffs and rocks along the river that serves as the border between the two families. In its midst, the two lovers reunite and try to make their escape on horseback across the river. As Mounts catches sight of them midstream and takes aim at them, Devil Anse raises his rifle and shoots Mounts in the back, killing him before he can fire a shot. That signals what's at least a temporary cease-fire—and thus a Hollywood happy ending—as Roseanna and Johnse ride off into the sunset, intercut with fleeting glimpses of both of their fathers witnessing their departure and smiling.

• • • • • •

The Hatfield-McCoy saga continued to play out on screens big and small, from satiric cartoon shorts to lackluster made-for-television dramas.[34] Certainly the most serious treatment of the feud (and most successful in terms of ratings and critical reception) is the most recent: a three-part miniseries produced by and aired on the History Channel in May 2012, titled simply *Hatfields & McCoys*. At over five hours in length, this production had the luxury of ample screen time in order to offer far fuller coverage of the multiple incidents that collectively defined the iconic conflict over its two-decade span. While it doesn't acknowledge any source material beyond three screenwriters, it is obvious that those three took advantage of the scholarly advances on the topic, particularly the most definitive and detailed account to date: Altina Waller's now classic 1988 chronicle, *Feud*. While one can admire the production's adherence to the historical record, some reviewers found the final screenplay to be too much of a good thing, or rather that the filmmakers took their subject matter a bit too seriously. According to the *Los Angeles Times*' critic, "It isn't a perfect piece; when faced between historical detail and story, *Hatfields & McCoys* errs on the side of detail, which is both the series' greatest strength and weakness."[35] (Given Hollywood's frequent disregard for historical truth, this is not a complaint often heard about a film's quest for accuracy at the expense of entertainment value.)

The miniseries was produced by Kevin Costner, who saw it as a star vehicle for himself as the senior (and far more sympathetic) of the two family patriarchs, Anse Hatfield. Costner also made the decision to pitch the project as a television production rather than a feature film, for the advantages inherent in spreading the story over multiple episodes (and perhaps due to his waning clout as a film presence, both in front of and behind the camera). Directed by Kevin Reynolds, with whom Costner had worked before, it was cast with top-tier actors, several of whom, including Costner, give strong, noteworthy performances. Yet the sheer number of named characters and their relations to each other can be perplexing to viewers either unfamiliar with the kinship complexities of how the two sides sorted themselves out or unaware of the legal machinations the conflict entailed.

Almost as much of the story plays out in courtrooms, lawyers' offices, and jail cells as it does on family farms and in the timber-rich wilderness, most of which was filmed in Romania (taking a cue from the producers of *Cold Mountain*, who a decade earlier had made the Carpathian Mountains double as western North Carolina). Much of it seems to be staged as a western, in the traditional Hollywood version of a strip town set, with hitching posts and a spacious, gaudy saloon complete with poker games, barmaids, and honky-tonk piano music; more than one shoot-out takes place either in the bar or on the street outside it. While the feud did frequently involve legal and social interactions in the two county seats (Pikeville, Kentucky, and Logan, West Virginia), the two seem indistinguishable onscreen, both more fitting for stereotypical western towns than for Appalachian villages. (An article on Costner's 2018 series, *Yellowstone*, listed other westerns that featured "Cowboy Costner," including *Hatfields & McCoys*.)[36]

Yet while a historian might complain that it is, at times, both too complex and too oversimplified, *Hatfields & McCoys*' filmmakers on the whole make an admirable attempt at adhering to the historical record, certainly more so than most made-for-television docudramas, and certainly when compared with any other screen version of this most familiar—or notorious—of all American feuds. Unlike other film depictions of these clannish clashes, this one does not dodge the crucial issue of how the conflict started; rather, it offers multiple explanations of its origin and regeneration that are viable, if not fully tenable, based on current scholarly assessments.

The series opens on an unnamed Civil War battlefield in West Virginia in 1863, in which both Anse Hatfield (Costner) and Randall McCoy (Bill Paxton) serve together in a Confederate company. At the end of an intense attack by Union troops, Captain Hatfield takes heroic action to minimize the onslaught's damage to his men. Immediately afterward, he confides to McCoy—at that point a close friend—that he's deserting the army and going home, acknowledging Confederate prospects as a "lost cause." McCoy tries to dissuade him but offers little more than reminders that they swore "death before dishonor" and that "God hates deserters," by which point Anse has mounted his horse and headed off. (Historically, Hatfield and at least two of his nephews did desert in 1863, purportedly to form a guerrilla band back home.)[37]

The film's following sequence is also based on historical fact. Although the actual details remain sketchy, it's dramatized quite credibly. In 1863, Harmon McCoy, Randall's brother, is publicly taunted at a saloon in Mate's Creek (later renamed Matewan) by Anse's uncle Jim Vance (a gruff, heavy-set Tom Berenger), who takes offense at the "Yankee" blue jacket worn by Harmon, one of few in the area with Union sympathies. The exchange turns into a bitter spat, with Harmon spewing reckless insults and accusations at Vance. Harmon realizes he's in trouble and goes into hiding; a month or so later, he is hunted down at Vance's behest by two younger Hatfields and killed, thus becoming the first death suffered by one family at the hands of the other. (Factually, Vance himself could have been Harmon's killer.) Yet Waller argues, quite logically, that Civil War loyalties were not the major impetus for the feud, given that it was thirteen years later, in 1878, when the next incident pitting Hatfields against McCoys occurred. She also notes, as does the film, that most members of both families were Confederate sympathizers all along.[38] Nevertheless, the screenwriters took seriously the war and the personal and local animosities it stirred, choosing to depict them as long lingering.

At the same time, in ways far more subtle and sophisticated than is true of most historically based films, the writers adeptly work in yet another causal factor—indeed one that Waller argues is crucial—as connective narrative tissue, even if the chronology is a bit skewed. Anse wastes no time upon his return home to take on a new business venture: timber. He says as much when news of the war's end spreads. In response to a bystander's comment, "It won't be over for some," Hatfield replies, "War's a goddamn waste; I don't intend to waste the peace."

On film, Randall McCoy is captured and spends the war's latter months as a prisoner at Ohio's Camp Chase. As he trudges home, months after the war ends, he passes a busy crew of timber cutters working a nearly barren mountainside and bitterly observes that they are being supervised by Anse, saw in hand. He expresses his resentment when the two meet the next day at church (of all places). While Anse greets him as his old friend, Randall confronts him again for deserting and for his brother Harmon's death.

Newly licensed lawyer Perry Cline, a cousin of the McCoys, makes his first appearance with a legal challenge to Anse's right to the timber on land that he'd bought just before the war. The scene plays out with considerable specificity regarding the legitimacy of the deeds to the property in question. Through a series of legal maneuvers in court, Anse exposes fraudulent actions by Cline (Ronan Vibert) and ultimately forces him to give up the timber rights to five thousand acres of land Cline had just inherited from his father. This and subsequent courtroom contests not only provide genuine drama but also serve to highlight the economic impetus—control of land and its resources—that fueled much of the family vendetta to come and made Perry Cline such an important player in that struggle (and, in this version, one of its more villainous instigators).

Only then does the film take a leap forward chronologically to the incidents most associated with the actual feud, beginning with the infamous "hog trial" of 1878, in which McCoy catches a neighbor, Floyd Hatfield, in possession of his missing pig. Cline urges McCoy to sue and naturally serves as his lawyer when he does. The trial does little to actually fuel the feud, other than attract new attention—and ridicule—to it. Yet it is taken quite seriously by the filmmakers, plays out in considerable detail onscreen, and works quite well dramatically, as does its aftermath. It also serves to make clear the reality that the two sides were not necessarily determined by name or kinship. The judge who presides over the trial, Valentine Hatfield (Powers Boothe), is trusted by the McCoys as being fully neutral in his rulings (seeing the whole affair as unworthy of his time or that of the court), and both a witness and a jury member named Hatfield weigh in against the Hatfield defendant. In addition, the court scene brings the community together and serves to introduce a second generation of family members who have come of age since the war and will become active players in the feud's latter phases.

It's no surprise that the Roseanna McCoy–Johnse Hatfield romance also warrants extended screen time. This segment amounts to nearly a third of the miniseries' content, given how its implications both reflect and inflame the hostility between the two families, with plot developments encompassing far more people and emotional resonance than do other facets of the feud. The beginnings of their relationship play out much as they did in the more simplistic 1949 film, but then follow the factual record that goes well beyond the vague and misleading happy ending of the earlier film. Johnse's infidelity with Roseanna's cousin Nancy McCoy (Jena Malone), and Roseanna's abandonment by both families when it becomes apparent that she's pregnant, serve to deepen the ill will and resentment of McCoys and Hatfields alike and lead to tragic consequences for her (as the historical record vaguely indicates). It also brings out the staunch character of the two mothers—Sally McCoy (Mare Winningham, in a particularly moving performance) and Levicy Hatfield (a too-young Sarah Parish)—who are both thrust into more proactive roles in this and later phases of the ongoing conflict, though not necessarily as the arbiters and peacemakers that their maternal counterparts were consigned to play in earlier feud films.

The violence escalates in the final phase of the feud, which consists of those episodes that earned the two families' spat such national notoriety and which are reproduced fairly faithfully onscreen. Growing ever more retaliatory, the hostility between Anse and Randall and that of their followers plays out in various forms, with ever-increasing casualties. A carefully planned attack by the Hatfields on the McCoy home on New Year's Day 1888 (fleetingly referred to in *Roseanna McCoy*) is meticulously re-created here and stands as one of the film's most chilling episodes. Though Anse insists that Randall be their only target, the Hatfield sons set the house on fire, forcing Randall and his entire family to make a run for it as the Hatfields shoot them down, killing both a son and a daughter of Randall and seriously wounding his wife, Sally. The incident is especially sobering in that it has subjected household domains to the same level of destructive violence that had once been limited to men.

Later that year, the largest confrontation takes place as mounted contingents on both sides engage in open warfare—the so-called battle of Grapevine Creek—providing a full-scale spectacle as the feud, like the film,

A Hatfield family portrait, with patriarch Anse (Kevin Costner) and his wife, Levicy (Sarah Parish), at the center.

reaches its climax. Though there are few casualties, several Hatfields are captured and tried. Only one, Ellison Mounts—a mentally challenged youth identified vaguely as an illegitimate son of Anse—is actually sentenced to death for the shooting of McCoy's daughter on New Year's Day, thus becoming a sacrificial lamb for the sins of his more competent and manipulative kinfolk, three of whom are sentenced to life imprisonment.[39] Anse's son Cap urges his father to let him break those three out, but Anse declines his request, stating that he doesn't want the next generation to take this on. "You're going to have children someday," he tells his son, "and your children aren't going to care about our old grudges and slights from long ago. . . . It's time for us to move on." And so the story ends with the legal system reasserting control, with individuals on both sides—men and women alike—expressing their regrets over the waste, the destruction, and, in at least one case, the pointlessness of the many years of vindictiveness.

Scenes of building a gallows and the gathering of spectators around it are intercut with that of a family gathering of Hatfields, called together by

Anse at his home. As part of a growing crowd to see Mounts's hanging, a young woman asks her husband why they had to dress the children up and come all this way to see it, to which he responds, "Hatfields and McCoys are famous." "Famous for what?" she inquires. "Famous for killing each other," is his final word on the subject.

Simultaneously, at the Hatfield gathering, Anse announces that he's prepared a message he's going to send out to newspapers (many of which were already giving thorough coverage to the ongoing vendetta). More than once, Anse Hatfield had sought a quiet resolution to the feud, mainly directed to his patriarchal counterpart and former friend, Randall McCoy, but to no avail. His notice this time serves as a final pronouncement, which he reads aloud: "I do not wish to keep the old feud alive. I suppose that, like me, everyone is tired of the names Hatfield and McCoy, and border warfare in time of peace. The war spirit in me has abated and I sincerely rejoice in the prospect of peace."

Despite conciliatory gestures made by Costner's Anse, urging a much more obstinate and hate-filled Randall to end the feud, which he maintains (probably rightfully) that only the two of them could make happen, Randall, ten years younger than Anse, is far more unwavering in his hostility toward the Hatfields, much of it fueled by Perry Cline and others who had been, at one point or another, victims of the "Devil's" legal or business acumen. By complicating both characters and motives, *Hatfields & McCoys* offers a far more sophisticated and nuanced account of the actual struggle, driven as it was by multiple factors—socioeconomic, psychological, and emotional. Given fairly equal weight, all three factors serve to shape the loyalties of each side and mitigate the role of kinship as the sole—or even prevalent—determinant of one's allegiance. Such was well beyond the scope of earlier film treatments of feuding mountaineers, though thematically, they are all of a piece with the 2012 miniseries in more ways than one.

• • • • • •

Perhaps foremost, the family unit is integral to all four of these films, just as it is to the very definition of feuding; yet in both gendered and generational terms, those relationships play out in a variety of ways. If more simplistically rendered in the first three films discussed, one clan in each claimed the audience's sympathies far more than the other. *Tol'able David*'s ultimately heroic title character, David Kinemon, is obviously the most sympathetic figure in that 1921 film, but equally significant is the fact that he is part of a full family—two parents and their three children—who are victimized by caricatured villains consisting of the all-male Hatburn clan. It is the disabling of the family that forces young David to step up and single-handedly fight these foes, ultimately (if improbably) killing them all—thus making this the most short-lived feud, with both a clear-cut beginning (and cause) and an equally finite end, in which good clearly triumphs over evil.

The Trail of the Lonesome Pine begins with two families already long at war with each other. As with its silent predecessor thirteen years earlier, the 1936 film depicts one family, the Falins, as all male—a father and several adult sons—and implicitly malevolent, while the Tollivers are far more sympathetic and interesting, in part because of the vital presence of a forceful, outspoken mother presiding over the household, and a daughter who's even more so. Further exacerbating the age-old hostility between the two families is the onset of modernization and the extent to which outside forces—railroads and coal companies—offer new opportunities and better lives to the mountain people. (By implication, such advances will serve to overcome the primitiveness and backwardness of their current lives, of which feuding is the most tangible manifestation; and yet there's no sense of prescience regarding the long-term impact of these "advances" on the land itself or on the locals living on it.) The Tollivers embrace these outside enterprises while the Falins shun them, suggesting that the lack of class differences in the two families will soon change, as the former come to profit considerably from the deal they've made, though they will pay dearly for their newfound fortune—in multiple deaths, including that of an eight-year-old.

Both of the Hatfield and McCoy films portray two full-fledged, two-parent households as the heart of their stories, though only the later miniseries completes that portrait by acknowledging the crucial, often entangled roles played by extended family members. Class prejudices—based on subtle and fluid differences—are evident in both films as well. In *Roseanna McCoy*, the McCoys live comfortably on what seems to be a productive farm, while the Hatfields live more remotely and modestly, depicting enough of a contrast in lifestyles to suggest a long-brewing contempt between farmers and hunters that was at least an underlying factor in the otherwise unexplained feud. In *Hatfields & McCoys*, produced some six decades later, the tables are turned. The Hatfields are, for the most part, more sympathetic characters than the McCoys—or at least Anse outshines Randall as a committed family man. Anse's timber business makes him the more enterprising and prosperous of the two—and the source of much of the McCoy family's resentment (not to mention what drew several McCoys to associate themselves with the Hatfields)—yet such a ranking is complicated by the fact that members of a so-called county-seat elite, including Perry Cline, Wall Hatfield, and other McCoy partisans, prove a considerable advantage as the legal struggle becomes more integral to the latter phase of the feud.

In short, screen treatments of Appalachian-based feuds from 1921 to 2012 share much more in common than might be evident at first glance. Their characters all feature strong personalities that determine how and why they are caught up in these family vendettas—whether as perpetrators, victims, or opponents—thus offering a spectrum, often only subtly implied, of socioeconomic circumstances that combine with more blatant human foibles—envy, revenge, power, greed, illicit romance—to complicate and contextualize late nineteenth-century southern highland society beyond the simplistic and sensationalistic treatment of mere "hillbillies" shooting at each other, which had been perpetuated in other forms of popular culture for so long.[40]

All of these films feature considerable interaction between spouses, siblings, and parents and their children, who are sometimes drawn closer and occasionally pulled apart by the clan-based vendettas in which they become entangled. Feuds are quite rightly conveyed as functions of decidedly patriarchal households (even though, among these four films, only the two Hatfield-McCoy films cast those patriarchs as the dominant—or most domineering—characters). Women, on the other hand, take on more varied roles. They often prove to be victims (even casualties) of the violence perpetrated by their menfolk, yet on occasion they find—or make—themselves active participants in (even instigators of) the actions taken by their husbands or others in their households.[41] Most of the matriarchal figures are portrayed by formidable character actresses and, more often than not, show at least as much fortitude as and often more moral judgment than their husbands or children. It is no coincidence that the two feuding clans that are exclusively male (the Hatburns and the Falins) are the most one-dimensional and least sympathetic of the eight families featured in these four films.

And, of course, women (or girls) are integral to the romances that serve as catalysts in all four of these sagas, where again they could be as assertive (June Tolliver) or as manipulative (Nancy McCoy) as their male counterparts. Those relationships, like all the others embraced by these narratives, served to humanize mountain people in situations brought on by a range of circumstances to which both leading and supporting participants reacted in a variety of ways. While the distinctions between the feuding families in each film—and the sheer number of characters each comprised—allow for varied levels of approval or disapproval, empathy, and admiration or revulsion among viewers, they also serve to individualize and complicate those highlanders who had for so often been stereotyped and stigmatized for the very behaviors on which these films focus.

Yet one cannot dismiss the range of violence and lawlessness that proved so endemic to these vendettas or the senseless loss of human life inflicted by these families on each other. From the full-scale shoot-outs (such as that between the Tollivers and the Falins that opens *The Trail of the Lonesome Pine* or the "battle" of Grapevine Creek in the *Hatfields & McCoys* miniseries) to ambushes, arson, execution-style shootings, fistfights, wrestling matches, barroom brawls, and even explosives, killing takes many forms and a wide array of victims. Perhaps most shocking are the deaths of young people—such as eight-year-old Buddy Tolliver and twelve-year-old Rand McCoy—or the two older sons (one Hatfield and one Falin) shot by their own fathers.

Yet none of these films characterize mountain people exclusively by these actions, as vital as they were to both the purpose and the entertainment value of each production. The eight feuding families depicted in these four films (counting two sets of Hatfields and McCoys) differ in subtle and not-so-subtle ways that go well beyond their roles in perpetuating or reacting to this violence. These include differences of class, education, aspirations, values, lifestyles, work ethics, and temperaments. In some ways, they defy stereotypes; in other ways, they confirm them. As Kathleen Blee and Dwight Billings so aptly described the creation of those stereotypes around the turn of the century: "Through the lens of those who rushed to the southern mountains to chronicle the region, it was a curious people who inhabited the land of newfound riches. Whether portrayed as savage, primitive, treacherous, or bloodthirsty, mountaineers were definitely cast as the other, radically and essentially different from the rest of American society."[42] Yet for Hollywood and its subsequent depictions of Appalachia's feuding families, from silent films through recent television miniseries, such imagery was only part of the far more mixed, multifaceted, and ultimately human portraits conveyed onscreen.

5 Women on a Mission

The "discovery" of Appalachia in the late nineteenth and early twentieth centuries has always loomed large in the vast and growing scholarship on the region. As missionaries, educators, social workers, and academics moved into the southern highlands in increasing numbers, the issue of "cultural otherness"—as David Whisnant has termed it—became central to how Americans came to see and understand Appalachia.[1] More specifically, it was an era in which, to quote Whisnant again, "mostly educated, urban, middle- and upper-class, liberal 'culture workers' perceived, manipulated, . . . and projected the culture of mostly rural, lower-class working people in the southern mountains during the half-century after 1890."[2] Much of the appeal of this particular constituency for such largesse is the fact that these southern highlanders were, for all the cultural otherness they embodied, white.[3]

The fact that women were front and center among these so-called benevolent workers has attracted much of the historical and literary work produced on Appalachia's "age of discovery."[4] Given the dramatic possibilities inherent in white women working heroically among strange and often exotic new peoples, it should come as no surprise that such stories attracted the attention of Hollywood, which produced a number of high-profile films based on this formula during the 1940s and 1950s. In 1951, Katharine Hepburn appeared in *The African Queen* as an American missionary to the Congo who joins forces with rogue Humphrey Bogart to combat Germans during World War I; a few years later, Ingrid Bergman starred as Gladys Aylward, a British woman who served in a remote Chinese orphanage in the 1930s, in *The Inn of the Sixth Happiness* (1958); and British widow Anna Leonowens's experience as a tutor to the children of the king of Siam in the 1960s resulted in two films: *Anna and the King of Siam* in 1946, and its musical adaptation, Rodgers and Hammerstein's *The King and I*, a decade later. Nuns as foreign mission workers were the subject of *Black Narcissus* (1947), with Deborah Kerr as the head of an order based in the Tibetan Himalayas, and *The Nun's Story* (1959), in which Audrey Hepburn plays a Belgian sister who joins a medical mission in Africa. All these films were based on novels except *The Inn of the Sixth Happiness*, which was inspired by a biography of Aylward.[5]

Along with such sagas of American and European women on missions to enlighten nonwhite peoples in Africa and Asia are several films that dramatize the same dynamic by American women reaching out to fellow Americans (and fellow whites) whose otherness provides fully as much of a culture clash as that experienced by the foreign-mission workers. Three films portray such encounters between outsiders and Appalachian residents, though only the first falls within the time frame of the trend just described, the other two having been made nearly a half century later. Each film centers on the experiences of individual women who, for different reasons and under different circumstances, move into the southern mountains with a mission. One came as the wife of a Methodist minister, one as a mission-school teacher, and one as a musicologist collecting mountain ballads. As such, they reflect three of the most basic and universal incentives behind these outreach efforts: religion, education, and culture brokering.

Though heavily fictionalized, each of these films is based on the experiences of real women. Corra Harris's loosely autobiographical account of her experience with her husband's first pastorate in the north Georgia mountains in the 1880s, *A Circuit Rider's Wife* (1910), inspired the film *I'd Climb the Highest Mountain* in 1951. Catherine Marshall, wife of celebrated preacher Peter Marshall, produced a best-selling novel, *Christy* (1967), based on her Asheville-born mother, Leonora Wood, and her first year as a teacher at a mission school across the state line in Tennessee's Great Smoky Mountains in 1910. It was made into a television movie in 1994, which served as the pilot for a short-lived series on CBS. Finally, *Songcatcher* (2000) is an independently produced film drawn in large part from the experiences of Olive Dame Campbell and her academic quest in 1907 to capture the English ballads and other music of North Carolina's Blue Ridge Mountains.

In one way or another, all three films treat what Whisnant saw as the central issue of this age of Appalachian discovery: "how people perceive each other across cultural boundaries." How these particular women engaged the Georgia, Tennessee, and Carolina highlanders they encountered in their missions and how those highlanders responded to them serve as a promising means of gauging Hollywood's shifting treatment of Appalachia and its people. Equally significant are the depictions of the female protagonists themselves. The rapport they establish with the highlanders they serve proves to be transformative to one degree or another, and they leave the region with a very different sense of who they are and what they are capable of. The varied nature of those particular messages, or morals of their stories, tells us as much about the eras in which these films were produced as they do about the historical realities they seek to re-create.

• • • • • •

Corra Harris was a prolific Georgia writer, whose "highly publicized experience in backwoods Protestantism," as one biographer termed it, began as a serial in the *Saturday Evening Post* in 1908, which was then pulled together and published as a novel in 1910.[6] While loosely based on the first year of her marriage to Lundy Harris in 1887 and his itinerant ministry in Hart County in northeastern Georgia (adjacent to her home county of Elbert), *A Circuit Rider's Wife* was as far from that reality of some twenty-three years earlier as the film version was from the novel. In actuality, Corra White was only seventeen years old when she married Harris, her senior by over a decade, and she moved only twenty-two miles from her hometown of Elberton to begin that ministry at three Hart County churches, as assigned by the Methodist's North Georgia Conference. The Harrises served but a single troubled year in that assignment before Lundy was offered a teaching position at Emory College in Atlanta, much to the relief of both husband and wife.[7]

When Harris made that yearlong experience the basis of her later writings, she extended both the time frame (covering many years) and her geographical base. William and Mary Thompson, the fictional counterparts of Lundy and herself, were appointed to several circuits, including one or two in more mountainous areas than the Redwine Circuit, which was the sole appointment actually served by the Harrises. It was in one of those highland settings, Harris wrote, that the Thompsons found themselves in "desperate straits," given that the people in the Blue Ridge Mountains had "no money at all except that which they received for a few loads of tanbark and with which they paid their taxes."[8] Relief came in the form of Christmas boxes of clothing and other necessities sent by "the women in a rich city church," one of which the Thompsons were fortunate enough to receive, which allowed William to make "a splendid appearance in the cast-off dinner suit of a certain rich but wicked Congressman."[9]

One biographer termed Harris's book more of a spiritual autobiography than a novel.[10] Given that Lundy was dying after years of alcoholism and mental instability as Corra was writing her book (he committed suicide later in 1910, after its publication), her tone was far darker than anything suggested in its screen adaptation. More episodic and rambling than plot-driven, the narrative focuses on how hard those years were for the couple, both ill-equipped for the arduous life of a circuit-riding ministry. Harris conveys real bitterness at the Methodist establishment that provided them—and other itinerant pastors—with little support and forced them to endure financial hardship.[11] The book is also a chronicle of a marriage in which Mary Thompson gradually learns that she has married a complex and sometimes tortured man, who wrestles with conflicts between church doctrine and governance and his theological beliefs. That somber tone is alleviated by what Harris's editor once called her "pithy little stories about southern country folk" for whom the couple display a genuine affection.[12] One critic summed up the common thread running through much of her work and the key to its appeal: "She was . . . an unapologetic champion of wives and mothers, telling their stories and celebrating their courage in homely, small-town settings that were being threatened by the ravages of fast-growing cities, swift industrialization, foreign ideologies, and rapidly changing morals."[13] To that, he could have added the obvious: her subjects were multigenerational Americans, and they were white.

It was those qualities that first attracted Atlanta native Lamar Trotti, one of Hollywood's most prolific screenwriters from the late 1930s through the early 1950s, to Harris's fiction; as early as 1945, he attempted to put together a film project based on *A Circuit Rider's Wife*. (Harris herself had tried to sell her books to film producers in the 1910s and 1920s, but she abandoned such efforts well before her death in 1935.)[14] While likely coincidental, the project came to fruition at a time when Hollywood was producing other films focused on white women mission workers, as noted at the start of this chapter. Beyond its domestic—or home mission—setting, *I'd Climb the Highest Mountain* stands apart from those films in that its focus is on a marriage and on a woman coming to terms with her duty as a wife. As such, it is probably more reflective of the 1950s than were those sagas of heroic—or merely plucky—women operating independently (or in league with other women) in far more remote and dangerous foreign cultures.

Trotti's adaptation, which ultimately went before the cameras in 1950, made significant revisions to Harris's novel. He minimized its angry tone, shifted William's spiritual doubts onto Mary, and made them far more fleeting incidents than the serious and sustained struggles with which William grappled in the novel. According to actor Alexander Knox, who appeared in the film, "Trotti may have an unfortunate talent for the mild, 'folksy' kind of sentiment which makes him the victim of certain kinds of story," and it was certainly those qualities in Harris's work that he chose to forefront.[15] One commentator noted that "tableau after tableau might serve as a *Saturday Evening Post* cover, which after all, were often quite charming in their old-oaken-bucket appeal."[16] Trotti also shifted the story's time frame from the early 1880s, at the beginning of the Harrises' marriage, to 1910, the year it ended so tragically (though of course Lundy's suicide was never referred to, or even hinted at, in his screenplay).

Equally important was his decision to set the story entirely in the mountains and within a single congregation and community, decisions that in turn forced a change in the title—from *A Circuit Rider's Wife* (since the circuit riding was scuttled) to *I'd Climb the Highest Mountain*. Nearly all of the film was made on location in Habersham and White Counties in north Georgia, much of it in the scenic Nacoochee Valley, using such quaint locales as chapels, railroad stations, farmhouses, ponds, streams, red clay roads, and vast cornfields in and around Helen, Demorest, Clarkesville, and Tallulah Falls. All of the extras and several minor character roles were given to local residents. (Some twenty Georgians had speaking parts, and over five hundred Georgians were employed in other roles on the production.) Trotti assured them that "the picture would poke no *Tobacco Road* fun at them," and joked that "we'll hang the first Yankee actor who tries to fake a southern accent." That commitment to accuracy and the respect shown to the local community (quite a contrast to the set of *Deliverance*, filmed twenty years later and only a couple of counties away) paid off in immense goodwill throughout the state and an enthusiastic reception for the film when it premiered in Georgia a year later.[17]

While the mountain setting, photographed in vivid Technicolor, quickly became—and remains—one of the film's chief assets, the local people to whom the Thompsons minister are anything but backwoods hillbillies. Trotti, who served as producer as well as screenwriter, hired Hollywood veteran Henry King to direct the film, and he too saw this as far more a story of rural America than of Appalachia, a term never mentioned in the film (and beyond its use in the title, the word "mountain" was rarely used in promoting the film or in analysis of it since). "It was a film about people who had never been seen in motion pictures," King later recalled in explaining its appeal to him. "I thought it was a story worth telling, a story of America, real Americana."[18] Surprisingly, the spiritual dimension of the story was fully preserved onscreen, with much discussion of faith, belief, and spirit, and quite a few scenes set in church. This led King to note that while the film was a success in the United States, "it did nothing abroad, because they don't know anything about Protestantism outside the United States."[19]

It was, as were most Hollywood productions of that era, a star-driven vehicle. When the original female lead, Jeanne Crain, had to drop out due to a pregnancy, an even bigger star, Susan Hayward, stepped into the role. (The role of William was played by a B actor, William Lundigan, whose casting was said to have irritated Hayward.) Though "wife" had come out of the film's title, it remained very much the film's central theme, opening on the day of Mary's wedding to William and covering their first three years of married life, as they bond with each other while dealing with the various challenges and occasional crises in the highland community they serve.

In the opening lines of a voice-over narration by Hayward that runs throughout the film, she articulates these dual themes: "It was like stepping through a doorway into a new world; a world I'd never seen before, a world I never knew existed." She continues: "My family and friends had warned me. I was a city girl, they'd said; I had no idea what it would be like living in the hills among strangers who knew nothing of the things I'd been brought up with." And then comes the kicker: "But they'd overlooked the one thing that made all the difference in the world—the fact that I love William and that nothing, no power on earth, was going to keep me from his side." Unlike any other film of this era or the two other films to be discussed here, Mary Thompson sees herself as a wife first and a mission worker (or even minister's partner) second, which makes the film as much a story of newlyweds adjusting to each other as it is of outsiders adjusting to mountain society. In short, Mary came to the mountains with no agenda, no sense of mission or service; she was there merely because that was where her new husband was assigned.

From the church services to various social activities—potluck suppers; shopping at the general store; a church picnic with hayride, baseball game, sack race, and sing-along—there's little in the film that suggests anything distinctively Appalachian, which in effect means that Mary is simply a city girl having to adjust to rural life. The local men dress in coat and tie and flat-topped straw hats (boaters); they live in two-story wood-framed farmhouses (for the most part) and ride in horse and buggies or carriages. There's nothing in their speech patterns that suggest Appalachian dialects, nor is the music they make distinctively regional—songs range from "In the Good Old Summertime" to mainstream hymns like "When the Saints Go Marching In," "How Firm a Foundation," and traditional Christmas carols. We see nary a farmer, tenant, moonshiner, or feuding family here. Nearly all the highlanders with whom the Thompsons interact are professionals or businessmen—a doctor, a merchant who also serves as the church's influential lay leader, and a snobbish wealthy woman who summers at a nearby lake and rides in a chauffeur-driven Model T. Curiously, the poorest household in the community—as indicated by an unkempt front porch and barefoot and overall-clad children—is headed by a Harvard-educated and book-reading atheist, Mr. Salter, who serves as the Thompsons' biggest challenge as they attempt to get his children to Sunday school.

Like the novel, the film consists of loosely woven incidents, some humorous and others more serious. The Thompsons encourage a courtship between a dapper young rogue and the daughter of a merchant who disapproves of this ne'er-do-well but good-hearted suitor. (He threatens to separate the couple by sending his daughter off to Wesleyan College in Macon, an option not open to many mountaineers.) When an unspecified "epidemic" breaks out, both William and Mary pitch in and help the local doctor by turning their church into a hospital. While it seems to end once William prays hard enough, that comes only after Mary has had to watch several of their new congregants die, which leads her to her first crisis of faith. She declares to William: "I'm going home. I'm not fitted for this sort of life; I had no business coming here in the first place. It's ugly and awful and a lie. I don't pretend to understand your God and never did." William forces her to stay, reminding her, "You wanted to come here; you accepted this life of your own free will." Quickly sobered and duly penitent, Mary states in a voice-over: "In spite of my weakness, I survived my first crisis. In a way, I'd grown up. I'd become, in fact, my husband's wife."

Further tragedy strikes shortly thereafter. When they take the Salter children to the church picnic, a first sign of progress in winning over this godless family, the oldest son accidentally drowns. That, along with Mary's loss of a premature baby—her first—throws her into a deep depression, after which she reveals the source of her greatest remorse: "In the selfishness of my grief," she proclaims, "I'd begun to commit the greatest sin a woman can commit against her husband: I ceased to care how I looked—I let myself go." As laughable as that statement sounds to us now (and as hard as it is to imagine Susan Hayward ever looking bad—only a plain gray dress suggests she has lost her looks), she is rudely awakened to the problem only when Mrs. Billywith, who summers on a lake nearby and who Mary calls "the most exquisitely groomed woman I'd ever seen," shows up at church one Sunday in all her finery. She immediately sets her sights on William, insisting that he counsel her on certain Old Testament passages that she can't quite understand. Sensing more feminine wiles than theological concerns, Mary tells her off in one of the film's best-written scenes and one of the few moments in which we see real spunk—and humor—in Hayward's character. Once the sputtering temptress makes her exit, Mary heads for the general store, buys some flowery pink cloth, and makes a dress that not only indicates that her grief is over but signifies that her good looks have been restored and her husband is all hers. (It is noteworthy that it took an affluent outsider, rather than a local mountain woman, to pose any threat, however remote, to Preacher Thompson's fidelity.)

Mary mounts a campaign to provide Christmas gifts to the needier children "in the hills" and rallies all the women in the community to help. In depositing toys on the porch of the Salter house, the obstinate father seems to appreciate the joy they bring the children (even if it's his wife who points out to him how happy they are), thus leading to a curious sort of religious conversion brought on by Santa Claus. (There's a certain irony in Trotti's inclusion of this scene, given Harris's reference in *A Circuit Rider's Wife* to the fact that the Thompsons themselves were actually the recipients of—and dependent on—such Christmas generosity from their congregants to supplement their meager income during their year on the circuit.)

The film concludes with the Thompsons' departure from the mountains after three years to take up a new appointment in Atlanta. The full community gathers to bid them farewell, and the camera pans those particular residents whose lives they seem to have most affected. Mary and William make one last visit to the grave of their dead baby, where she tells William that she has learned to love the mountains and their life there. In addition, she confesses, "[I have] come to understand that I was jealous of your God, your work, and you." She concludes by embracing him and quoting Ruth: "Thy people shall be my people; thy God my God; and whither thou goest, I shall go." After assuring his congregation that "part of our hearts remain here in the red clay of your hills," they drive off on the same red clay road by which they'd first arrived in the film's opening, with the swelling strains of a full choir singing "The Lord's Prayer" as the camera rises to pan a white cloud-covered sky. The film ends with a far rosier view of where this marriage is headed and the impact of their mountain ministry on it than was the case in either real life or in Harris's novel.

• • • • • •

In December 1909, Leonora Whitaker—nineteen years old and thus two years older than Corra Harris was when she began her mountain mission work—left her family in Asheville, North Carolina, and took a six-hour train trip just across the state line into Tennessee's Great Smokies, where she got off at Del Rio, a few miles east of Newport in Cocke County. Arriving just after a major snowstorm, she had to wait another day before she could find someone (the local postman) to escort her seven more miles on foot over the mountain to a remote cove called Morgan Gap, where she was to take on the sole teaching position at the newly established Ebenezer Mission School. That incident, as related by Leonora to her daughter Catherine Marshall, makes up the opening pages of the latter's novel *Christy* and the opening scene of its television dramatization in 1994.[20]

In a prologue to her novel, Marshall explains that the impetus for the novel was a visit with her mother in 1958 to Del Rio and Ebenezer, where Leonora reminisced about the two pivotal years she had spent there a half century earlier. By the time she left the area at the end of 1911, she was Mrs. John Wood, having married Catherine's father, a young minister serving the same community. The site was completely deserted during their visit, with only abandoned buildings or shells of buildings offering tangible prompts to Leonora's memories. According to Marshall, Leonora stated that "the story aches to be told. . . . But Catherine, I'm not the one to put it on paper. You know, sometimes the dreams of the parents must be fulfilled in the children."[21] Marshall took the hint and realized that the story could only be told through her mother's eyes yet would have to be adapted into fictional form. Extensive interviews with her mother provided the basis for what ultimately became her "imagined story" of Leonora Whitaker (renamed Christy Huddleston) and her first year at Ebenezer (renamed Cutter Gap); the result was a nearly five-hundred-page novel, published as *Christy* in 1967.[22] It spent ten months on the *New York Times* best-seller list, joining *A Man Called Peter* (1951)—Marshall's biography of her late husband, a renowned evangelist and chaplain of the U.S. Senate—as the most successful of her multiple books.[23]

Leonora, like Christy, was part of an affluent Presbyterian family in Asheville. In nearby Montreat, where the family spent a month every summer, Leonora heard Dr. Edward O. Guerrant speak about the newest of more than fifty mission schools he had established for poor mountain children in Kentucky and Tennessee since 1897, through an organization he founded and called the Society of Soul Winners.[24] Like her fictional counterpart, Leonora volunteered her services as a teacher on the spot, and within a year, despite her parents' reservations, she arrived at Ebenezer, a nineteen-year-old with a year and a half of college education from Flora MacDonald College in eastern North Carolina.

Given the book's popularity, it is hard to understand why it took so long—nearly three decades—to adapt it to film. MGM studios bought the film rights to it from Marshall in the late 1960s but let it languish until its option expired in 1986. At that point, producer Ken Wales bought the rights and approached CBS about turning it into a TV series, selling it as a wholesome family drama that could replicate the appeal of earlier series such as *The Waltons, Little House on the Prairie*, and *Dr. Quinn, Medicine Woman*. The network gave Wales the go-ahead to develop a twenty-episode series, which he developed over the next few years. In the meantime, a musical version of the book was produced for a regional theater company in Lancaster, Pennsylvania, in 1992 and soon thereafter played to large audiences in summer theaters in Tennessee, including one in Townsend, with the Smokies forming a natural backdrop for the action on stage.[25]

By then, CBS was ready to move into production and selected Townsend, just on the edge of the Great Smoky Mountains National Park, about fifty miles south of Knoxville, as the site where it would be filmed; Del Rio was considered too remote for a film crew. Wales leased a four-hundred-acre farm for the duration of the production and had some twenty-four buildings constructed on the property, all based on meticulous research as to what a 1910s-era Appalachian community would look like. Filming took place in the fall of 1993, with many of the minor roles filled by area residents (as was true of both of the other films under discussion here). Although Catherine Marshall died in 1983, her family maintained a strong interest in the project, and many of them gathered in Townsend to celebrate Thanksgiving with the cast and crew. Peter Marshall Jr. delivered a sermon for them all at a small Baptist church there.[26]

The series aired in 1994 and 1995, with the two-hour pilot debuting on Easter Sunday to huge ratings for CBS. Although the network chose not to extend the series beyond its original run, it was soon picked up by the Family Network, which re-aired the entire series over the next few months. The series was much lauded by evangelical Christian organizations, like the Christian Film and Television Commission and the National Religious Broadcasters, and quickly acquired a cult following that led to multiple websites, online fan clubs, and rebroadcasts of the series on Christian networks, as well as newly produced special holiday movies. In 2001, a new miniseries, called *Christy: Return to Cutter Gap*, was produced on the PAX network, at least in part the result of an aggressive online campaign by fans of the original series who wanted to see more. Since 1997, an annual gathering of fans, known as ChristyFest, has been held in either Del Rio or Townsend.[27]

The pilot, which will be the focus here, showcased its setting from the start. Such authenticity of place was still a bit unusual for a television production, and it added much to its appeal. The film opens with a vast panorama of the mountains and Christy's voice-over: "The Great Smokies. . . . Nothing in my life prepared me for the wonder of those mountains. Smoke blue and serene, folded one behind the other; I counted eleven ranges rising up against the vault of the sky," which seems an odd statement for someone who grew up in equally mountainous Asheville. A caption simply reads "Tennessee, 1912," though it is never made clear why the filmmakers shifted the date forward from the novel's 1910–11 time frame.

Following the train ride and her grueling hike over to Cutter Gap, Christy (played by eighteen-year-old Kellie Martin), is suddenly thrust into the drama of highland life. Her postman escort tells her "to either warn your neighbors of your presence or take a chance of being greeted with the barrel of a rifle," an ominous introduction to the world she is about to enter. While visiting the first family along the postman's route, a man with a serious head wound, Tom Allen, is brought to their door, followed shortly by the imposing Dr. McNeill on horseback, who, in a Scottish brogue, insists on operating immediately. As the distraught wife of the then comatose man arrives and debates with the doctor whether or not surgery is necessary, certain themes of mountain life are introduced—from superstitions (Mrs. Allen swings an ax into the floor to cut her husband's pain) and religious fatalism ("it's in God's hands") to distrust of outsiders and their modern ways—all of which Christy will find herself combating in other circumstances over the coming months. There's also the first reference to a family feud in the community, with one onlooker suggesting that the patient may not have been the victim of a mere accident, given the Allens' long-standing antipathy toward the Taylors. (It seems a bit gratuitous on the part of both Marshall and the filmmakers to have inserted a family feud into the plot, given that the scholarship on feuding confirms that it was largely confined to eastern Kentucky rather than Southern Appalachia as a whole.)[28]

Christy is quickly taken under the wing of Alice Henderson, a middle-aged Quaker missionary from Pennsylvania, who is in charge of the Cutter Gap school and serves as the young teacher's mentor and sounding board. Although there seems to be no mention of a historical counterpart to Miss Alice, as she's called (Leonora Wood never mentions any such female supervisor or mentor in her factual account of her years at Ebenezer), she does represent a mainstay of the mission school movement in the southern

The character of Christy Huddleston (played by eighteen-year-old Kellie Martin) in *Christy* was loosely based on author Catherine Marshall's mother and her two-year mission experience in a Tennessee mountain community.

highlands at the time: the many strong, take-charge women who headed up several of the Guerrant schools and others in Kentucky, North Carolina, and elsewhere in the highlands in the early twentieth century.[29] Miss Alice is one of the novel's most compelling characters and a commanding presence in the film, as embodied by Tyne Daly (who won an Emmy for the role). Yet her actual function is a rather enigmatic one in that she seems to float above the actual operation of the school, offering little tangible relief in the classroom despite how overburdened and in need of help Christy is. (Christy usually encounters Miss Alice when she's strolling across the open fields.)

An equally pivotal character is the young minister, David Grantland (Randall Batinkoff), modeled on Marshall's father, John Wood. While physically attractive, as Christy notes early on, he remains rather aloof and humorless with everyone in the community except Christy, to whom he's obviously attracted. He seems to relish his role as her mentor and guide into this strange new culture, but unlike his more nuanced characterization in Marshall's book, he appears to have little sympathy for the highlanders he has come to serve. His judgmental and rigid approach to reforming their ways and saving their souls wins him few friends (certainly far less than does Christy's sympathetic and empathetic approach to the same constituency) and makes him a far less appealing character in the pilot, though he softens up some in certain episodes that follow. The contrast in their approaches and the rapport each develops with the local highlanders probably reflect the actual range of successes and failures, or perhaps the range of actual benevolence demonstrated by the many so-called benevolent workers, both male and female, who touted those roles throughout Southern Appalachia at the turn of the century.

It is Christy's role as teacher and her trial-and-error approach to the challenges of relating to her mountain pupils that forms the core of the pilot's plot, as it does of Marshall's novel. Christy faces a large class of eager pupils in a still partially built, single-room schoolhouse; they range in age from five to grown boys her own age. Here she appears both naive and inept as she attempts to bring order to the class while distracted by the smell—and sound—of hogs rooting under the floorboards and the pet raccoon one young student keeps in his desk. The children are too cute by half, with one, full of self-assurance, proclaiming, "Teacher, I've come to see you and swap howdies," and others making equally disarming comments, reflecting not only the quaintness of mountain speech but also the otherworldliness of this society—for both Christy and the viewer. While taking roll, she asks for each student's name and address, the latter a term most have never heard. Once she explains, one young boy responds with a long rambling set of directions that ends with something like, "At the third fork in the trail, you scoot under the fence and head for Pigeon Roost Hollow. Then ye spy our cabin and pull into our place."

In this scene and others early in the film, Christy comes off as far more innocent and inexperienced than does the Mary Thompson character in *I'd Climb the Highest Mountain*. In part, this is because Susan Hayward was in her mid-thirties and Kellie Martin was only eighteen when they made their respective films, and Hayward, one of the big screen's more forceful personalities, could only go so far in acting demure and innocent. One of the strengths of *Christy* on film along with later episodes in the series is the dramatic arc that traces her growing self-confidence and maturity as she continues to wear down local opposition to both the school and the outsiders seeking to change their mountain ways. Almost all of this resistance comes from adult males, and it is clear throughout that this is a far more patriarchal than matriarchal society.

While some of mountain mothers seem willing to stand up for their children's welfare, the film never flinches from the reality that wives and daughters were often intimidated and even abused by husbands and fathers, and were cowed by men in general, a truth that Christy finds as troubling as the dire poverty she sees wherever she looks; she feels powerless to address either problem in any meaningful way. She visits the home of one of her youngest students, Mountie, who seems to be mute, to ask the parents about the girl's problem and what can be done about it. Only the mother is at home, and she seems not only fatalistic about her daughter's speech defect ("I reckon if the Lord wants Mountie to talk, she will") but also deferential to her husband on the matter of seeking some sort of treatment or counseling ("My man wouldn't like it—he don't believe in fussing over no girls").

Moonshine soon comes into play, as bottles of liquor are discovered hidden under the school, and the self-righteous young reverend and Christy herself stand bound and determined to turn over to authorities Bird's-Eye Taylor, the head of that clan and "the most likely culprit . . . a notorious moonshiner who had nothing but contempt for our mission," according to Christy's voice-over. This sets off what is by Hollywood standards a rather enlightened debate on the subject, as Dr. MacNeill, the elderly Scottish physician long based in the community, lectures the young preacher and teacher on their high-minded moralism. He offers a spirited defense of why corn liquor is in effect their only "cash crop" and, as such, an economic necessity for the people of the cove. After he launches into a treatise on the Whiskey Rebellion, Christy retorts, "This is 1912, not 1794," to which the Scottish doctor responds, "These people *still* scratch out a bare living," and selling liquor is their only source of money in this cash-poor economy. Reverend Grantland insists that "it's still the Devil's work" and the cause of many quarrels and killings, but MacNeill insists, "I'm warning you, they don't see it that way." It's hard to think of another film that addresses this issue so fully and robustly and in much the same terms that mission workers would have faced at the time.[30]

Like *I'd Climb the Highest Mountain*, Christy's story as dramatized for television did not shy away from a strong spiritual context. On several occasions, she (like Mary Thompson) experiences moments of self-doubt and crises of faith. The first comes after her visit to Mountie's home, where she first witnesses the extreme poverty (she comments on the stench of the cabin's interior) and the mother's reluctance to buck her callous husband and seek help for her daughter. Christy is discouraged enough to declare to Miss Alice that she doesn't belong there and should return home. Alice (in Tyne Daly's finest moment in the film) lectures her on the inner light that's so central to Quaker faith and service, and tells Christy that "that light will only come when you open your eyes to the pain and grief around you." She challenges Christy, now fully exposed to the harsh realities of mountain life, to decide: "Were you meant to come here and serve and work or were you only running away from home?" Christy later prays about her motives and tells God that yes, she may first have come for fun and adventure, "but I think you had something different in mind. You can use me in this cove. Well, God, here I am." (It's no wonder that the Christian media have embraced the film and the series as ardently as they have for so long.)

To the film's credit (like Marshall's book), the problems endemic to this highland society and the attitudes of those perpetuating them are never solved by Christy or her coworkers, and there are few, if any, individual conversions or repentances that allow for a feel-good conclusion to either the film or the series that followed. What little impact these benevolent workers have is modest and achieved only incrementally, while the major issues of poverty, moonshine, and feuding remain as daunting as ever by film's end.

The climax comes shortly thereafter. Christy is doing paperwork at her schoolhouse desk at night (a bit odd but convenient plot-wise) when several men sneak up to the building and set it on fire. She is knocked out by a flaming beam and awakens the next morning in bed, where she tells Miss Alice that she suspects that the Taylors, the moonshining father and son, are behind the arson. In short, she's made no headway on that front. Miss Alice urges her to forgive them, if they are indeed the culprits, and to break the cycle of violence (though of course it's never been cyclical, given that the same culprits have perpetuated it all on the same target throughout). Christy finds it harder to forgive and decides to slip away without notice to anyone. But as she stops by the school for one final look, she is overwhelmed by memories of the children. When Mountie arrives, quite conveniently, and speaks her first word, Christy naturally changes her mind (in a scene far too reminiscent of Julie Andrews and her brood of Von Trapp children in *The Sound of Music*). As the film ends, all the children gather around her as Mountie recites the alphabet to her beaming teacher. Miss Alice arrives at the front steps, witnesses the warm scene inside, and proclaims, "Christy Huddleston, I think thee will do."

That final scene, while resolving little other than Christy's own determination to stay and her confidence that she can make a difference in these children's lives, serves as an effective launching pad for the series to come, which takes a variety of directions and allows for more fully developed interactions with other characters in Cutter Gap, all in one-hour episodes. Christy is usually at the center of both the problems they confront and the solutions with which those problems are conveniently resolved at the end of each episode, with her growth and increasing effectiveness serving as the running theme throughout the series.

• • • • • •

In 2000, six years after *Christy* had its television debut, the feature film *Songcatcher* appeared in theaters. Certainly the most ambitious and sophisticated screen treatment of "culture brokers" in Southern Appalachia, this independently produced film, written and directed by Maggie Greenwald, suggested more complex dynamics in play in terms of how outsiders interacted with insiders and the impact of that interaction on both. Filmed almost entirely in Madison County, North Carolina, just north of Asheville, Greenwald loosely based her story on Olive Dame Campbell's experience in discovering and collecting Old English ballads in the North Carolina mountains, a venture that began with her first trip through the region with her husband, John C. Campbell, in 1908 and 1909. Greenwald stated in an interview that her initial interest in the subject was the origins of country music and the much earlier mountain ballads and folk music from which it evolved. She and her husband, David Mansfield—a musician and her collaborator on the film—put the music front and center and went to great pains to recruit local and regional performers as consultants in both selecting the songs and accurately performing them. The relationship they formed with the renowned Madison County ballad singer and banjo player Sheila Kay Adams opened a number of doors among local residents, who were initially skeptical of the intent of filmmakers moving into the area.[31]

Greenwald was also intrigued that it was primarily women, as teachers and missionaries moving into the southern mountains, who first discovered and initiated efforts at collecting and preserving that music. "They soon came to the realization," she said, "that these were not backward, ignorant people, but people with an incredible culture, rooted in the music."[32] Thus, along with their agenda of re-creating the music and the culture it reflected, Greenwald was equally intent on using a largely feminist framework through which to relate its discovery and preservation. (It is telling that of the story's eight principal characters, six of them are female.)[33]

Greenwald candidly acknowledged that Olive Dame Campbell served as the basis for Lily Penleric, though reviews and commentary by several Appalachian scholars suggest that traces of a variety of other historical figures are also evident in the character, from writers and teachers to academics and musicologists.[34] Greenwald sets the film in 1907, the year before the Campbells' first venture into the southern highlands and the year in which Olive first hears a mountain version of the British ballad "Barbara Allen"—a song that until then she had known only as an English ballad—sung to her by a student at the Hindman Settlement School in Kentucky.

Olive Dame Campbell was not a professor or a musicologist as is her cinematic counterpart, Lily Penleric; nor was she single. She was a Massachusetts native who moved south with her new husband, educator and minister John C. Campbell (his second marriage), as he undertook an extensive study of Appalachian society and culture by traveling through the region, from Kentucky and Virginia through Tennessee, North Carolina, and Georgia. After discovering this regional version of English, Scottish, and Scots Irish ballads and folk songs, Olive began collecting and documenting this music, meticulously copying words and transcribing the tunes on a piano. From 1908 to 1915, Campbell collected over seventy ballads. In Boston in 1915, she met and shared her findings with Cecil Sharp, the eminent British authority on folk songs and dance, and in 1917, they jointly published a selection of those songs (thirty-nine) in a seminal volume titled *English Folk Songs from the Southern Appalachians.*[35]

Greenwald uses much of this scenario in the film she wrote, including a character named Cyrus Whittle, based on Sharp, who is referred to early on as a potential academic rival but appears as a character only in the movie's final scene. The film opens with Penleric being denied full professorship at an unnamed New England college, which leads her to beat a quick retreat to the mountains of North Carolina, lured there not by a husband but by her younger sister. Elna Penleric is one of two teachers who run the Clover Settlement School, which seems to be for girls, though we never see any students or classes in session. A teenage girl, Deladis (Emmy Rossum), lives with the two and sings "Barbara Allen" to their northern guest on her first night there. As was the case with Campbell, this performance sets Lily onto the realization that the Appalachians are a repository of early British folk music, and she's quick to begin an intense effort at collecting and recording as many such songs as she can. (One of several anachronisms in the film is the fact that she uses a large phonograph to record what the mountain residents sing onto small wax cylinders, an innovation that wouldn't come about—certainly in that region—for more than a decade.)[36]

Songcatcher benefits from a much more tightly woven plot than do either of the two films previously discussed, as Lily confronts, befriends, and alienates a number of local residents, who react in a variety of ways to her “meddlin’,” especially her attempts to exploit or capitalize on (as some see it) their culture. Lily is stiff, uptight, and uncomfortable upon her arrival in the region, and also somewhat condescending, even dismissive, toward the first residents she encounters. It is only with her discovery of their rich musical heritage that her attitude begins to change, and she comes to appreciate and to advocate for them (especially women) and their way of life.

The issues of “cultural brokering” are explored far more astutely here than in either of the other two films. A pivotal exchange between Lily and a skeptical Tom Bledsoe (Aidan Quinn), whose “granny” Viney Butler (wonderfully played by Pat Carroll) has been won over by Lily and agreed to let her record her singing, suggests the stakes at play:

Lily: I believe you can win public sentiment with your music. When my book is published, I believe the mountain people will be seen in a very different light.

Tom: What light is that, may I ask?

Lily: Well, the common view is that there is no culture here and that the people are dirty, ignorant savages.

Tom: You forgot illiterate and inbred. . . . The only way to preserve our way of life up here is to keep your way of life down there.

Lily: That is the way you kill something, by shutting it out.

Tom: What you don’t understand and never will is that we just want to be left alone.

Lily: Then the mountain ways will die.

Tom: We’ll see.

Among the historical issues Greenwald inserts into her film is a subplot involving a coal mining company trying to buy up local farmland; this is of course one of her most egregious factual flaws, given that there’s no coal in the North Carolina mountains. But it does provoke several confrontations between Lily and the unscrupulous agent of the company, Earl Giddens, that suggest the self-awareness of at least some highlanders in terms of how they’re perceived by outsiders. Giddens is actually from the region and knows all these people personally, though he makes a point of letting any and all know that he has a college degree from Chapel Hill. When Viney Butler threatens to shoot him if he doesn’t get out of her yard, Giddens tells her, “Viney, that kind of talk gives city folk a terrible impression of us hillbillies.” Introduced to “Dr.” Lily Penleric, he lets her know that he too is educated. “It’s fine to see an outsider appreciate the charms of our local music," he tells her, but "I much prefer the elegant perfection of the compositions of Mr. Johann Sebastian Bach." Lily responds that "such comparisons don't benefit either tradition—they are apples and oranges." He turns back to Mrs. Butler, telling her how much better off she'd be by spending her later years in a town, where, he says, "you might even learn to read and write." She snaps back, "I was born on this mountain and I'm going to die on it . . . and so are you." She then cocks her rifle and yells, "Get goin', Giddens!" and he scurries off.

When Giddens later succeeds in bilking a local family out of its farm at a pittance of a price, Lily declares that what he's doing is criminal; in response, he offers the standard rationale: "The only way these folks are going to better themselves is to get the hell off this mountain and give up their backward ways," to which she retorts, "Is that what your education taught you—to hate your own people?" In making Giddens a local resident, Greenwald is taking what Hollywood often depicted as a sharp dichotomy between outsiders and insiders and offering instead, through Giddens's encounters with Lily, a more complex and morally ambivalent scenario of the role played by both locals and outsiders in terms of who's defending the mountain way of life and who's undermining it.

One of *Songcatcher*'s more remarkable scenes comes midway through, when the coal company's owner and his refined and overdressed society wife attend a tea party given by Elna and another schoolteacher. In something of a tour de force, Greenwald uses them and the presence of a Baptist preacher to address, if only fleetingly, a variety of issues regarding the role of educators and culture brokers in the region. Just three lines of dialogue in this extended scene suggest the range of attitudes and approaches to the education of mountain people by outsiders. The wife of the coal owner states, with utter naivete: "I endorse the English idea; we must educate by example. If we teach these ruffians to serve tea properly, they will want refinement, will seek it out." Elna stifles her disdain at such a premise and says simply, "I believe we must ask the mountain people what they want and what they need," to which the mine owner himself retorts, "Educating these savages is a waste of money. If you want to help these children, you should get them out of their hovels and put them to work."

There's much more to the scene, including a discussion of the pros and cons of coal mining's impact on highland communities, both economically and culturally, and another on the burgeoning folk arts movement, which was bringing Southern Appalachian culture to light in northeastern markets and could pay off handsomely for local artists and craftspeople. Given the mere lip service these issues receive, it's easy to write off such scenes as attempts to cram far too much into what's already a very issue-oriented narrative. On the other hand, no other film before (or since) has made any effort to even acknowledge these conflicting ideas, much less dramatize them in the deft but fleeting way Greenwald does here.

The film moves too rapidly through a series of rather unlikely climaxes, as the teachers—who are lesbian lovers—are spied in an affectionate embrace by a young man (Deladis's beau, whom Lily recruited to assist her with her recordings). The young man is repulsed, and he recruits a handful of his cronies to burn down their house and the school, which destroys the discs of the songs Lily had worked so hard to record. Even more implausibly, a woman storms into the local church during a Sunday service and guns down her lover, a man whom Lily had persuaded to return to his wife and many children. This too comes across as gratuitous, as if any Appalachian-based story must include at least one such murderous vendetta. (In this case, it recalls Frankie Silvers, whose celebrated murder of her husband took place some eighty years earlier and only a couple of counties away.)

The movie's conclusion also fails to ring true. With much of her work destroyed, Lily declines her sister's proposal that she stay and help her rebuild the school. Instead, Lily, having fallen in love with Tom Bledsoe, decides to move to an unnamed big city with Tom and Deladis, and make a new start recording and marketing mountain music—another anachronism, given that there would be no viable recording industry for another decade at least. As they move down a steep mountain road toward their new life, they just happen to run into, of all people, Cyrus Whittle, who has come to North Carolina to seek her out. After a brief exchange, she hands him all of her surviving notations, thus passing the torch to him. He promises that any publication that comes out of his work will appear under both their names. As the threesome continues down the road, the final credits roll as yet a third version of "Barbara Allen" is heard, this one a contemporary, upbeat rendition sung by Emmylou Harris.

For all of its historical inaccuracies, overstuffed plot points—many of which are left unresolved at film's end—and fleeting lip service to certain issues, *Songcatcher* is nevertheless the most serious and sophisticated treatment of Southern Appalachia ever captured in a feature film. To her considerable credit, Maggie Greenwald is unusually attuned to the many implications of the region's discovery by the outside world, realizing that there were no easy answers in terms of the problems such exposure brought, nor easy judgments as to the good or ill done by those with even the best of intentions in terms of what they thought they were doing for the highlanders in whose midst they put themselves.

• • • • • •

These films' three protagonists came to the mountains under different circumstances. It is curious that two of these three women did not travel far from home to the mountain missions they served—Corra Harris (Mary Thompson) moves only a few counties away in Georgia; Leonora Whitaker (Christy Huddleston) merely crosses the state line from highland North Carolina to highland Tennessee—and yet their respective films depict them as being exposed to a society and culture as foreign to them as it was to New Englander Lily Penleric. As exaggerated as this clash of cultures may seem as laid out in both fiction and film, those interactions and negotiations made across cultural boundaries provide much of the thematic thrust and dramatic conflict so crucial to both genres. Yet this too has a basis in fact; like Harris and Whitaker, many of the region's benevolent workers—Mary Martin Sloop, Martha Berry, May Stone, and Katherine Pettit, for example—came into the highlands from other parts of their own states (sometimes nearby), and approached the people and problems they found there in much the same way as those who traveled much farther to do so.

Each of the three leads is meant to be a sympathetic character, though in the case of Lily Penleric, she is decidedly less so at the beginning, but becomes more appealing as her attitude and behavior improve over the course of the film. The basis for that improvement is quite simply her growing appreciation for the highland people and their culture. Upon her arrival, Lily asks her sister if she really feels safe among "these savages" and then is interested only in their music; when her sister asks her what she thinks of their school, she has nothing to say. Only gradually does she come to appreciate the people as individuals and their culture as a whole, and by the film's end, she treats them all with genuine affection and respect. Likewise, to a lesser degree, do Mary Thompson and Christy Huddleston, though they seem to enter the region with fewer preconceived ideas and far less animosity toward mountain people; the dramatic arcs in their stories have more to do with overcoming their own insecurities and self-doubt as we watch them mature, grow, and ultimately emerge as giving, self-assured women.

It is their goodwill, affection, respect, and advocacy for their congregants, students, or research subjects that makes these women so appealing and ultimately admirable characters for us as viewers, which in turn suggests that the filmmakers expect us to see mountain people in the same light (made easier perhaps because they're all white). In *I'd Climb the Highest Mountain*, they are good-hearted, country people, more reflective of wholesome Americana than of Appalachia, given that anything suggesting regional otherness has been carefully excised. *Christy* seriously conveys the problems that plague the region, while still giving most of the mountain characters some sense of dignity and certainly sympathy (in part by keeping the children front and center). *Songcatcher* does much the same, but it adds to that a sense of savvy, self-awareness, and pride on the part of highlanders, who refuse to let themselves become mere pawns for those coming in to "uplift" them. Not coincidentally, it is almost exclusively mountain men whom Hollywood scriptwriters see in real need of reform, and each film features one or two menacing figures—a feuder, a moonshiner, a schemer, and even a two-timing husband or beau—to make the point.

In all three films, mountain people remain basically supporting players, who serve primarily to provide the enlightenment or fulfillment for the female leads; the former seem to exist in order for the latter to leave the mountains as better people than when they arrived. And yet all three also refute the claim of Henry Shapiro and others that these types of benevolent workers had much to do with creating community in the mountain South. He stated that "the absence of community [was] the principal characteristic of Appalachian otherness" and credited the "benevolent workers" coming into the region as creating not only "desirable institutions, but also . . . a social system and a sense of community necessary to sustain them."[37] Such creations were never part of the mission for these women onscreen. While in the latter two films they are responsible for establishing schools and thus formalized education (schools play no part in *I'd Climb the Highest Mountain*), Mary Thompson, Christy Huddleston, and Lily Penleric all move into what are already well-formed social systems and fully functioning communities. This may be less a conscious statement about the region on the part of the filmmakers, given that such constructions serve other functions for both fictional and film narrative.

The Cutter Gap community into which Christy moves is perhaps less well defined, with only the presence of the schoolchildren and a fleeting open-air cornhusking indicative of any collective activity among the cove's scattered populace. A Saturday night barn dance in *Songcatcher* serves not only to highlight the music and musicians performing it but also to bring nearly all the characters together in what would have been a typical entertainment throughout the region at the time, while the church picnic in *I'd*

Climb the Highest Mountain serves much the same purpose. All three films feature church services during which key plot developments take place. Nevertheless, the remoteness of these mountain societies is fully evident. We never see a town or a village of any substance in any of the three; not even a store appears in *Christy* or *Songcatcher.*

Finally, it is easy to trace an increasingly feminist approach in the treatment of both the benevolent workers and the mountain residents they come to serve over the half-century span covered by these films' production. It is not surprising that in a 1951 film based on a 1910 novel, the protagonist is first and foremost a helpmate to her husband, and that pleasing him becomes as much a goal as serving the Appalachian Georgians she's been brought there to serve. While local women are very much in evidence throughout, not one of them emerges as a formidable force or memorable character in the film.

In the 1994 film, which draws largely on the emerging feminist sensibilities of the late 1960s novel on which it is based, Christy is not only single but a mere nineteen years old. She has a strong sense of purpose—if less so of self—and is mentored by a very wise, independent, and forceful woman who can handle a rifle as well as any man who challenges her. Among the Tennesseans to whom they reach out are several key female characters who are far from liberated in terms of the deference they give—and occasional abuse they suffer—in this decidedly patriarchal and chauvinistic society. And while Christy is courted by two eligible young men in both the book and the film, it's probably due to a 1990s sensibility that she's still single when the film, and even the series, ends, although her real-life counterpart left as a bride.

Finally, the one film created by a woman and unveiled at the turn of the twenty-first century presents us with three willful, independent career women, two of them in a lesbian relationship, the third almost defiantly single as she struggles in what was still a very masculine world of academic research. All three, but especially Lily, interact with a range of North Carolina mountain women and girls, coming to the defense of those oppressed or wronged, and cheering on those with minds and wills of their own, from an elderly granny to their own adolescent protégé. For the most part, these women are portrayed as willful and self-assured enough to stand up to the men misbehaving around them. In perhaps the scene that most stretches credibility, a spurned lover shoots the man who'd deserted her. (It suggests, one supposes, that mountain women could also have violent tempers and that mountain men could be redeemed—the man shot had just returned to his wife and children—though in this case, the redemption came at a high cost.)

Cratis Williams, one of the first scholars to write on the clash between southern mountaineers and these benevolent workers, wrote in his seminal 1961 dissertation, "The Southern Mountaineer in Fact and Fiction": "'Missionaries' dedicated their efforts to the salvation of [the mountaineer's] soul and to changing his social behavior patterns and his standard of living to preconceived patterns and standards that were often unlike anything that had ever been on land or sea but that helped to 'lift' him from the stagnation of the eighteenth century into the standardization of the twentieth."[38]

While that was indeed the intent of many of those missionaries, among these three films that description can be applied only to *Christy*. There is very little going on in either *I'd Climb the Highest Mountain* or *Songcatcher* that suggests Hollywood had succumbed to that particular formula in its depiction of the mountain people with whom Mary Thompson and Lily Penleric interact. If the first minimizes the cultural differences of northern Georgians, thus suggesting there's little need for "uplift," the latter embraces and even romanticizes that mountain culture as one to be valued and preserved. In both—indeed, in all three—films, Appalachians are, for the most part, treated with dignity and respect, though it must be said that the women—both outsiders and insiders—come off far better than do their male counterparts.[39]

6 Coal, Conflict, and Community

From Wales to West Virginia

No aspect of Appalachia's social and economic character has generated more of a comparative perspective to another part of the world than have the coalfields of central Appalachia and those of South Wales. Thanks to the groundbreaking work of several of Appalachia's most eminent scholars and activists over the past four decades—most notably Helen Lewis, John Gaventa, Ronald Lewis, Patricia Beaver, and Tom Hansell—miners from both regions have come together in a variety of ways to explore the commonalities and differences in their experiences, past and present.[1] Hansell, a documentary filmmaker, noted in his 2016 documentary, *After Coal*, that one of his most striking observations in traveling through Wales was that its "industrial history . . . had created a coal-mining culture not unlike Appalachia's [which] gave rise to community spirit."[2] Helen Lewis quoted a local Welsh labor leader who had elaborated on that reality in the 1970s: "The miners live together in small mining villages," he stated. "They marry girls from the same village. The children are brought up in the same village, in the same valley. The disasters they share together. The fatal accidents they share together. Because everyone knows one another in the mining valleys. It's a community in the right spirit."[3]

That strong sense of community has indeed been a vital element of the coal culture that evolved in both regions, though it has not always been central to the scholarly treatment of either. In his book *Coal Towns* (1991), Crandall Shifflett reports that over five hundred such towns sprang up throughout central Appalachian coalfields from the 1880s through the mid-1920s. And yet, he notes, for all the scholarly attention given to the coal industry by labor and business historians, few if any up to that point had focused on the social entities that formed around the mines—whether as communities, as households, or as families.[4] Although that void has since been filled by a number of single-community studies conducted by historians and sociologists, this seems to be one area in which the film industries—of both Hollywood and Great Britain—have been well ahead of the academic curve, in that their depictions of coal miners onscreen are often rendered in localized and intimate terms.

The social and economic hardships inherent in coal mining communities in Kentucky, West Virginia, and Pennsylvania have rendered several of the most effective and realistic screen depictions of Appalachia and its people at various points over the course of the twentieth century. Yet far more films have centered on the lives of Welsh (and other British) coal workers, in no small part due to the more extensive documentation on South Wales mining life—in the form of autobiographies, novels, and oral histories—to be drawn from as source material than exists for its Appalachian counterparts.[5]

While the social dynamics laid out in these films are defined by local mining operations and are affected by company policies and practices, the primary drama in which they're engaged takes place far more above ground than below, making communities and households their central playing fields or framing devices. Given the fact that such communities were by and large single-industry towns that existed primarily because of the "black gold" that lay beneath their surfaces, options were limited for those who came of age in those generally oppressive settings, and more often than not, the mere decision to stay or to leave served as the central plot thread in the very human stories told through these movies.

The few such films set in Appalachian coal towns have made their way to the screen only in more recent decades (specifically the 1980s and 1990s). Whether consciously or subconsciously, these were built on a much older and richer tradition of British-based or British-produced films set in the United Kingdom's own coal country. Before moving this chapter back to its Appalachian focal point, three products of that earlier tradition are worth a closer look for the precedents and parallels they establish in terms of content, theme, and character. Two of the three are set in Wales, and one in England; two were filmed in Britain (and largely on location), while the third was produced in Hollywood; coincidentally, all three were released within a year and a half—in 1940 and 1941.

The demand for coal and thus the scope of the mining industry dominated Britain far more than it did its counterpart in the United States from the late nineteenth century through much of the twentieth. In 1920, more than 1.2 million miners worked in collieries scattered across the island. Given that miners were such a substantial segment of the British working class, the struggles they faced from the 1920s through the Depression era, in particular, were more deeply seared into the national consciousness than was ever the case in the United States. As an English mine leader declares in one of the films discussed in this chapter, "Coal is the foundation on which our nation is built. . . . It's our great buried treasure."[6]

One indication of the integral role played by coal and those who mined it lies in the sheer number of British-based films on the subject—both features and documentaries—produced throughout the first half of the twentieth century and beyond.[7] The tone of these films varies considerably. Several focus on the plight of miners and their families, as they demonstrate how deteriorating working conditions, safety concerns and health hazards, pay cuts and layoffs, and conflicts with antagonistic or apathetic managers forced large numbers of miners to abandon the mines in search of employment opportunities elsewhere. By 1939, some fifty thousand people had moved away from Wales's once thriving Rhondda valley.[8] Yet other films offer a more nostalgic and romanticized treatment of daily life in colliery communities and celebrate the perseverance and resilience of its residents. The three films discussed here embrace this full range of realities and sentiments. Two of them, *The Stars Look Down* and *The Proud Valley*, opened in London within a month of each other in early 1940. *How Green Was My Valley* premiered in Hollywood in the fall of 1941.

• • • • • •

The Stars Look Down was based on the second of a series of popular novels by a Scottish physician, A. J. Cronin, who drew from his experiences as a medical inspector of mines in South Wales in the 1920s.[9] Shifting his fictional setting to northern England, Cronin published *The Stars Look Down* in 1935, but it would be another five years before his sprawling seven-hundred-page narrative would be adapted to the screen. Along the way, it was compressed into a much tighter screenplay, with significant reductions to its vast chronological sweep and its large cast of characters. Generously financed by a British distributing company, much of it was filmed on location in the mining country of Northumberland. This was the first serious film to be entrusted to young director Carol Reed, who would go on to become one of Britain's most accomplished filmmakers; major roles were assigned to young British actors on the rise, such as Michael Redgrave, Margaret Lockwood, and Welsh native Emlyn Williams.[10]

The Stars Look Down was unusually topical for a British film; one critic noted that "it was one of few English films before the 1960s with a strong contemporary subject" (though the same could be said of *The Proud Valley*). It opens abruptly with a standoff by miners in the fictional town of Sleescale, declaring their defiance of both the mine owner and their own union. (Implicating the union as well as the owner proved somewhat controversial, but it may well have warded off British censors, who were wary of dramatizing pro-labor activity during the late Depression years.)[11] At the instigation of a longtime miner, Rob Fenwick, and a few of his elderly colleagues, the coal workers stage a walkout after both the owner and union leaders refuse to acknowledge the perceived threat of massive flooding in the mine pit due to a water buildup behind an unstable coalface. The workers follow Fenwick in a protest that leads to an eight-week closure of the mine.

Several weeks into the strike we see its impact through the Fenwick family's nearly empty cupboards and his wife's complaints about her inability to adequately feed her two grown sons, both miners themselves. When Mrs. Fenwick approaches the local butcher to ask for meat scraps, he refuses her, snarling of her husband that "maybe an empty belly will make him think twice before he calls another strike." Idle workers lounging on the street observe the butcher's same callous refusal to other wives and mothers and quickly galvanize into a mob of both men and women, who attack the shop and make off with all the meat. Several, including the elderly Fenwick, are arrested and spend several days in jail for their role in the melee.

All the while, Fenwick's idealistic older son David (Redgrave) aspires to an education at a nearby university that will enable him to advocate either politically or legally on behalf of the miners, "to fight," he says, "for my own kind." Joe Gowlan (Williams), a disreputable friend and fellow miner, also attends the university but with more pecuniary ambitions: he studies accounting in order to profit from collusion with the local mine owner over questionable contracts with industries seeking underhanded deals on the coal supplied them. A romantic triangle manipulated by Joe leads to a loveless marriage for David to the shallow Jenny (Lockwood), which in turn forces him to give up his quest for a law degree and return home with his bride to become a schoolteacher, a decidedly lower rung in terms of salary and social status, as his restless wife is quick to point out. Nevertheless, he continues to push his father's efforts at holding mine owners accountable for unsafe working conditions, delivering impassioned speeches on behalf of nationalization of mining operations, along with continued pleas to unresponsive—and corrupt—local union leaders to take up their members' cause.

Further complicating matters is the presence of the mine owner, Mr. Barras, who is made a viable character who interacts at a personal level with his employees far more than is usually the case in these films.

He's much resented by the idle workers, though some insist they won't work even if he reopens the pits. "I'm not going to drown myself to keep Barras fat," declares Joe at one point. Yet Barras's greed overrides any personal concern for his workers, and despite some qualms, he resumes his mining operation without resolving the potential for flooding that instigated the walkout in the first place. Without the backing of the union, most in the village—having barely survived the devastating consequences of the mine's earlier closure—have little choice but to return to work.

Soon enough, the inevitable happens. In an extended sequence in the mine shaft, floodwaters burst through the coalface as predicted, which in turn triggers a gas explosion. The focus narrows to five trapped miners, which include David's father and younger brother and Gowlan's father, all of whom succumb in drawn-out, heartrending death scenes that span six days of futile attempts by both a rescue party headed by David and more last-ditch efforts by Barras, who himself collapses and dies of heart failure in the mine. These shots are intercut with those of anxious women and children waiting above for word of their loved ones' fate. The film ends on a somber note, as David accompanies his grieving mother back home. Oddly it dispenses with the novel's conclusion, in which David is elected to Parliament, where he can begin to effect real reform in the coal industry. This, among other deletions, led its director, Reed, to dismiss the film as "a gloomy little piece."[12]

Despite its bleak tone, tragic ending, and blatantly politicized message, *The Stars Look Down* was a box-office success in Britain, drawing large appreciative audiences even as the opening throes of war with Germany threatened to divert interest in miners' causes, again a credit to how integral the coal industry continued to be to the national economy.

• • • • • •

While *The Stars Look Down* was the more acclaimed and more popular of this pair of films that appeared one after the other in 1940, it was the second, *The Proud Valley*, that has proven more historically significant and commanded more attention in recent years. This is due largely to the involvement of the man behind its production—the iconic Paul Robeson. Robeson was at the height of his success as a singer, an actor, and a political activist at the end of the 1930s. As America's most internationally acclaimed African American, he and his wife spent most of the 1930s living in London and much of the latter part of the decade performing on concert stages throughout Europe, including the Soviet Union. Robeson's sympathies extended to Welsh mine workers—whom he'd first come to know in the 1920s through concert tours, and again much later, in 1938, while fundraising for the republican forces in Spain during the civil war there. In his memoir, *Here I Stand*, he wrote of the latter experience: "The miners of Wales, who gave great support to the anti-fascist movement, welcomed me when I came to sing in behalf of aid to Spain and invited me into their union halls and into their homes. The Welsh miners . . . made it clear that there was a closer bond between us than the general struggle to preserve democracy from its fascist foes. At the heart of the conflict, they pointed out, was a class division, and although I was famous and wealthy, the fact was I came from a working-class people like themselves."[13] This mutual admiration society was based on their affinity for each other's music as much as it was on their political leanings. As Paul's granddaughter, Susan Robeson, wrote many years later: "The Welsh people were great lovers of my grandfather and his music. [They] are a struggling people with music in their souls, and they felt a deep bond with the sufferings and hopes expressed in the Negro spirituals Paul sang. He, in turn, was amazed to feel a kinship with the traditional folk music of the Welsh."[14]

It was soon after his 1938 tour that Robeson decided to use film to bring to light the plight of Welsh workers; not surprisingly, music would play a central role in the story he wanted to tell. Long a Communist sympathizer who'd spent time in the Soviet Union, Robeson and his wife became close friends with Herbert Marshall, a London-based writer, filmmaker, and theater director of the Old Vic, who had also spent considerable time in Russia. Over the summer of 1939, Marshall (in close collaboration with Robeson) wrote a screenplay, originally titled *David Goliath*, that was rushed into production in August and overseen by a young director, Pen Tennyson, the great-grandson of the poet Alfred, Lord Tennyson. Much of the movie was filmed on location in the Rhondda valley, which had been hit particularly hard over the Depression decade. Most of the exteriors were shot there, and much of the cast and crew, including Robeson, stayed in miners' homes for their duration of the filming. While visiting a local mine, Robeson made an impromptu suggestion that the film's title be changed to *The Proud Valley*, which met with hearty approval from the miners gathered around him.[15]

Robeson plays David Goliath—whose name suggests both his underdog status and his great physical stature and strength. He's a wayfaring sailor who put ashore at Cardiff and took to wandering the Welsh countryside; when he tells a fellow hobo that he had once worked as a miner in West

Paul Robeson (left) demonstrated his affinity for Welsh coal miners through his involvement in the conception and production of *The Proud Valley*, in which he played the central role of itinerant miner David Goliath.

Virginia, his new companion responds that he'd heard of possible work for blacks in Wales's southern coalfields. Ironically, it's music that paves the way for David's employment as a miner. As the two men enter the village of Blaendy, they overhear a male choir practicing in an open-windowed second-floor room, and David joins in from the street below. Dick Parry, the choirmaster, who's also a miner, is taken with David's voice and invites him to come home with him, telling his wife, "He's got a bottom bass like an organ . . . that floated through the hall like thunder from the distance." Given that the choir is preparing for a national choral competition, and realizing what an asset David's rich bass would be to Blaendy's chances of winning, Parry convinces this towering American to stay with his family, get a job in the colliery, and, most importantly, join the choir.

There's only slight resistance from the other miners to having a black man join their underground team, to which Parry responds, "Why, damn and blast it, aren't we all black down in that pit?" More objections are raised by members of rival choirs, who, during a shift change in the mine, confront Parry and his team for having taken on this "big stranger" not so much to work as to provide an unfair advantage to their choir. Parry again comes to his defense, and David's own jovial nature helps to quell the resentment. As they emerge from the lift to enter the mine, he breaks into "All through the Night" and is soon accompanied by his new, perfectly pitched coworkers in one of several authentic Welsh hymns and folk songs they perform over the course of the film.

A month later, just before the national festival, a gas explosion in the mine results in a fire that takes Parry as its only casualty, despite a heroic attempt by David to rescue him from the flames. He carries his dying host out of the shaft and lays him before his grieving family, including his adult son, Emlyn, a mining engineer. Rather than compete as planned, the Blaendy Male Choir, with David as its spokesman, pays tribute to its fallen leader, and David, to his benefactor; he concludes by singing a moving rendition of "Deep River," an African American spiritual, thus incorporating onscreen the two musical traditions for which Robeson credited much of his affinity for Welsh workers.

The scene shifts back to Blaendy, where, in a striking visual, the miners—including David Goliath and Emlyn Parry—trudge across the side of a giant slag heap, reduced to collecting coal remnants in the face of the mine's closure by its London-based owner. The men much resent that they're being paid such a pittance ("on the dole") for grunt work, especially since the owners repeatedly refuse a plan devised by Emlyn to repair and reopen the section affected. He and four other miners, including Goliath, march to London to confront the owners in person; en route, they learn that Britain, along with France, have just declared war on Nazi Germany. By the time they reach London and confront the owner, they overhear that he has just committed the company to provide the government with forty thousand tons of coal for the war effort. Taking full advantage of their impeccable timing, Emlyn makes a patriotic speech about the role they can play, stating, "Coal is as important to our national defense as guns or anything else, so why not let us take our chance in our pit?" He then presents specific plans and calculations as to how they can safely reopen the mine, and the owner grants permission for them to proceed.

In fact, the outbreak of World War II actually occurred just a week or so after filming of the production got underway late in August 1939, thus prompting Marshall and Robeson to quickly write this sequence, providing a logical resolution for getting the colliery reopened and the miners back to work while still condemning British mine owners for their trepidation and neglect of workers' interests up to that point. (Until war policy forced this shift in the company's complacency, Marshall's script had settled for a far less plausible scenario: the workers' takeover of the colliery and its operation.)[16]

Yet even with the owner's capitulation in reopening the mine, a happy ending is not assured. What follows is the most extended underground sequence in any of these films—nearly twenty minutes of an agonizing, suspense-filled return into the collapsed mine. A small group of gas-masked miners—including David Goliath and Emlyn Parry, move carefully through the rubble, setting up explosives to clear it out. Forcing open an iron door, they face a burst of full flames followed by a cave-in that leaves several miners trapped. Five men draw lots to see which one will risk staying behind to set the short-fused charge; Emlyn loses, but David tries to convince him that he should think of his widowed mother (and a fiancée) and step aside to let him, the loner, take on this "suicide mission" instead. When Emlyn refuses, his black guardian knocks him out and drags him a safe distance away, then moves forward to set the charge himself. His fellow miners bring Emlyn back to consciousness and hear an explosion that soon leads to the realization that it did indeed kill David while opening fresh air currents for the rest of them.

Then, to the soaring voices of the men's chorus, the camera pulls back to show a fully reactivated mining operation and large trucks brimming over with coal being rolled out of the shafts, as the full community stands ready to move forward together. With that rousing change of fortune, the scene dissolves into a close-up of Robeson singing the unofficial anthem "Wales." (It's worth noting that there's little or no reference to union or organized activity on the part of miners; rather, and perhaps far more effectively, their solidarity is conveyed throughout by their vocal harmonizing.)

With the war underway and London under siege, production of *The Proud Valley* was accelerated, with filming remarkably completed by September 25, only a month after it began. When it opened in Britain in early 1940, it was well received by critics and audiences alike (though oddly not as successful on either front as *The Stars Look Down*). Robeson had returned to the United States by then and had to wait for over a year—May 1941—to see it distributed there (and retitled yet again, this time as *The Tunnel*). His granddaughter later wrote that of all his film work, "this one satisfied him most, both politically and artistically."[17] A major reason for his satisfaction was the uniqueness of his role as a caring, competent, even heroic protagonist. According to an African American newspaper critic, "Hollywood has never produced a picture in which a colored actor has been cast as Robeson is in *The Proud Valley*. . . . Millions of movie-goers have been waiting to see a colored man cast as a man."[18] Soon, however, both films were overshadowed by yet a third film focused on British coal miners.

. . . . . .

Hot on the heels of the two relatively modest British productions came *How Green Was My Valley*, a prestigious Hollywood-based saga of life in a

Welsh coal town, which appeared on American screens late in 1941. Darryl F. Zanuck, the head of 20th Century Fox, paid top dollar to Welsh writer Richard Llewellyn for the rights to his best-selling novel soon after its publication in 1939. Although originally assigned to director William Wyler, who planned to film on location in Wales, the outbreak of war in Europe—in particular Germany's escalating air attacks on Britain in 1940—forced the studio to move the project back to California and to replace Wyler with director John Ford. The imposing set—a full-scale village consisting of a long line of quaint but sturdy stone row houses clinging to a hillside, capped by a smoke-churning colliery spread across its top—was constructed in the Santa Monica mountains and remains one of the film's most defining features. (That those mountains were more brown than green forced the decision to film in black and white rather than Technicolor, as had been originally planned.) There's a certain irony in the fact that this California-shot film, the only one of the three films not produced on location, projects the strongest and most sharply defined sense of place, yet it's hardly surprising. Enjoying the full backing of the Hollywood studio system's expertise and resources during what were still its golden years, *How Green Was My Valley* represents a far more polished, sophisticated production than its smaller-scale British counterparts, from its direction and screenplay to its photography and editing.[19]

As its director, John Ford proved a most appropriate fit for this material, given that this would be his third collaboration with Zanuck over the past year and a half in adapting popular novels to the screen—following *The Grapes of Wrath* (1940) and *Tobacco Road* (1941)—all three of which dramatized the plight of poor families, though each in very different circumstances and tone. *How Green Was My Valley* was remarkably well-received by American audiences and most critics. It ranked second only to *Sergeant York* as the year's biggest box-office draw, and it was rewarded with five Academy Awards, including Best Picture and Best Director (making it Ford's third Oscar, including one the previous year for *The Grapes of Wrath*).[20]

Like Llewellyn's novel, the Welsh-based saga onscreen was less plot-driven and more of an episodic slice-of-life, tracing the travails of a large family of coal miners over the course of the late nineteenth and early twentieth centuries. A recent critic called it "a devastating study of loss—of a family destroyed, a romance interrupted and an idyllic, rural community obliterated by industrialization and corporate greed."[21] While all this is true, what's most striking about this film—and what sets it apart from nearly every other screen treatment of coal miners—is the veneer of sentimentality and nostalgia in which that "study of loss" is wrapped. Screenwriter Philip Dunne followed Zanuck's lead in downplaying the specifics of labor unrest and exploitation that propelled the novel forward over time, noting that unlike its source material, he chose to emphasize the human over the sociological. Even though one critic dismissed the result as "a monstrous slurry of tears and coal dust," the forces behind this deterioration of both household and community often seem to be underdeveloped and unexplained.[22] (By contrast, *The Grapes of Wrath* and its dust bowl migrants make for a far more somber saga of similar themes, despite its tacked-on optimistic conclusion: Ma Joad's much quoted "We are the people!" speech.)

In part, the feel-good tone in *How Green Was My Valley* can be attributed to the fact that the story is framed as childhood memories of the youngest member of this large family, Huw Morgan (twelve-year-old Roddy McDowell in a star-making performance). In a voice-over narrative that serves as both connective tissue and social commentary throughout the film, the ten-year-old Huw recounts the daily rituals of his parents and his adult siblings—five brothers and a sister. The vast majority of the action takes place within the Morgans' unusually spacious house or on the town's steeply stepped thoroughfare, which fronts the sizable house. Huw's father (an Oscar-winning performance by Donald Crisp) and brothers all work in the colliery perched at the top of the hill; until the film's conclusion, we only see the miners going to or coming from it, dozens of them singing in perfect harmony, and thus get no real sense of what their work underground consists of.

The first of Huw's memories depicted is a lighthearted procession of sons arriving home on payday and dropping their few coins into their mother's apron, which she holds open as they pass into the house. From there, they move to the backyard for thorough scrubbings; only their father—called "Dada"—gets the luxury of a full tub bath. In short order, we've learned how dirty their work is and how little they're paid to do it, and yet they all seem to accept their lot cheerfully. "Coal miners were my father and brothers, and proud they were of their trade," Huw exudes in his opening voice-over. As for the scrubbings, he further expounds on that coal dust: "Most would come off, but some would stay for life. It was the honorable badge of the coal miner, and I envied it on my father and grown-up brothers."

Yet in that same monologue, Huw sets the stage for what's to come: "In those days, the black slag had only begun to cover the side of our hill, not yet enough to mar the countryside, nor the beauty of our village." As the slag spreads over the course of the film, it often seems to be more a function of scenic design than of human drama. The latter minimizes the downturns and setbacks for the Morgans and other mining families; from an ill-conceived and divisive attempt at unionizing to lowered wages and increasing layoffs, working conditions are treated only fleetingly—sometimes addressed merely by Huw's narration. As Zanuck acknowledged after the film's Academy Award triumph, "When I think of what I got away with, it really is astonishing. . . . Not only did we drop five or six characters, we eliminated the most controversial element in the book, the labor-vs.-capital battle in connection with the strike."[23]

Only in its direct impact on the Morgans does the mine merit a full place in the narrative. Most acutely, it forces the breakup of the family. The lack of work—particularly for more experienced, and thus more costly, miners—ultimately forces four of the five brothers to leave the country. The departure of the first two to America plays out in a moving series of farewell scenes, as does the film's most poignant moment—Mrs. Morgan's mournful contemplation of her family's global diaspora as Huw points out on a map of the world the destination of each of her boys: America, South Africa, Canada, and New Zealand. Such a scenario may well have resonated with both British and American audiences in 1941 as they contemplated where this new world war might carry their own loved ones.

Class tensions serve to complicate the Morgan saga, most notably the forced—and ultimately failed—marriage of the sole daughter (nineteen-year-old Maureen O'Hara) to the mine owner's son, despite her strong attraction for the local preacher (Walter Pidgeon), and her humiliating return alone to live as the mistress of the owner's mansion, which makes her the subject of malicious gossip by the women of the village. Huw alone seems to have scholarly potential but is made to endure much bullying and belittling by both teacher and more socially elite students at his one shot at formal schooling in a neighboring village. Perhaps because of that treatment he decides to follow in the family tradition and work in the mine—thus ignoring his despairing father, who points out, "It was different in our day. There was good money and fair play for all," and frets, "Why take brains down in a coal-mine?" The filmmakers seem of mixed mind regarding what seems to us an obviously mistaken decision on Huw's part—though one he never rethought; while they do nothing to glorify or soft-pedal the hardship of a life spent underground, they also fail to amplify the tragic waste expressed in Dada's question.

A poster for *How Green Was My Valley* highlights its central romance between Angharad (Maureen O'Hara) and Mr. Gruffydd (Walter Pidgeon), and the star-making debut of twelve-year-old Roddy McDowall as Huw.

The accidental mining deaths of one of the Morgan brothers (the only one who'd married) and, at the end, the father as well reflect sobering realities that the filmmakers could hardly avoid. Dada dies following a mine explosion—just after a futile effort by a rescue team that includes Huw (which provides the film's only substantive action in the coal shafts). In its final full sequence, the only remaining Morgans—all women, two of whom are widowed, one of whom is divorced—along with what seems to be the town's entire female populace, anxiously gather at the entrance to the mine, where they'll learn the fate of their menfolk. (This, by now, seems to have become an obligatory scenario in these films, although neither of the preceding two movies stage it nearly so effectively.) Slowly, the elevator's final platform rises to the surface to reveal Mr. Morgan's corpse, with Huw cradling his head. But even that final blow to the Morgan family is offset by a nostalgic coda in which the older Huw recalls all the good times of those early years, and closes with father and son, strolling arm in arm, through a thick field of daffodils.

• • • • • •

As distinctive as each of these three films is, it is no surprise that they share much in common in terms of theme and content. Perhaps most notably, all of them focus on family dynamics; in each, a single household serves as the linchpin for both plot and tone, centered to varying degrees on the multigenerational nature of their relationships with the mines and the industry's impact on them. In *The Stars Look Down*, the Fenwick family—elderly parents and two grown sons—holds center stage in the drama surrounding the walkout (led by its patriarch, Rob) and then the shutdown of the colliery; the clash with a local merchant involves both husband and wife (Martha) in their desperation for food as the shutdown drags on. Martha's stern and bitter manner makes the home front a gloomy retreat for her husband and sons, especially David, for whose quest for an education she holds nothing but contempt; and only slightly less so for that of her spirited younger son, who sees a soccer scholarship as his ticket out of a lifetime in the mines. Mother and older son only come together after the deaths of the other two family members, as she agrees to go with him when he returns to the university.

In *The Proud Valley*, we enter the Parry household as they become the host family for David Goliath, and follow the local struggles with a distant mine owner through the proactive roles played by the father and elder son Emlyn until the former's untimely death at around the film's midpoint. From then on, Goliath's die-hard loyalty to Mrs. Parry and to the welfare of her sizable brood of young children drive much of the plot, including its climax—the suicidal sacrifice this gentle giant makes to spare Emlyn for the sake of his mother, siblings, and fiancée.[24]

As noted previously, much of *How Green Was My Valley*'s immense appeal lies in its episodic, nearly plotless narrative, constructed around the Morgan family over time. Framed primarily through the youngest son's coming of age, their lives are driven by romance, rivalries, comings and goings, illness and health, and setbacks and successes, much of which is defined by the colliery operation that dominates their world. It is perhaps coincidental, perhaps not, that in all three of these films, the father of each household and one of his sons are killed in mining accidents—certainly the most explicit examples of the impact of this dangerous enterprise on families. (In two of the three, it is other sons who carry or cradle their father's dead or dying bodies as they emerge from the mine to face anxiously waiting wives, mothers, and children; in the third, *Proud Valley*, it is surrogate son David Goliath who bears Dick Parry out of the mine.)

Moving beyond households, the sense of community plays out somewhat differently from film to film. In *The Stars Look Down*, the local working class isn't nearly as united as it is in the other two—it's the only film in which miners initiate a strike against the owner, and do so without the input, much less consent, of their union (whose leadership is as complacent as that of the owners regarding unsafe conditions underground). Tensions run high otherwise, as evident in the mob outbreak in the butcher shop, and even former classmates end up clashing violently in a subplot of marital discord and infidelity.

The sense of a united community is more pervasive and more positive in the two Welsh-based films. In *The Proud Valley*, community identity and esprit de corps are strongly tied to the local men's choir, which (given that the film is built around Robeson's presence as a singer), becomes the focal point of both plot and character. It provides the (almost) credible explanation for what makes the town so racially color-blind in its embrace of this outsider—and the anomaly that an American black man could be so much a part of the vibrant civic pride with which Blaendy residents rally around their much anticipated national music competition.

Even as the Morgan family provides the axis around which *How Green Was My Valley* revolves, the town (never named) and its communal interactions are the most pronounced and multifaceted of the three films, ranging from church to school to shops to frequent street scenes, all taking full advantage of the magnificent showcase of sets provided by Hollywood prowess and resources. It too features male voices raised in song, though the perfect harmonizing by miners trudging home from work feels somewhat more contrived than those bursts of vocalizing built into *The Proud Valley*'s narrative. The same civic pride comes to the fore in *How Green Was My Valley* when one of the older Morgan sons receives an invitation for his men's choir (mentioned then for the first and last time) to sing for Queen Victoria at Windsor Castle. Cheering villagers gather in front of the Morgan home as the choir falls into formation and sings a stirring rendition of "God Save the Queen," which in 1941 may have been an added salute to British patriotism with the war underway.

Finally, the theme of young people getting out, escaping the fate of their elders and the working lives they've spent underground, plays out in different ways in these films—just as it does in their Appalachian-based counterparts, as we shall see. In *The Stars Look Down,* the two Fenwick brothers demonstrate mixed motives for making their way out—one far loftier than the other. While the younger boy simply sees soccer as his ticket out of the colliery and Sleescale, the idealistic David views his university degree as a means of empowerment for his mining community in combating the formidable forces that either ignore or work against their interests. When his marriage forces him to discontinue his studies and return home to teach school, David encourages his students to use their education as an escape hatch from life in the pits. Yet he faces considerable pushback from parents and other townspeople, who resent his putting such ideas into their children's heads. One especially contemptuous mother taunts David that for all his grand talk and aspirations, he himself has landed back in town as a "mere" teacher, making far less than her son will make as a miner. This complacency—which they may well have seen as facing facts—reflected what was likely a common attitude among mining families of two generations, both in what parents wanted for their children and in what those children aspired to—or not. *The Stars Look Down* is quite adept in embracing both points of view, through the encouragement of David by his father, who tells him, "Someday you're going to do something about this industry; the men have great faith in you," and his mother's disapproval of his leaving home at all.

In *The Proud Valley,* the focus falls on only one young person, Emlyn Parry, and though he's a mining engineer, he is committed to the community and helping fellow miners (politically as well as technically). Despite the mass exodus of miners and their families from the Rhondda valley in the 1930s, Paul Robeson's sentiments lay with those still there, and he was reluctant to use his film to push the notion that better lives could only be achieved elsewhere. Like David Fenwick in *The Stars Look Down,* Emlyn Parry represents the idea of an education as a laudable goal, but less as an escape hatch from the collieries than as a means of improving conditions and terms for his fellow workers, which has much to do with Goliath's willingness to give his own life to save that of this dedicated young engineer.

Finally, in *How Green Was My Valley,* the Morgan sons' decisions to leave are forced upon them by the downsizing of the workforce. If they are not dismissed outright, notified by authorities as they stand in line for what will be their final weekly wages, they must decide on their own, as their aging status among the available workforce means a reduction in pay for what few hours they are granted. Thus, Huw's fate seems so painful an irony, as the son with the best mind and greatest potential to move on to what his father calls "a more respectable profession" elsewhere (to which an indignant Mrs. Morgan takes issue, retorting, "Respectable? Are you and all his brothers a bunch of jailbirds, then?"). Yet Huw chooses to spend most of his life in a mine, supporting his otherwise abandoned mother and leaving only when she dies, as we learn in the film's opening lines, a voice-over narration by the then middle-aged Huw, who states simply, "I am packing my belongings in the shawl my mother used to wear when she went to market. I'm going from my valley. And this time I shall never return."

• • • • • •

As noted earlier, it was only much later that Appalachian coal mining fully attracted Hollywood's attention. Three films—*Matewan* (1987), *Coal Miner's Daughter* (1980), and *October Sky* (1999)—deal with themes and issues similar to those confronted in the earlier British films just discussed, but there are considerable differences as well. Most significant, perhaps, is that the latter films are all based on fact (and will be addressed in order of historical chronology rather than by date of production): first, John Sayles's independently produced treatment of a well-documented showdown between miners and mine owners that played out in Matewan, West Virginia, in 1920, followed by two coming-of-age sagas based on popular autobiographies by the children of coal miners—Loretta Lynn's in Butcher Hollow, Kentucky, in the late 1940s, and Homer Hickam's in Coalwood, West Virginia, in the late 1950s—and the circumstances that took them out of those environments.

Matewan is the most ambitious and sophisticated attempt by a filmmaker to portray the historical reality of the coal wars of the 1910s and 1920s, despite its low budget and the relatively small scale of the story it tells. John Sayles had first taken an interest in the mining conflicts during the late 1960s while hitchhiking through central Appalachia and hearing stories from miners and descendants of miners of those early conflicts, as he noted in a book he wrote on the making of *Matewan* in 1987, the same year as the film itself was released.[25] A decade after his initial "on the road" exposure to the region, Sayles wrote a novel, *Union Dues* (1977), in which a West Virginia adolescent runs away to Boston in 1969; becomes embroiled in a commune, with its radical politics and counterculture lifestyle; and must then confront his coal miner father, who comes north to find him and take him home. In researching the Appalachian background of his two lead characters, Sayles became even more intrigued with the region's earlier labor organizing efforts and ensuing violence in Matewan, a small coal town on the Tug River, as a means of conveying that larger history through a concise, complex, and cinematically compelling reenactment of the events leading up to that incident.[26]

For all the richly delineated characterizations throughout, the sense of place, so often a strength of these films, falls a little short here. Sayles was determined to make the film on location in West Virginia, but as Matewan itself had grown and modernized too much to return it to its early twentieth-century look, he and his production team chose Thurmond, West Virginia—a nearly abandoned old town on the New River, about a hundred miles east of Matewan—as its stand-in. The problem lies in the fact that Thurmond comes across as a near ghost town on screen, with the shells of buildings still looking like shells, with mere signage and window dressing failing to disguise a sparse-looking, underpopulated main street. More effective are the dramatic mountainside woodlands that are used to good effect in establishing an authentic sense of place, much of the credit for which belongs to veteran cinematographer Haskell Wexler, who earned an Academy Award nomination for his work here.[27]

The film opens with fast cuts of fleeting movements as word spreads among the miners that they're walking out on their employer, the Stone Mountain Coal Company, for dropping their wages (which were calculated on the tonnage of coal brought out per week). A voice-over by a middle-aged miner—identified only as Pappy—provides a minimal explanation in distant hindsight, stating, "Hit were 1920 in the southwest field and things was tough." He says simply that the miners were trying to bring the union to West Virginia, and "the coal operators and their gun thugs was set on keepin' 'em out." At the mine entrance, two guards armed with a sandbagged machine gun stand watch as men come pouring out of the mine into the daylight. "Them was hard people, your coal miners then," Pappy continues. "So push comes to shove and pretty soon we had us a war down there in Mingo County, which in them days was known as 'Bloody Mingo.'"[28]

With the stage thus set (and the time frame much compressed), the scene shifts to an oncoming train bringing outsiders who will raise tensions even higher. These include Joe Kenehan (Chris Cooper), a fictional composite of a United Mine Workers of America (UMWA) organizer—and a pacifist at that—and a boxcar crowded with strikebreaking African Americans from Alabama, led by the historically based figure nicknamed Few Clothes, embodied by the formidable James Earl Jones. The latter are attacked by local miners as soon as they step off the train, leading Kenehan to begin damage control and attempt to convince the Matewan strikers to join the Alabama "scabs," along with a group of "fresh-off-the-boat" Italian immigrants brought in by the company as well. This proves to be the first of a continuous chain of violent encounters—ambushes, set explosions, open attacks, and counterattacks—that escalate throughout the film until the infamous "massacre," which brings it all to an almost-too-abrupt conclusion.

The impetus for most of this violence comes from mining company officials—represented by a sinister pair of agents from the Baldwin-Felts Detective Agency—who arrive on the scene shortly after the strike begins. They quickly make their contempt for the mountains and its people known, with snide remarks about the "mountain trash" they're dealing with and doing what they need to do quickly so that they can get out of "this shit-hole."[29] In evicting the strikers from their company housing, the Baldwin "thugs" clash with Matewan town officials—the mayor, Cabell Testerman (Josh Mostel), and the police chief, Sid Hatfield (David Strathairn)—over who has jurisdiction over those houses. Even after both groups of outsiders agree to join the union and the strike, further tensions—largely based on mutual cultural prejudices among the black Alabamians, the Italian families, and the Appalachian locals—play out in the makeshift encampment they must share in the nearby woods.

Sayles made much of the fact that his ensemble cast reflects the multicultural context of the story he tells. Such ensembles were a hallmark of his films, he once noted: "One thing I've tried to do in all [my] movies," he explained, "is to have a world populated by more than one or two people, to present a community. I'm more interested in how individual and political acts affect communities of people—parents, friends, children, co-workers. To pull this off, to have all these characters seem three-dimensional, they need not only more screen time than is usually provided but also more depth of character."[30]

While *Matewan* provides as full-bodied a portrait of an Appalachian community as any onscreen, family and household settings are less prevalent than they are in most of the other films discussed here. We see little of marriage or two-parent households in Matewan. There are only three female characters of any substance (all of whom seem to be fictional creations); all are widows, made so by a mine explosion several years earlier. Two of the three are mothers of adolescent sons. One of these, Elma Radnor (Mary McDonnell), is a strong, capable woman who runs a company-owned boardinghouse and emerges as a pivotal character in that she must play host to both Joe Kenehan and the two Baldwin-Felts agents while trying to rein in her outspoken son, Danny, in the midst of strained encounters with the agents. Another is an older woman, Mrs. Elkins (Jo Henderson), who has a son slightly older than Danny named Hillard; the Elkinses are barely making ends meet as part of the strikers' tent camp they must share—quite grudgingly—with the Italian delegation. Mrs. Elkins must endure the most painful moments of the film—the excruciating murder of her son at the hands of company thugs, and his subsequent burial service deep in the woods. The third female is Bridey Mae (Nancy Mette), a flirtatious and naive young woman who becomes a pawn in the surreptitious machinations of the company agents to expose Kenehan and other union leaders. (She's the target of the Baldwin-Felts agent's comment on "mountain trash.")

Another, more marginal element of the Matewan community—one that might have been lost in less sensitive hands than Sayles's—is one that is rarely acknowledged in most treatments of Appalachia's coal country. These are the so-called hill people, local woodsmen (perhaps once small farmers) who are not employed by the coal company but continue to live off the land in the surrounding wilderness. In *Matewan*, they appear as bearded hunters who stumble upon the tent-dwelling strikers who have just moved onto their turf, as they're under attack by the company agents. They're sympathetic with the strikers' plight and fire several rifle shots to drive away the company agents, with one declaring, "Now you all get in that machine [car] and get back into town where you belong. Hain't but one law here, and that's the law a nature."

Once Baldwin's "hit men" have grudgingly done as they were told and departed, the same obliging hunter addresses the tenters: "You folks try to keep the noise down here, you'll do fine. Help yourself to bird and rabbit, but you see any hogs they's probly ours and we'd appreciate it if you leave 'em be." As he nods and heads back into the woods with his companions, Joe Kenehan asks, "Who were those people? They miners?" to which Mrs. Elkins responds, "Never find them folks near a hole. They had most of their land stole by the company." When Bridey Mae adds, "They's hill people," Mrs. Elkins corrects her: "Foothill people really. Your genuwine hill people, they can be dangerous." While much of this sequence rings true and delineates social if not true class distinctions (which give way to the most benign form of stereotyping), the brief exchange also denotes an inherent sense of decency and justice in the woodsmen's response to the plight of the beleaguered coal workers who have been forced to take refuge in their woodland domain.

Though fully an ensemble work, it's noteworthy that Sayles makes a fourteen-year-old boy one of the linchpins of the story and among his more intriguing characters. Danny Radnor, Elma's son, is fictional (as are roughly half of the movie's characters) and played by Will Oldham, a young actor discovered at a regional theater in Louisville. Like so many of the other films that feature young people as pivotal figures, one of the more manageable approaches to analyzing *Matewan* is through the role of this adolescent and the multiple ways in which Sayles builds much of his story around or through Danny's presence. Clearly a prodigy of sorts, wise well beyond his years, Danny is a miner (and already an experienced one, it seems), a preacher, and—by midway through the film—a union activist.

When Joe Kenehan takes a room in his mother's boardinghouse, Danny begins to bond with the union organizer and comes to admire both the man and his mission. He helps his mother in supplying food to those evicted from company housing, and sounds the alarm when he overhears the Baldwin-Felts agents discussing a mole they've planted in the strikers' midst. We hear him deliver two hard-hitting sermons—one for the Free Will Baptists and the other for the Missionary Baptists—in which he uses biblical analogies—one Old Testament, one New—to convey thinly disguised pro-union messages to his adult congregants, including explicit warnings of the coal company's nefarious methods to bring them down.

Perhaps it's his familiarity with the people he's grown up among that makes Danny skeptical of Kenehan's pacifist approach to resisting the company's bullying ways; the brutal killing of his companion Hillard pushes him toward more militant tactics. Following a moving eulogy at his burial ("He was a good miner, a good union member, and good to his mama"), Danny is emboldened enough to take rifle in hand. Kenehan approaches and states simply, "I came here to help." Danny lashes out in anger over how empty that phrase has become to Matewan residents: "Sure you did. First people come in here to help us with money, and next we know we got no land. Now you come in and want to help us bring in the new day. Well Hillard ain't gonna see no new day. We had about as much help as we can stand. We got to take care of ourselves."

The following day brings the showdown toward which such tensions have been building. As Baldwin-Felts reinforcements head into Matewan to enforce evictions from company-owned houses, a veteran of the "gun thugs" sets the tone for what's to come when he asks a new recruit beside him if he'd ever heard of the Hatfields and McCoys. "This here is their stomping ground," he declares. "They'll put a bullet in your brain as sure as look at you."[31] (This is Sayles's only nod to the popular notion that the incident was part of a tradition of mountain violence and vengeance entrenched

The shoot-out between battling strikebreaking agents and local officials serves as the climax of *Matewan*.

in the region.) A standoff between the gunmen and the mayor and chief of police on May 19, 1920, on Matewan's main street triggers the so-called massacre. While effectively staged, filmed, and edited (the whole thing transpires in less than five minutes of screen time), Sayles only loosely recreates the actual melee, given that he fully integrates his fictional characters into the action, giving them key moments. These include Kenehan being fatally shot and Danny's mother, Elma—in a more contrived but dramatically satisfying scene—blasting the more sinister of her Baldwin-Felts boarders while shielded by her freshly hung laundry. The ten actual fatalities that day included the mayor, seven of the twelve Baldwin-Felts agents on-site, and two unarmed miners.[32] Historically, no black miners were involved in the incident, which Sayles handles simply by having Few Clothes say the day before, "Best to stay out of town tomorrow. . . . You know how white folks get when they get excited."[33]

Sayles also provides Danny with a final face-to-face confrontation that allows for his own redemption of sorts. After kneeling beside the dying body of his mentor, Joe Kenehan, the young preacher encounters a young

Baldwin-Felts recruit seeking to run away from the "battlefield" and, unarmed, begs Danny to spare his life. After a moment's hesitation, Danny lowers his rifle, allowing the lad to leap into the Tug River and swim to safety on the Kentucky side. Obviously he has absorbed, at long last, something of Joe's nonviolent principles. In short, this bloody climax resolves several plot issues while remaining true to the spirit of events that transpired in Matewan on May 19, 1920.

As the camera pulls back, the narrator's voice returns to describe the aftermath of the massacre, as the image onscreen is of a lone miner walking along a dark shaft. As he approaches the camera, we see that it's Danny, and it only then becomes obvious that it's been a middle-age version of his voice that we've heard frame the story from the start. Among other things, he states, "That were the start of the great Coalfield War, and us miners took the worst of it like Joe said we would. 'Hit's just one big union, the whole world over,' Joe Kenehan used to say, and from the day of the Matewan massacre, that's what I preached. That was my religion."

At that point one wonders if Sayles has taken his cue from the Huw Morgan character in *How Green Was My Valley*, in that much of *Matewan*'s story has been viewed through the eyes of the fourteen-year-old Danny and framed in hindsight by a much older version of that self. Danny, like Huw, chose to stay in the mines. Curiously, as bright and spirited as he obviously is, no one ever mentions the possibility of formal education for Danny, nor is there any indication that he craves it, as was the case for so many other young people in these films, whether as an escape from the miner's life or as a means of serving their fellow miners in other ways. Regardless of what little schooling he may have had, Danny's final narration suggests that he did commit to serve his fellow workers by using his preaching skills to spread a new gospel—that of the union. In that sense, he echoes the more mission-driven sons from *The Stars Look Down* and *The Proud Valley*—one a schoolteacher and one a mining engineer—who return to serve their own mining communities. Yet for *Matewan*, it seems merely an afterthought or a vague coda that puzzles more than clarifies, in terms of both the message of the film and the fate of its most intriguing character.

• • • • • •

When Loretta Lynn published her plain-spoken and disarmingly candid autobiography, *Coal Miner's Daughter*, in 1976, her status as a country music star was at its peak, and her book became a national best seller.[34] Both of these facts, plus the appeal of almost any all-American rags-to-riches saga, meant that Hollywood saw in the Kentucky native's life story great potential for a screen adaptation. Though Lynn turned down an offer to produce it as a made-for-television movie, she sold the rights to her book to Universal Studios with few strings attached in terms of content. She simply urged executives to be as true to the book as possible, and expressed less concern over how she would be characterized than on how they would portray her volatile, often hard-drinking husband, Doolittle Lynn. She campaigned hard for a reluctant young Texas actress, Sissy Spacek, to play her on-screen, and was equally persistent in urging producers to hire another Texan, Tommy Lee Jones, to play Doolittle. She collaborated closely with screenwriter Tom Rickman in adapting the book to film, and as a result, the final product in 1980, directed with great sensitivity by Michael Apted, who was from a coal mining area in England, has an aura of authenticity—in both character and setting—that's exceptional for a screen biography. (It compares favorably with *Sergeant York* in terms of filmmakers' commitment to a truthful depiction and respect for Appalachian residents, though the screen version of Alvin York's story exudes far more sentimentality and romanticized characterizations than does Loretta Lynn's.)[35]

As the only film to use the term "coal"—or, for that matter, "miner"—in its title, that way of life as experienced in Appalachia in the late 1940s is meticulously, if quite succinctly, chronicled in its opening scenes. (The Kentucky-based scenes make up approximately the first third of the film.) By the late 1970s, once-remote Butcher Hollow (like Matewan) was too marred with telephone poles and electrical wires to be used for location filming; thus, most of the mountain and coal mining scenes were shot about seventy miles south, in and around Wise, Virginia (with the interiors shot in an abandoned Piggly Wiggly grocery store in Hazard, Kentucky).[36]

Lynn herself was very much a presence during filming. She acknowledged in a later interview (in 1985) that she had never lost touch with her roots. "Something hit me last year," she mused, "when I went back to the house [in which I'd grown up] in Kentucky, and I said to myself, 'How did I get out of here?' Memories everywhere. Doo got me out; if he hadn't, I doubt I'd ever have left. There was only a path out of Butcher Hollow, wasn't no dirt road, just a path. And it hit me last year, and kind of made me sad."[37]

This is the thrust of the film's early scenes—how Doolittle Lynn, a recent World War II veteran, courted and married fourteen-year-old Loretta Webb and provided her a path out of Appalachia and into a new and very different life (even if she did follow his lead rather reluctantly). Coal was fully at

Fourteen-year-old Loretta Webb (Sissy Spacek) and her father (Levon Helm) as he ends his shift underground in the opening sequence of *Coal Miner's Daughter*.

the center of the life into which she was born. The film's opening sequence, depicting several men setting explosives deep in a mine, is intercut with Loretta and her little brother riding a horse along a highland ridge to meet their father, Ted Webb (Levon Helm), one of those miners, as he gets off work. They proceed to the company store, where they first encounter the cocky veteran, Doolittle Lynn, in a red jeep. Ted asks, "Who's the soldier boy out there strutting around like a bantam rooster?" and is told by the storekeeper that he's "old man Red Lynn's boy, come back from the army acting like a wild heathen. But he'll calm down as soon as they slap a coal shovel in his hand." Thus, a prime lesson of life in coal country: mining as the means of taming youthful exuberance and energy, and the efforts of those with both to escape its ruinous clutches.

Also wedged into this packed opening sequence is a moonshiner, hawking his self-made wares from jars stacked on his flatbed truck. A friend of Doolittle's, he takes bets from the gathering crowd that Doo can't get his jeep to the top of a steep slag heap without it rolling over and "killing hisself." He manages to reach the top with himself and his jeep intact and, in so doing, earns the admiration of Loretta, who happens to attract his attention for the first time as well. Jones was thirty-three years old when he played the twenty-one-year-old Lynn, and while not nearly as convincing as thirty-year-old Spacek is as a fourteen-year-old, he still managed to convey the youthful swagger that Loretta described so vividly in her autobiography. (According to a birth certificate later found, she was actually fifteen at the time of their courtship and marriage in 1948, having been born in 1932.)[38]

Doolittle's friend attempts to talk him into partnering with him in his illicit operation, telling him what he already knows: "You born in the mountains, you got three choices: coal mine, moonshine, or movin' on down the line." Corrupt dealings by this ne'er-do-well lead to a shoot-out that's heard from the Webb house, soon followed by the sight of Doo walking by with the corpse of his would-be partner slung over a horse. The film cuts to a scene that reveals that Doo has been pushed into the option he most wanted to avoid—shoveling coal deep underground and looking very discontented.

The "pie social" at which Doolittle and Loretta first make real contact is drawn almost verbatim from her book and launches a whirlwind romance in which we fully see other sides of Doo's character and his serious aspirations for a better life. He tells her of his war experience and the wider world to which it exposed him. "So I ain't about to spend my life buried in no coal mine, either. Ain't no future in it, and that's what I'm interested in, the future." He and his jeep seem to sweep her off her feet, but they face a real barrier in her parents.

Spacek shines, as do Helm and Phyllis Boyens as her parents (both musicians acting for the first time on film), in their scenes at home as a family, which ring particularly true in terms of physical setting, the interactions among family members, and the speech patterns all built into a masterful script. As sparse an existence as is on display in their home, it is obviously a happy household of caring adults and seemingly well-adjusted children. Loretta is the second oldest of nine children and the first to contemplate matrimony, thus causing the only familial friction we see among the Webbs. Her father actually gives her a switching "for running off with that wild boy and worrying everybody to death," and her mother orders her to stay away from him, or "I'll do even worse than what your daddy did," even as she offers her some salve for her legs.

In another iconic scene, Doo comes to the house late one night and makes a formal request for her hand. After prolonged exchanges with Loretta and her parents, each in different rooms, and several heartfelt promises from the eager suitor as to how much he loves and will care for their daughter, her father capitulates. But he extracts two other promises from his soon-to-be son-in-law: that he'll never hit her and that he won't take her far from home. Doo promises both, and they get married the next in a nearly empty mountainside church, at the door of which Mr. Webb makes a brief appearance. (Other than the pie social, there's little sense of a collective community in Butcher Hollow, in itself a sharp contrast from the other films discussed here.) Following several rocky weeks of less than wedded bliss, Doo announces that he's leaving Kentucky and heading west, where he'll look for farmwork he's seen advertised in Washington State. "There's nothing for me here," he declares, "just a chest full of coal dust and bein' an old man by the time I'm forty." Loretta tells him she's pregnant, and he says he'll soon earn enough money to send for her.

In a heartrending scene at the depot several weeks later, her father waits with Loretta for the train that will take her across the country and out of their lives. She weighs herself on a scale, then urges her daddy to do the same. He insists it would do no good, since he "wouldn't know how much was me and how much was all that coal dust I swallowed." Knowing he probably doesn't have long to live, he tells her, "I ain't never goin' to see you again. Them years have been robbed from me, like a thief broke in and robbed them." The train pulls up, and we get a sudden shift several years forward to a farm in Washington and Loretta (at age eighteen) in full mode as a housewife and mother of four.

The only other scene set in Kentucky is the family's return for her father's funeral. (He was fifty-one when he finally succumbed to black lung disease and high blood pressure in 1959.)[39] Though his funeral and burial were indeed in Kentucky, making for some poignant moments onscreen and a turning point in his daughter's life and in the film, the latter skirts the fact that he had lost his job in the mines several years before, and the Webbs, like many Kentucky highlanders, had moved to Wabash, Indiana, where Loretta's mother became the chief breadwinner at a drive-in restaurant, where she earned sixty-five cents an hour.[40]

The film ends with Spacek on stage at Nashville's Ryman Auditorium, sporting Loretta's voluminous hairdo and frilly floor-length gown and belting out her signature anthem, "Coal Miner's Daughter," while a montage of clips from her early years in Kentucky flashes by onscreen (a film narrative convention that dates back at least to *How Green Was My Valley*). In her lyrics for this most autobiographical of her many songs (and her prose version of her life story), Lynn didn't shy away from remembering the poverty and material deprivations she experienced as a child, yet she also expressed her appreciation for a loving life with caring parents who made very real sacrifices for their children. There's no mention in the song of why she left, but the film, like her memoir, makes it clear that the initiative to leave was clearly Doolittle's, and that his innocent fourteen-year-old wife merely followed his lead, her only comment being, "You promised Daddy you'd never take me away from home."

Apted's film fully captures the spirit of both Lynn's book and song. More than almost any other film set in Appalachia, it balances genuine nostalgia for a place and time with the grim realities so integral to life there, with little acknowledgment of the contradictions in such sentiments by those who've left the region. Though never soft-peddling the hardships (and health hazards) that coal imposed on life in Butcher Hollow and, by extension, throughout central Appalachia, *Coal Miner's Daughter* makes fully understandable Lynn's affection for the place, a place that for her is more defined by family ties and family life than by any broader community or mountain environment. Much of that perspective stems from her sheer youth, which Sissy Spacek renders so convincingly and with such appeal; when a husband replaces her father as the authority figure in her early adolescence, Loretta dutifully crosses the country to begin a whole new life with him. Thus, her memories of the Kentucky mountains are those of a young girl, not an adult. And yet Lynn worked to preserve—indeed to celebrate—her origins as a coal miner's daughter and made them central to her identity, in no small part because Hollywood embraced her rags-to-riches saga on its own terms—and on hers. (Only Dolly Parton has done more to publicly—and profitably—document her poverty-stricken Appalachian upbringing in such a multimedia mode, though she's often soft-pedaled that poverty more than Lynn has.)

• • • • • •

Homer Hickam's memoir of life in Coalwood, West Virginia, in the late 1950s chronicles yet another means of an adolescent escape from a coal miner's life—this one far more calculated and hard-fought than was Loretta Lynn's. About a hundred miles east of Butcher Hollow, Kentucky, Coalwood was a company-owned town, where Hickam's father served as the superintendent of a large mining operation in the 1950s, which provided the family a more comfortable middle-class life than the Webb family had known (including access to a full-fledged high school education). Hickam's *Rocket Boys*, published in 1998, chronicled his efforts and those of several classmates to experiment with building and launching jet-propulsion rockets. While at once a commentary on the impact of the 1957 launch of the Soviet Union's first satellite, Sputnik, on America's Cold War fears and dreams of space travel, such dreams for these particular students were also tied to a more immediate goal: college scholarships that would provide their tickets out of coal country and beyond lives as coal miners.

As a NASA engineer working in Huntsville, Alabama, in the 1990s, Hickam wrote an article-length version of his high school project, playfully titled "The Big Creek Missile Agency"; it appeared in the Smithsonian's *Air and Space* magazine in 1994 and caused enough of a stir to generate interest from both Hollywood producers and New York publishers. Ultimately, simultaneous deals on both fronts led to an unusual timetable in which the film was in production at the same time Hickam wrote and revised his memoir. This led to several significant discrepancies in the versions of the story each told, including the compression on film of a nearly three-year span between Sputnik's launch in 1957 and the National Science Fair in the spring of 1960 into a single school year.[41] While the filmmakers stuck with their tightened time frame, they did correct a more serious problem Hickam had with their script: its depiction of Appalachia and its people. The first draft of the screenplay, he wrote, "confirmed all my unspoken fears. It was one stereotype after another. Coalwood was filthy, its people toothless and barefoot, the boys foul-mouthed, my father violent, my mother spineless."[42] Individual scenes proved just as offensive, including striking miners "storming up and down the mean, gritty streets of Coalwood carrying torches" (which brought to mind the addled villagers in pursuit of the monster at loose in *Frankenstein*), and a kitchen table scene in which his mother "worried where our next meal was coming from, as if we were refugees from *The Grapes of Wrath*."[43] Hickam was forceful in his objections, and presumably due to his persistence, we're presented instead with perhaps the most identifiable and "all-American" working-class group of Appalachian miners ever to appear on movie screens.

Hickam had hoped that the movie could have been filmed on location in Coalwood, but its remoteness and the sheer topography of the town, whose surrounding mountains blocked sunlight for most of the day, worked against it, according to the director, Joe Johnston. Instead, the producers found the town of Petros, Tennessee, in a more modest mining district near Oak Ridge, and thus near Knoxville, making it far more accessible to the Hollywood crew.[44] Film production actually began before Hickam completed his book, based on a "treatment" of the story he laid out. *Rocket Boys* appeared in print in September 1998, after the film had completed production and before it was released in February 1999 with its new title, *October Sky* (an anagram of *Rocket Boys*, a reference to the month of Sputnik's appearance, and apparently a more marketable title for middle-aged women filmgoers).

Escape is as central to Hickam's story as it is for any of the films discussed here, if not more so. As we've seen, the impulse to leave often proves a source of conflict between generations or between parents. The latter is very much at the heart of this story, which Hickam makes clear in the first sentence on the first page of his book: "Until I began to build and launch rockets, I didn't know my hometown was at war with itself over its children and that my parents were locked in a kind of bloodless combat over how my brother and I would live our lives."[45] Unlike disagreements between parents in earlier films, such as *The Stars Look Down* and *How Green Was My Valley*, in which fathers rather than mothers champion their sons moving on to better lives elsewhere, in Hickam's case, it's his mother who takes that stand against the strong opposition of her husband, the boys' father. Homer Sr., in fact, stands out not only among his fellow miners in Coalwood but also from those in the other films discussed. Having advanced into a supervisory capacity, he is not merely resigned to his job and its accompanying hardships but genuinely loves it and believes others—especially his sons—would as well if they'd just give it a chance; no other character in a coal-based film is more aggressive in proselytizing the benefits of a mining life than Homer's father.

The stakes are laid out early in the film. Homer (a star-making turn by sixteen-year-old Jake Gyllenhaal) is repeatedly knocked down at football practice, proving he's not the athlete his older brother Jim is and leading his father (Chris Cooper) to crack, "Well, I told you if you'd spent the summer shoveling coal, you'd be playing linebacker next fall." Other miners tease Homer, including a lingerer who gets in the last word, which he intends as encouragement: "Buck up, Homer. You're a Coalwood boy. You get down in that mine and get that coal shovel in your hand, it'll be as natural to you as a tick on a dog."

Homer, however, is far more interested in the hoopla over Sputnik, which inspires him to seek out information on rocket science. He then joins forces with three classmates to see if they can construct a workable rocket. They seek the help of a welder for the coal company, to whom Homer confides the excitement of seeing the Russian satellite streaking across the sky overhead on October 5 (hence the film's new title). "Anyone in the world could have looked up and seen what I saw," he exudes. "For once, it felt like Coalwood was part of the outside world." The more resigned welder responds simply, "Homer, believe me, there are much worse places than Coalwood in this world."

The boys' chemistry teacher, Miss Riley (Laura Dern), is excited to see her students so suddenly inspired by scientific endeavors, and she encourages them to make it a project for a regional science fair. This perks Homer's interest only when she tells them that those who advance to the nationals can win scholarships to colleges all over the world. "You can't just dream your way out of Coalwood," she tells Homer.[46] She later gives him a book on the higher mathematics behind rocket science; the school principal sees this and lectures her afterward: "Our jobs are to give these kids an education, not false hopes. . . . Once in a while," he says, "a lucky one will get out on a football scholarship. The rest of them work in the mines." She responds, "How about I believe in the unlucky ones, hmm? I have to, or I'd go out of my mind." With Miss Riley as inspiration and resource, young Hickam and his schoolmates begin hit-or-miss experimentation with rocket launches.

One such effort sends a missile hurtling through the mining property, causing panic and embarrassment to Mr. Hickam, who's meeting with company owners at that moment. This leads to a showdown between father and son. The latter tells his mother that his dad loves the mine more than he loves the family, and for what? "All the mine's given him is a spot on his lung the size of a quarter." Mr. Hickam arrives home, overhears that pronouncement, and shouts back to his son, "You don't know what the mine gives me. You don't know because you're a boy, but by golly, you're going to find out soon enough." Homer stomps off to the basement, where he finds all of his "rocket stuff" gone; his father has thrown it out with the trash and bans him from using company property for his experimentation—which means that the entire town and well beyond are off limits.

It takes a good deal of prodding for Homer to get his friends to recommit to the project, leading to a revealing debate on the pointlessness of a "bunch of hillbillies" thinking they can win a science fair and, regardless of such a win, the inevitability of their futures in mining coal. "I know I'm going to be a miner," says one, matter-of-factly. "I've known my entire life. What the hell's so bad about mining coal?" Homer responds by citing the deaths it's caused of men they knew and noting the reason so many others were among "the biggest drunks in West Virginia." His argument resonates with his friends, and they resume their experiments in full force, using a vast slag dump well beyond the bounds of Coaltown as their base of operations.

Homer Hickam (Jake Gyllenhaal) clashes with his father (Chris Cooper), a coal mine supervisor, over Homer's future as a miner in *October Sky*.

As encouragement, Homer's mother arranges for an autographed photograph and note from Wernher von Braun for his birthday; he's thrilled, but his father spoils the moment, saying, "Boy, you better take an interest in your own damn town instead of worrying about Von Braun and Cape Canaveral!"

As their rocket launches prove more successful, more townspeople and fellow students rally around the boys, treating them almost like football players, as one observes. But other setbacks serve to complicate the plot: Homer offers to work in the mine after his father suffers an eye injury in a mine explosion, and the two bond when his father recovers and they find themselves working side by side underground. His father asks him, "Well, is mining coal as terrible as you figured it'd be?" to which Homer replies, "I guess not . . . but almost." He's troubled by more delusional observations from his dad later on, such as when he tells him, "Homer, I was born for this; I guess it shouldn't surprise me that you are too." Even the principal, in signing the school release that allows him to go to work, assures him that "mining coal is an honorable trade, Mr. Hickam. Nothing to be ashamed of."

At one point, not clearly explained, Homer decides to stick with mining and not return to school, which leads his mother to step forward and insist that he not throw away all the promise of his work-in-progress and the academic opportunities beckoning. (According to Hickam, the whole premise of his leaving school to work in the mine was invented by the screenwriters and not based on fact.)[47] Yet only when Miss Riley, who's found out she has Hodgkin's disease (she died at age thirty-one), tells Homer that her life might have counted for something if the boys had followed through and gone to college does he see the light, return to the book she'd given him, quit the mine, and stand up to his father when he tries to talk him into coming back.

In an overpacked conclusion, the boys win the regional science fair, and Homer alone goes on to the national fair in Indianapolis. Simultaneously, Mr. Hickam has to contend with a UMWA strike of his workers (which makes for an interesting role reversal for Chris Cooper, whose first major film role was as a union organizer in *Matewan* twelve years earlier). There's much celebration among Coalwood residents when Homer returns home with a first-place trophy, his father meets worker demands and settles the strike, and father and son are reconciled. It's all a bit too contrived—in both Hickam's memoir and the film—but it does serve as an effective means to wrap up the various plot points and to play up the local bonds that held Coalwood, and many coal towns like it, together, despite the stresses and strains that challenged its inhabitants.

Next to *Matewan*, perhaps, but in very different ways, *October Sky* provides the most full-bodied portrait of a community of any film discussed in this chapter. The credit for this must go primarily to Homer Hickam, whose memoir sets his travails and triumphs firmly within a community framework. The fact that much of it centers on high school activities and interactions (as no other film does) provides a more communal dynamic. As one reviewer of the book noted, "Coalwood is the real star here. Teachers, clergy, machinists, town gossips, union, management, everyone become co-conspirators in the explosive three-year project."[48] The success of the "rocket boys" provided a boost of civic pride in much the same way that men's choirs or soccer teams did in other such communities onscreen. Yet in this film, more than most others, one is also aware that the town is dying a slow death along with the mine. At the film's end, a list of facts describes the later lives of the major characters—most of which were success stories that played out elsewhere—and concludes with the most sobering fact of all: "In 1965, the town of Coalwood was sold off and the mine was closed forever."[49]

• • • • • •

Donald Trump made the rejuvenation of the coal mining industry and of the miners dependent on it a signature issue of his 2016 presidential campaign. And yet his contempt for those miners was made clear in an earlier

Playboy interview (where apparently there was little chance of coal miners reading it). "The coal miner gets black-lung disease, his son gets it, then *his* son," Trump pontificated in 2008. "If *I* had been the son of a coal miner, I would have left the damn mines. But most people don't have the imagination—or whatever—to leave their mine. They don't have it."[50]

The movies have, for the most part, demonstrated otherwise. With the exception of *Matewan*, the films discussed here, whether set in Britain or in Appalachia, in Wales or West Virginia, have taken seriously the notion that the impulse to escape, to establish better lives elsewhere, is a universal one. Those yearnings account for much of what allows audiences to identify, to sympathize, and to root for particular characters in each. (At the same time, most of these films also acknowledge in more marginal respects other, more communal forms of resistance to the industry and to the abuses that generated such hostility on the part of its workers.)

Yet the narrative thrust in five of these six films lies in the varied circumstances through which young people sought to break out of the underground traps that so fully ensnared their fathers, brothers, and fellow townsmen. They met varying degrees of pushback to their efforts from a variety of sources; for some of these protagonists, push factors prevailed over pull factors in driving or drawing them away, and not all are success stories when judged on these terms. One factor all share is the primacy of family and community as the readily identifiable frameworks within which filmmakers chose to ground these very human stories. The central dramas in most play out much more in homes (or on streets, in schoolrooms, in churches) than they do in the mines themselves. Yet not much happens in any of these settings that's not directly or indirectly due to circumstances imposed by either mine owners or working conditions in the mines. Perhaps the most common denominator of these six coal-based sagas is that they celebrate the role of individuals (sometimes with the support of families or communities, sometimes not) and how they ultimately responded to those challenges and, in various ways and to various degrees, triumphed over them.

Acknowledgments

My first written analysis of an Appalachian-based film—or, for that matter, any film—came from an invitation from Jerry Williamson, then editor of the *Appalachian Journal*, to critique *The Journey of August King*, soon after it was released to theaters in 1995. He paired my positive response (based on how well I thought it captured certain historical realities of race and racism in early western North Carolina) with a much more critical, and more astute, assessment by Jack Wright of Appalshop. It was also in 1995 that *Hillbillyland*, Jerry's own groundbreaking treatise on film depictions of the southern highlanders and their cultural kin, was published by the University of North Carolina Press. Ever since then, I've been the beneficiary of Jerry's bold and utterly original insights as a film scholar, his support of my work and the opportunities he long provided me while wearing his journal editor's cap, and, most recently, his sharp and very helpful critique of this manuscript before press. (I thank the other reader, who remains anonymous, for his or her good suggestions on multiple fronts as well.)

Sandy Ballard, who has so ably filled Jerry's shoes as editor of *Appalachian Journal* since he stepped down, has also been a much valued friend and supporter. She too has offered much useful feedback as my work on film expanded, and given me opportunities to continue to test my ideas on new ways of assessing screen depictions of the region and its history.

I've benefited much from the interactions I've had and the commentary I've received—including some sharp criticism and spirited debate—from conference sessions and published roundtables on the media representations of the region with other scholars, including Emily Satterwhite, Chip Arnold, Meredith McCarroll, Anna Creadick, Erica Locklear, and Darin Waters.

Summer teacher workshops also proved to be useful testing grounds for exploring films as pedagogical resources. I thank Kathy Newfont for including me in several Appalachian-focused National Endowment for the Humanities teacher institutes she hosted at Mars Hill College; Dan Pierce and Jamie Ross, who did the same in more recent years at the University of North Carolina–Asheville; and Pat Beaver and Sandy Ballard, with whom I teamed for a memorable week in beautiful Ashe County for a teacher workshop sponsored by the North Carolina Humanities Council. All of these proved to be valuable venues for exchanging ideas and raising questions about regional identity in multidisciplinary contexts, from which I learned much that's seeped into how I view the films under discussion here, both individually and collectively.

I thank Hugh Ruppersburg and Richard Neupert, film scholars and colleagues here at the University of Georgia; Matthew Bernstein at Emory; and other good friends who use films in their history classes and with whom I've long compared notes: George Justice, Warren Rogers, Christopher Lawton, and Bob Pratt.

One of the greatest pleasures of my career at the University of Georgia has been the wonderful array of graduate students I've worked with, many of whom took on Appalachia-related dissertation topics and most of whom have remained cherished friends since they've left Athens . . . or stayed. I don't dare try to name them all, but they know who they are. I do need to single out Matt Hulbert, who enticed me last year into compiling and coediting an essay collection on films focused on nineteenth-century America, which proved to be a most rewarding experience for us both.

I appreciate the University of North Carolina Press's support of this project, which began with David Perry years ago and continued with Mark Simpson-Vos. I've ended up in the very capable and committed hands of Lucas Church and Andrew Winters, and those of an excellent production editor Kirsten Elmer, with whom I've much enjoyed working on this book's final transition into print.

Finally, and most of all, I'm grateful to Jane, my wife of forty-three years, for all she means to me, all she does for me, and all she puts up with from me.

Notes

Introduction

1. *Roanoke (VA) Times*, quoted in Mike Myer, “Making a Film about Hillbillies,” *Wheeling Sunday News-Register*, May 5, 2019.

2. J. D. Vance, *Hillbilly Elegy: A Memoir of a Family and Culture in Crisis* (New York: Harper, 2016), 17–18, 21. Reactions by the Appalachian scholarly community were swift, including two highly critical books and a documentary film: Elizabeth Catte, *What You Are Getting Wrong about Appalachia* (Cleveland: Belt, 2018); Anthony Harkins and Meredith McCarroll, eds., *Appalachian Reckoning: A Region Responds to Hillbilly Elegy* (Morgantown: West Virginia University Press, 2019); *Hillbilly*, directed by Sally Rubin and Ashley York (Holler Home Productions, 2018).

3. Barbara Kingsolver, “By the Book,” interview, *New York Times Book Review*, October 28, 2018.

4. Kingsolver, “By the Book.”

5. Quoted in Anthony Harkins, *Hillbilly: A Cultural History of an American Icon* (New York: Oxford University Press, 2004), 56.

6. David E. Whisnant, *All That Is Native and Fine: The Politics of Culture in an American Region* (Chapel Hill: University of North Carolina Press, 1983), 110.

7. Anthony Harkins offers the fullest analysis of these early Appalachian-based films and how the concept of “hillbilly” gradually came to embody the genre and its characters in the late 1910s. Harkins, *Hillbilly*, 58–59. See also Sandra Ballard, “Where Did Hillbillies Come From?,” in *Confronting Appalachian Stereotypes: Back Talk from an American Region*, ed. Dwight B. Billings, Gurney Norman, and Katherine Ledford (Lexington: University Press of Kentucky, 1999), 138–52.

8. J. W. Williamson, *Southern Mountaineers in Silent Films: Plot Synopses of Movies about Moonshining, Feuding and Other Mountain Topics, 1904–1929* (Jefferson, NC: MacFarland, 1994). See also a more comprehensive filmography, compiled and edited by Laura Schuster and Sharyn McCrumb as “Appalachian Film List,” *Appalachian Journal* 11 (Summer 1984): 329–84.

9. In addition to Harkins’s *Hillbilly*, see also Scott von Doviak, *Hick Flicks: The Rise and Fall of Redneck Cinema* (Jefferson, NC: MacFarland, 2005); Emily Satterwhite, “The Politics of Hillbilly Horror,” in *Navigating Souths: Transdisciplinary Explorations of a U.S. Region*, ed. Michele Coffey and Jodi Skipper (Athens: University of Georgia Press, 2017), 227–45. For a broader sense of media treatments with only scattered references to Appalachia, see Nancy Isenberg, *White Trash: The 400-Year Untold History of Class in America* (New York: Viking, 2016), esp. chap. 11.

10. Robert Brent Toplin, *Reel History: In Defense of Hollywood* (Lawrence: University of Kansas Press, 2002), 1.

11. J. W. Williamson, *Hillbillyland: What the Movies Did to the Mountains and What the Mountains Did to the Movies* (Chapel Hill: University of North Carolina Press, 1995), ix, back cover.

12. Stephen L. Fisher, "Claiming Appalachia . . . and the Questions That Go with It," *Appalachian Journal* 38 (Winter 2010): 59. Fisher's essay is part of an excellent roundtable discussion on Appalachian identity (58–76).

13. Williamson, *Hillbillyland*, 157–58.

14. See "Whiteness and Racialization in Appalachia," special issue, *Journal of Appalachian Studies* 10 (Spring/Fall 2004), especially essays by Larry J. Griffin, Barbara Ellen Smith, John Hartigan Jr., and Mary K. Anglin; Harkins, *Hillbilly*, esp. chap. 2.

15. Quote from Samuel Tyndale Wilson, *The Southern Mountaineers* (New York: Presbyterian Home Missions, 1906), 42.

16. Both quotes from John C. Inscoe, "Race and Racism in Nineteenth-Century Southern Appalachia: Myths, Realities, and Ambiguities," in *Appalachia in the Making: The Mountain South in the Nineteenth Century*, ed. Mary Beth Pudup, Dwight B. Billings, and Altina L. Waller (Chapel Hill: University of North Carolina Press, 1995), 105–6; Vance, *Hillbilly Elegy*, introduction; Catte, *What You Are Getting Wrong*, 64–71.

17. Meredith McCarroll, *Un-White: Appalachia, Race, and Film* (Athens: University of Georgia Press, 2018).

18. On such patterns elsewhere, see David R. Roediger, *The Wages of Whiteness: Race and the Making of the American Working Class* (New York: Verso, 1991); essays in "Whiteness and Racialization in Appalachia" (see note 14).

19. Edward J. Cabbell, "Black Invisibility and Racism in Appalachia: An Informal Survey," in *Blacks in Appalachia*, ed. Edward J. Cabbell and William H. Turner (Lexington: University Press of Kentucky, 1985), 11.

20. For broad studies of women in the region, see Kathi Kahn, *Hillbilly Women* (New York: Doubleday, 1973); Wilma A. Dunaway, *Women, Work, and Family in the Antebellum Mountain South* (Cambridge: Cambridge University Press, 2008); Connie Park Rice and Marie Tedesco, eds., *Women of the Mountain South: Identity, Work, and Activism* (Athens: Ohio University Press, 2015); Erica Abrams Locklear, *Negotiating a Perilous Empowerment: Appalachian Women's Literacies* (Athens: Ohio University Press, 2011); "Appalachian Women," special issue, *Appalachian Journal* 37 (Spring/Summer 2010); Barbara Ellen Smith, "Beyond the Mountains: The Paradox of Women's Place in Appalachian History," *National Women's Studies Association Journal* 11 (Fall 1999): 1–17. On Appalachian women in film, see Williamson, *Hillbillyland*, chap. 8; McCarroll, *Un-White*, chap. 2, appendix.

21. For a recent essay collection on the subject, with over a third of the essays based on Appalachian communities, see Steven E. Nash and Bruce E. Stewart, eds., *Southern Communities: Identity, Conflict, and Memory in the American South* (Athens: University of Georgia Press, 2019). All essays in this book are by my former graduate students.

22. Beyond the references made here, I don't discuss *Deliverance* in the body of this book, though I did teach it regularly. (My students have generally been Georgians, after all.) It's probably the most seen, and most discussed, of any Appalachian-based film, with one of the most perceptive critiques that of Williamson in *Hillbillyland* in a chapter titled "More Than Dogpatch: The Mountains as Monstrous" (157–67). For other notable analyses, see McCarroll, *Un-White*, chap. 1, in which she draws parallels between the four canoers and cinematic tropes of American Indians; Scott Von Doviak, *Hick Flicks: The Rise and Fall of Redneck Cinema* (Jefferson, NC: MacFarland, 2005), chap. 13; John Lane, *Chattooga: Descending into the Myth of the Deliverance River* (Athens: University of Georgia Press, 2004); Anna Creadick, "Banjo Boy: Masculinity, Disability, and Difference in Deliverance," *Southern Cultures* 23 (Spring 2017): 63–78; Christopher Dickey's memoir of the filming of his father's novel, *Summer of Deliverance* (New York: Touchstone, 1999); Charles Bethea, "Mountain Men: An Oral History of *Deliverance*," *Atlanta Magazine*, September 2011, www.atlantamagazine.com/great-reads/deliverance.

23. Quoted in John C. Inscoe, "Northeast Georgia: Appalachian Otherness, Real and Perceived," *The New Georgia Guide* (Athens: University of Georgia Press, 1996), 168.

24. Allen Batteau, *The Invention of Appalachia* (Tucson: University of Arizona Press, 1990), 17–18.

25. David D. Lee, *Sergeant York: An American Hero* (Lexington: University Press of Kentucky, 1985), 104.

26. Toplin, *Reel History*, 204.

Chapter One

1. Cratis D. Williams, "Who Are the Southern Mountaineers?," in *Voices from the Hills: Selected Readings of Southern Appalachia*, ed. Robert J. Higgs and Ambrose N. Manning (New York: Frederick Unger, 1975), 496.

2. John C. Campbell, *The Southern Highlander and His Homeland* (New York: Russell Sage Foundation, 1921), quoted in Allen W. Batteau, *The Invention of Appalachia* (Tucson: University of Arizona Press, 1990), 81. See especially Batteau, chap. 4, in which he credits Kentucky novelist John Fox and Berea College president William Frost with establishing this concept of Appalachia as a repository of rural American values. See also Henry D. Shapiro, *Appalachia on Our Mind: The Southern Mountains and Mountaineers in the American Consciousness, 1870–1920* (Chapel Hill: University of North Carolina Press, 1978), esp. chap. 5.

3. Campbell, *The Southern Highlander and His Homeland*, 12.

4. Batteau, *Invention of Appalachia*, 17–18.

5. For the broader context of the film industry's impact on American interventionist sentiments on the eve and early months of World War II, see John Whiteclay Chambers II, "The Peace, Isolationist, and Anti-interventionist Movement in Interwar Hollywood," in *Why We Fought: America's Wars in Film and History*, ed. Peter C. Rollins and John E. O'Connor (Lexington: University Press of Kentucky, 2008), 196–225.

6. *Sergeant York: Of God and Country*, written and directed by John Mulholland (MODA Entertainment, 2006).

7. David B. Lee, *Sergeant York: An American Hero* (Lexington: University Press of Kentucky, 1985), x. Chapter 6 of Lee's book, along with J. W. Williamson's *Hillbillyland: What the Movies Did to the Mountains and What the Mountains Did to the Movies* (Chapel Hill: University of North Carolina Press, 1995), chap. 7, and *Sergeant York: Of God and Country*, offer the fullest treatments of York and his role in the production of the film.

8. Bosley Crowther review of *Sergeant York*, quoted in Homer Dickens, *The Films of Gary Cooper* (New York: Citadel Press, 1970), 183.

9. Batteau, *The Invention of Appalachia*, 17–18. See also Nina Silber, "'What Does America Need So Much as Americans?': Race and Northern Reconciliation with Southern Appalachia, 1870–1900," in *Appalachians and Race: The Mountain South from Slavery to Segregation*, ed. John C. Inscoe (Lexington: University Press of Kentucky, 2001), 245–58.

10. Sam K. Cowan, *Sergeant York and His People* (New York: Funk and Wagnalls, 1922); Tom Skeyhill, ed., *Sergeant York: His Own Life Story and War Diary* (Garden City, NY: Doubleday, Doran, 1928). Skeyhill's subtitle and designation as editor, not author, belies the fact that he supplied the text himself but did so in the guise of first-person narration by York. See Lee, *Sergeant York*, 94–95.

11. Quote from Cowan, *Sergeant York and His People*, 12. See table of contents for both Cowan, *Sergeant York and His People*, and Skeyhill, *Sergeant York*.

12. Lee, *Sergeant York*, 97.

13. Lee, 105–6. Alvin York turned thirty years old in December 1917, while Gary Cooper turned forty during the production of the film in 1941.

14. Williamson, *Hillbillyland*, 216–17.

15. On the DVD of *Sergeant York*, nineteen of the thirty-two segments into which the film is divided take place at home in Tennessee.

16. The film makes no mention of Alvin's two older brothers, both of whom had left home and established families of their own before their father's death after being kicked by a mule in 1911, thus making Alvin the titular head of the household despite his mother's clearly dominant role. Cowan, *Sergeant York and His People*, 143–47; Douglas V. Mastriano, *Alvin York: A New Biography of the Hero of the Argonne* (Lexington: University Press of Kentucky, 2014), 14–15.

17. *Sergeant York: Of God and Country.*

18. Skeyhill, *Sergeant York*, 144.

19. Skeyhill, 174–77; Lee, *Sergeant York*, 19.

20. Williamson, *Hillbillyland*, 207.

21. Michael Birdwell commentary in *Sergeant York: Of God and Country*. Birdwell is a historian at Tennessee Tech, the curator of the Alvin York Papers, and part of the project team of the online Sergeant Alvin C. York Project. See www.sergeantyork.com.

22. One of the film's harshest critics said of these two key developments, "No writer would ever willingly begin with such difficult premises," which he called "a challenge at best, a real handicap at worst." These "non-sequiturs," as he calls

them, are botched by the team of screenwriters, who fail to make sense of their inherent contradictions, or to rationalize the otherworldly premises on which they are built. Donald C. Willis, *The Films of Howard Hawks* (Metuchen, NJ: Scarecrow Press, 1975), 169. See also Robin Wood, *Howard Hawks* (London: BFI, 1981), 168, who takes a far more positive view of the film as a whole but calls the treatment of York's pacifism and the religious basis for it "a crippling weakness."

23. Skeyhill, *Sergeant York*, chap. 17.

24. Skeyhill includes a lengthy description of Alvin's courtship of Gracie in his own words, to most of which the film faithfully adheres, deviating only by making their courtship the prime motivation for his quest for the piece of bottomland. Skeyhill, *Sergeant York*, 147–51.

25. Jerry Williamson provides an inspired, if almost tongue-in-cheek, interpretation of Alvin as a "mama's boy," thus making the saintly role of Ma York pivotal and—in so doing—saying much about the gendered dimensions of the film and of highland society at large. Williamson, *Hillbillyland*, 218–22. Her role in Alvin's reform also draws directly on the earlier narratives, particularly that of Skeyhill, who in York's own voice lays it out in consecutive chapters, one called "Hogwild" and the next, "Mother." Skeyhill, *Sergeant York*, chaps. 15–16. See also Cowan, *Sergeant York and His People*, 174–75.

26. Lee, *Sergeant York*, 71–72. Curiously, Skeyhill's "autobiographical" account of York's life avoids any mention of this gift at all in its chapter on York's return home. Skeyhill, *Sergeant York*, chap. 30.

27. *Sergeant York: Of God and Country.*

28. Haeja K. Chung, introduction to *Harriette Simpson Arnow: Critical Essays on Her Work*, ed. Haeja K. Chung (East Lansing: Michigan State University Press, 1995), 3; Glenda Hobbs, "Harriette Arnow's Kentucky Novels," in Chung, *Harriette Simpson Arnow*, 65. Other essays in this volume that focus on *The Dollmaker* include those by Sandra L. Ballard, Linda Wagner-Martin, Kathleen Walsh, and Kathleen R. Parker.

29. Haeja K. Chung, "Fictional Characters Come to Life: An Interview [with Harriette Arnow]," in Chung, *Harriette Simpson Arnow*, 266. For biographical treatments of Arnow, see Wilton Eckley, *Harriette Arnow* (New York: Twayne, 1974), chap. 1; Sandra L. Ballard, "Harriette Simpson Arnow's Life as a Writer," in Chung, *Harriette Simpson Arnow*, 15–31.

30. Patricia Bosworth, *Jane Fonda: The Private Life of a Public Woman* (Boston: Houghton-Mifflin-Harcourt, 2011), 482. Several reviewers of the film noted the parallels between the fictional migrants Tom Joad and Gertie Nevels.

31. Michael Freedland, *Jane Fonda: A Biography* (New York: St. Martin's Press, 1988), 235. See also Martha Bayles's *Wall Street Journal* review, and Tom Shales's *Washington Post* review, both reprinted in *Appalachian Journal* 12 (Fall 1984): 7–10.

32. Freedland, *Jane Fonda*; Jane Fonda, *My Life So Far* (New York: Random House, 2005), 416–19. Fonda provides an extended description of her stay with the Johnsons and concludes by stating, "I felt privileged to have been permitted for a time to know this world and its people . . . a world that as late as 1984 was probably not so different from that of my own pioneer ancestors" (419). Some reviewers

felt that Fonda remained physically unconvincing in the role, despite the few extra pounds she'd gained. As one critic put it, "Arnow's Gertie is a physically huge and homely woman. Slim, attractive superstar Fonda, with aerobic-toned body, perfect teeth and high cheekbones, looks nothing like Arnow's conception." Quoted in Betty Krause, "*The Dollmaker,* Film and Novel: Narrative Structure and Personal Mythology," *Journal of Appalachian Studies* 5 (Fall 1997): 274.

33. According to user reviews on IMDb, *The Dollmaker* has the highest favorable rating of any Jane Fonda movie.

34. Linda Wagner-Martin, "Harriett Arnow's Cumberland Women," in Chung, *Harriette Simpson Arnow,* 78.

35. Unless otherwise indicated, all quoted dialogue is from the film rather than the novel.

36. Eckley, *Harriette Arnow,* 90; Wagner-Martin, "Harriette Arnow's Cumberland Women," 82.

37. Harriette Arnow, *The Dollmaker* (New York: Macmillan, 1954; Lexington: University Press of Kentucky, 1985), 149.

38. The meaning of the cherrywood Christ and its destruction has generated much discussion from literary critics and commentators. See especially essays by Barbara Baer, Glenda Hobbs, and Kathleen Walsh in Chung, *Harriette Simpson Arnow,* and Arnow's own explanation in her interview with Chung, "Fictional Characters Come to Life," 271–72.

39. Chung, "Fictional Characters Come to Life," *Harriette Simpson Arnow,* 269. After *The Dollmaker*'s TV airing introduced many readers to Arnow for the first time, she came to resent the fact that it was the only work of hers that had ever generated any interest. As Sandra Ballard notes in her introduction to a paperback edition of Arnow's 1949 novel *Hunter's Horn* (Lansing: Michigan State University Press, 1997), Arnow declared that she "did not want to be ridden to fame on Jane Fonda's coat-tails" (v).

40. Danny L. Miller, "Harriette Simpson and Harold Arnow in Cincinnati, 1935–1939," in Chung, *Harriette Simpson Arnow,* 35.

41. Arnow, quoted in Krause, "*The Dollmaker,* Film and Novel," 275–76.

42. Martha Billips Turner, "The Demise of Mountain Life: Harriette Arnow's Analysis," *Border States: Journal of the Kentucky-Tennessee American Studies Association* 8 (1991): 6–10, quote on p. 7. Turner maintains that far too much of the scholarly analysis of *The Dollmaker* suggests that Arnow set up "a relatively simplistic dichotomy between an edenic, pastoral world and a hellish, industrial one," a contrast fully embraced by the film as well (10).

43. Among the works covering the removal—or relocation—of Appalachian families by the federal government are Durwood Dunn, *Cade's Cove: The Life and Death of a Southern Appalachian Community, 1818–1937* (Knoxville: University of Tennessee Press, 1988), chap. 10; Anne Mitchell Whisnant, *Super-Scenic Motorway: A Blue Ridge Parkway History* (Chapel Hill: University of North Carolina Press, 2006), esp. chap. 3; Katrina M. Powell, *The Anguish of Displacement: A Politics of Literacy in the Letters of Mountain Families in the Shenandoah National Park* (Charlottesville: University Press of Virginia, 2007).

44. Ronald D. Eller, *Uneven Ground: Appalachia since 1945* (Lexington: University Press of Kentucky, 2008), 258.

45. In the 1950s alone, at the height of his career, over half of Kazan's output on both stage and screen took place in southern settings. In addition to *Wild River*, Kazan directed four other films set in the South—*A Streetcar Named Desire*, *Pinky*, *Panic in the Streets*, and *A Face in the Crowd*—though in content and theme, they could hardly have been more different. For a comprehensive listing of Kazan's work on both stage and screen, see Richard Schickel, *Elia Kazan: A Biography* (New York: HarperCollins, 2005), 457–65.

46. North Callahan, *TVA: Bridge over Troubled Waters* (Cranbury, NJ: A. S. Barnes, 1980), 45–51. For the fullest case study of relocation of farm families by the TVA, see Michael J. McDonald and John Muldowny, *TVA and the Dispossessed: The Resettlement of the Population of the Norris Dam Area* (Knoxville: University of Tennessee Press, 1982).

47. Elia Kazan, *A Life* (New York: Alfred A. Knopf, 1988), 596–97.

48. Schickel, *Elia Kazan*, 367.

49. Schickel, 364.

50. Michael Ciment, *Kazan on Kazan* (New York: Viking Press, 1974), 130.

51. The fullest discussion of "People of the Cumberland" is found in Schickel, *Elia Kazan*, 59–62.

52. Ciment, *Kazan on Kazan*, 23, 132.

53. Kazan, *A Life*, 597.

54. William Bradford Huie, *Mud on the Stars* (New York: L B. Fischer, 1942), 8.

55. Huie, *Mud on the Stars*, 20.

56. Huie, 51.

57. Huie, 131.

58. Huie, 131.

59. Huie, 184.

60. Ultimately, only Osborn received credit for the screenplay, though most accounts make it clear that Kazan himself contributed as much or more than did anyone else. Kazan, *A Life*, 596–97; Schickel, *Elia Kazan*, 366–69.

61. Borden Deal, *Dunbar's Cove* (New York: Charles Scribner's Sons, 1957), 28.

62. Kazan, *A Life*, 597.

63. Kazan, 600.

64. Jeff Young, ed., *Kazan: The Master Director Discusses His Films—Interviews with Elia Kazan* (New York: Newmarket Press, 1999), 258–59.

65. Ciment, *Kazan on Kazan*, 131. Kazan also noted that several of his screenwriting collaborators opposed the idea of a Jewish protagonist.

66. Quoted in Schickel, *Elia Kazan*, 368. Jo Van Fleet was a difficult actress but one who Kazan valued greatly. She'd won an Academy Award under Kazan's direction for *East of Eden* in 1955. Only forty-five years old when *Wild River* was filmed, she was utterly convincing as the eighty-year-old Ella Garth, in a performance widely considered her best on film.

67. Allison Inman, "When Elia Kazan Came to East Tennessee," *Media Update* (blog), Nashville Public Radio, September 28, 2010, https://blogs.wnpt.org/mediaupdate

/2010/09/28/when-elia-kazan-came-to-east-tennessee. Inman was on-site in Charleston producing a modest documentary on the making of *Wild River,* based primarily through reminiscences with local residents. That film, completed a year later, was called *Mud on the Stars: Stories from Elia Kazan's "Wild River."*

68. Perhaps ironically, it is the only part of the film not shot in Tennessee; most likely Kazan used clips from Pare Lorentz's *The River,* which depicted flooding on the Mississippi and Ohio Rivers but not the Tennessee. Commentary by Richard Schickel on the DVD of *Wild River,* released for the first time in 2010, on the fiftieth anniversary of the film's release, and one of the last of Kazan's films made available on disc.

69. Ciment, *Kazan on Kazan,* 134–35.

70. Young, *Kazan,* 258, 260.

71. In one of few serious commentaries on *Wild River,* Allison Graham sees both Mrs. Garth's refusal to leave her island and the opposition of whites to the opportunities offered by the TVA to blacks as part of a spectrum of white resistance to modernization as imposed by an "outside agitator," thus providing the film with more relevancy in 1960 than is usually acknowledged. See Graham, *Framing the South,* 54–55. Chris Cagle makes a similar point in his essay "The Postwar Cinematic South," 109–10.

72. Young, *Kazan,* 258.

73. Kazan stated in the early 1970s, "I felt very affectionate toward that film when I made it, and I guess as I get older I feel even more affection for it." Young, *Kazan,* 261. In his autobiography, he called it "one of my favorites, possibly because of its social ambivalence." Kazan, *A Life,* 600.

74. On this curious juxtaposition, see Inscoe, "Appalachian Otherness, Real and Perceived," *The New Georgia Guide* (Athens: University of Georgia Press, 1996), 165–68. On the origins of Foxfire, see John L. Puckett, *Foxfire Reconsidered: A Twenty-Year Experiment in Progressive Education* (Urbana: University of Illinois Press, 1989), chap. 1; *New Georgia Encyclopedia,* s.v. "Foxfire," by Adrienn Mendonca, last edited November 2, 2015, www.georgiaencyclopedia.org/articles/education/foxfire.

75. "Aunt Arie," in *The Foxfire Book: Hog Dressing; Log Cabin Building; Mountain Crafts and Foods; Planting by the Signs; Snake Lore, Hunting Tales, Faith Healing; Moonshining; and Other Affairs of Plain Living,* ed. Eliot Wigginton (New York: Doubleday, 1972), 17.

76. All of these were shot on location in Georgia, including the latter, although the Fannie Flagg novel on which it was based was set in Alabama.

77. *Foxfire* entry, IMDb. See also Milly S. Barranger, *Jessica Tandy: A Bio-Bibliography* (Westport, CT: Greenwood Press, 1991); Hume Cronyn, *A Terrible Liar: A Memoir* (New York: William Morrow, 1991), 415–16. Cronyn extends his narrative only through the 1960s, with information on *Foxfire* as play and film limited to an appendix.

78. Wigginton, *The Foxfire Book,* 20–22.

79. Quotes from James Kilgo, *Inheritance of Horses* (Athens: University of Georgia Press, 1994), 26, 28–29. See also Inscoe, "Appalachian Otherness, Real and Per-

ceived," 201–2; John Alexander Williams, *Appalachia: A History* (Chapel Hill: University of North Carolina Press, 2002), 390–91. Williams notes that every north Georgia county considered Appalachian exceeded national norms and social indicators. "The peril in this prosperity," he wrote, "is that the entire region may become an appendage of the nearby metropolis [Atlanta]" (390).

80. Wendell Berry, "The Body and the Earth," in *The Unsettling of America: Culture and Agriculture* (San Francisco: Sierra Book Club, 1977), 97.

81. Batteau, *Invention of Appalachia*, 191.

82. Ronald D. Eller, *Miners, Millhands, and Mountaineers: Industrialization of the Appalachian South, 1880–1930*, 38.

83. Batteau, *Invention of Appalachia*, 17–18.

Chapter Two

1. J. W. Williamson, *Hillbillyland: What the Movies Did to the Mountains and What the Mountains Did to the Movies* (Chapel Hill: University of North Carolina Press, 1995); Thomas Cripps, *Slow Fade to Black: The Negro in American Film* (New York: Oxford University Press, 1977). Neither do other works on cinematic depictions of the South find anything to note on blacks as highlanders. See Edward D. C. Campbell Jr., *The Celluloid South: Hollywood and the Southern Myth* (Knoxville: University of Tennessee Press, 1981); Jack Temple Kirby, *Media-Made Dixie: The South in the American Imagination*, rev. ed. (Athens: University of Georgia Press, 1986).

2. William Brewer, "Moonshining in Georgia," *Cosmopolitan* 23 (June 1897): 132; Ellen Churchill Semple, "The Anglo-Saxons of the Kentucky Mountains: A Study of Anthropogeography," *Geographical Journal*, June 1901, both quoted in John C. Inscoe, "Slavery and Race in the Nineteenth Century," in *High Mountains Rising: Appalachia in Time and Place*, ed. Richard A. Straw and H. Tyler Blethen (Urbana: University of Illinois Press, 2004), 34.

3. John C. Campbell, *The Southern Highlander and His Homeland* (New York: Russell Sage Foundation, 1921), 94, quoted in Inscoe, "Slavery and Race in the Nineteenth Century," in Straw and Blethen, *High Mountains Rising*, 34.

4. Edward J. Cabbell, "Black Invisibility and Racism in Appalachia: An Informal Survey," in *Blacks in Appalachia*, ed. Edward J. Cabbell and William H. Turner (Lexington: University Press of Kentucky, 1985), 3.

5. Preface to Cabbell and Turner, *Blacks in Appalachia*, xiv.

6. William H. Turner, "The Demography of Black Appalachia: Past and Present," in Cabbell and Turner, *Blacks in Appalachia*, 238, table 21.1.

7. Three key treatments of assumptions of whiteness as the core of Appalachian exceptionalism include James C. Klotter, "The Black South and White Appalachia," *Journal of American History* 66 (March 1980): 832–49; Nina Silber, "'What Does America Need So Much as Americans?': Race and Northern Reconciliation with Southern Appalachia," in *Appalachians and Race: From Slavery to Segregation in the Mountain South*, ed. John C. Inscoe (Lexington: University Press of Kentucky, 2001), 244–58; William H. Turner, "Black Hillbillies Have No Time for Elegies," in

Appalachian Reckoning: A Region Responds to Hillbilly Elegy, ed. Anthony Harkins and Meredith McCarroll (Morgantown: West Virginia University Press, 2019), 229–44.

8. Three Civil War films discussed in chapter 3—*Little Shepherd of Kingdom Come* (1961), *Shenandoah* (1965), and *Cold Mountain* (2003)—each make brief references to slavery, yet they picture actual enslaved characters only fleetingly and, with only one exception, outside the highland region.

9. John Ehle, *The Journey of August King* (New York: Harper & Row, 1971). This is a modified version of an essay that appeared in *Appalachian Journal* as half of a "debate" with Jack Wright over the film's merits. *Appalachian Journal* 24 (Winter 1997): 204–15. For a far more critical assessment of the film, see Wright's essay, "How Monochrome Was Their Valley," *Appalachian Journal* 24 (Winter 1997): 193–204.

10. Borden Mace, interview by Steve Ward, *Appalachian Journal*, 23 (Fall 1995): 51. Much of this interview focuses on the production of *The Journey of August King*. See also John Ehle, interview by Carol Boggess, *Appalachian Journal* 31 (Fall 2006): 32–51.

11. Carter G. Woodson's seminal essay "Freedom and Slavery in Appalachian America," *Journal of Negro History* 1 (April 1916): 132–50, stood alone on the subject for several decades. More recent treatments of these topics include Richard B. Drake, "Slavery and Antislavery in Appalachia," *Appalachian Heritage* 14 (Winter 1986): 25–33; John C. Inscoe, *Mountain Masters: Slavery and the Sectional Crisis in Western North Carolina* (Knoxville: University of Tennessee Press, 1989); Kenneth W. Noe, *Southwest Virginia's Railroad: Modernization and the Sectional Crisis* (Urbana: University of Illinois Press, 1994), esp. chap. 4; Wilma A. Dunaway, *Slavery in the American Mountain South* (Cambridge: Cambridge University Press, 2003); Wilma A. Dunaway, *The African American Family in Slavery and Emancipation* (Cambridge: Cambridge University Press, 2003); and several essays in Cabbell and Turner, *Blacks in Appalachia*, and in Inscoe, *Appalachians and Race*.

12. A number of historians have wrestled with issues of connectedness and isolation and the dynamics of localism in early settlement patterns but, for the most part, merely confirm realities that John Ehle was already well aware of and conveyed in his novel with such insight much earlier. Robert D. Mitchell, *Commercialism and Frontier: Perspectives on the Early Shenandoah Valley* (Charlottesville: University Press of Virginia, 1977); Durwood Dunn, *Cade's Cove: The Life and Death of a Southern Appalachian Community, 1818–1937* (Knoxville: University of Tennessee Press, 1988); David Hsiung, *Two Worlds in the Tennessee Mountains: Exploring the Origins of Appalachian Stereotypes* (Lexington: University Press of Kentucky, 1997); Paul Salstrom, *Appalachia's Path to Dependency: Rethinking a Region's Economic History, 1730–1940* (Lexington: University Press of Kentucky, 1994); Wilma A. Dunaway, *The First American Frontier: Transition to Capitalism in Southern Appalachia, 1700–1860* (Chapel Hill: University of North Carolina Press, 1996).

13. See titles listed in note 11, none of which, other than Woodson's essay, were published before Ehle published his novel.

14. Turner, "Demography of Black Appalachia," 237–38.

15. John Baxter, interview by Maggie Lauterer, cited by Patricia D. Beaver, "African-American and Jewish Relations in Early Twentieth Century Asheville, North Carolina" (paper presented at Appalachian Studies Conference, Unicoi State Park, GA, March 1996).

16. John Brown and John Kagin, interview by Richard Hinton, August 1858, reprinted in *John Brown*, ed. Richard Warch and Jonathan F. Fauton (Englewood Cliffs, NJ: Prentice-Hall, 1973), 54.

17. Leon F. Williams, "The Vanishing Appalachian: How to 'Whiten' the Problem," in Turner and Cabbell, *Blacks in Appalachia*, 201. See also John C. Inscoe, "The Strength of the Hills: Representations of Appalachian Wilderness as Civil War Refuge," in *The Blue, The Gray, and the Green: Toward an Environmental History of the Civil War*, ed. Brian D. Drake (Athens: University of Georgia Press, 2015), 113–43.

18. Quoted in William H. Turner, "Between Berea (1904) and Birmingham (1908): The Rock and Hard Place for Blacks in Appalachia," in Turner and Cabbell, *Blacks in Appalachia*, 13. The whole notion of Appalachia as a center of Underground Railroad activity is suspect. Most major treatments of the Underground Railroad make no reference to routes in the southern highlands. See Larry Gara, *The Liberty Line: The Legend of the Underground Railroad* (Lexington: University Press of Kentucky, 1961); William Still, *The Underground Railroad* (Philadelphia: Porter and Coates, 1872); Eber M. Pettit, *Sketches in the History of the Underground Railroad* (Fredonia, NY: W. McKinstry, 1879). The only such account to even refer to the possibility that Appalachians provided regular routes is Wilbur H. Siebert, *The Underground Railroad from Slavery to Freedom* (New York: Macmillan, 1899), 118–19, but its map (facing p. 113) indicates no routes anywhere in the region.

19. For Ehle's explanation on this point, see Mace, interview by Steve Ward, 66.

20. Julian Ralph, "Our Appalachian Americans," *Harper's Monthly* 107 (June 1903): 37. The term "Holy Appalachia" comes from Allen Batteau, *The Invention of Appalachia* (Tucson: University of Arizona Press, 1992).

21. Harry M. Caudill, *Night Comes to the Cumberlands: A Biography of a Depressed Region* (Boston: Little, Brown, 1962), 38–39.

22. Woodson, "Freedom and Slavery in Appalachian America," 147.

23. Samuel Tyndale Wilson, *The Southern Mountaineers* (New York: J. J. Little and Ives, 1914), 57.

24. Inscoe, *Mountain Masters*, chap. 3; Noe, *Southwest Virginia's Railroad*, chap. 4; Ehle, *Journey of August King*, 139.

25. Frederick Law Olmsted, *A Journey through the Back Country in the Winter of 1853–54* (New York: Mission Brothers, 1860), 237–39. See also John C. Inscoe, "Olmsted in Appalachia: A Connecticut Yankee Encounters Slavery in the Southern Highlands, 1854," in *Race, War, and Remembrance in the Appalachian South* (Lexington: University Press of Kentucky, 2008), 65–79.

26. On abolitionist activity in Southern Appalachia, see Woodson, "Freedom and Slavery in Appalachian America"; Drake, "Slavery and Antislavery in Appalachia"; Asa Earl Martin, "The Anti-Slavery Societies of Tennessee," *Tennessee Historical Magazine* 1 (1915): 261–81; Gordon E. Finnie, "The Antislavery Movement in the

Upper South before 1840," *Journal of Southern History* 35 (1969): 319–42; Durwood Dunn, *An Abolitionist in the Appalachian South: Ezekiel Birdseye on Slavery, Capitalism, and Separate Statehood in East Tennessee, 1841–1846* (Knoxville: University of Tennessee Press, 1997).

27. In the film version of *Gone with the Wind*, the Klan label is not used (as it was in Margaret Mitchell's novel), though reference to the organization and its function are fully apparent.

28. The film appeared before the publication of Natalie Demon Davis's celebrated history of the case, *The Return of Martin Guerre* (Cambridge, MA: Harvard University Press, 1983), though Davis was a consultant on the film and contributed to its screenplay.

29. In fact, there's no evidence that anyone in Vine Hill other than the Sommersbys had owned slaves, which would have been in keeping with the racial demographics of the region. In 1860, only 9 percent of East Tennessee residents were slaves, and less than 3 percent of slaveholders were planters (defined as owning twenty slaves or more). John Cimprich, "Slavery's End in East Tennessee," in Inscoe, *Appalachians and Race*, 189.

30. Another film to do so is *Days of Heaven* (1978), Terrence Malick's aesthetically dazzling saga of migrant workers on wheat farms in the Texas panhandle, and the film that provided Gere with his first starring role.

31. Vincent Canby, review of *Sommersby*, directed by Jon Amiel, *New York Times*, February 5, 1993. See also a published lecture by Natalie Zemon Davis, "Remaking Impostors: From Martin Guerre to Sommersby," Hayes Robinson Lecture Series No. 1 (London: Royal Holloway, 1997), 20, in which Davis relates a similar reaction by James McPherson, with whom she first viewed the film. See also Tom Lee, "*Sommersby*: Identity, Imposture, and (Re)construction in the Post–Civil War South," in *Writing History with Lightning: Cinematic Representations of Nineteenth-Century America*, ed. Matthew C. Hulbert and John C. Inscoe (Baton Rouge: Louisiana State University Press, 2018), 217–27.

32. The fullest source on the Happy Land settlement is a pamphlet by Sadie Smathers Patton, "The Kingdom of the Happy Land," *Mountain Xpress*, February 9, 2007. See also Beth Beasley, "Settlement outside Tuxedo Was Home to Freed Slaves," *Hendersonville Times-News*, February 19, 2012, www.blueridgenow.com/article/NC/20120219/News/606020952/HT.

33. The fullest treatment of the colony is William Lynwood Montell, *The Saga of Coe Ridge: A Study in Early History* (Knoxville: University of Tennessee Press, 1970).

34. Montell, *Saga of Coe Ridge*, 64–65.

35. Steven E. Nash, *Reconstruction's Ragged Edge: The Politics of Postwar Life in the Southern Mountains* (Chapel Hill: University of North Carolina Press, 2016), 169–74. Billy Yeargin confirms this surge in tobacco production in *A History of Burley Tobacco in East Tennessee and Western North Carolina* (Charleston, SC: History Press, 2015), though he suggests that it was only in 1887 that burley came to take precedent over other types of tobacco as the major agricultural commodity of the southern mountains (6–10). See also Tom Lee, "Southern Appalachia's Nine-

teenth Century Bright Tobacco Boom: Industrialization, Urbanization, and the Culture of Tobacco," *Agricultural History* 88 (Spring 2014): 175–206; Drew A. Swanson, *Beyond the Mountains: Commodifying Appalachian Environments* (Athens: University of Georgia Press, 2018), esp. chap. 7.

36. Noel Fisher has stated that despite its origins in Pulaski, in south-central Tennessee, the Klan made little headway in the state's eastern counties, other than fleeting threats made in Knoxville and Chattanooga in 1868. Fisher, *War at Every Door: Partisan Politics and Guerrilla Violence in East Tennessee, 1860–1869* (Chapel Hill: University of North Carolina Press, 1997), 158–59. See also W. Todd Groce, *Mountain Rebels: East Tennessee Confederates and the Civil War, 1860–1870* (Knoxville: University of Tennessee Press, 1999), 128. In addition, the Klan is not acknowledged in East Tennessee, despite coverage of its activity in the Appalachian regions of other states. Andrew L. Slap, ed., *Reconstructing Appalachia: The Civil War's Aftermath* (Lexington: University Press of Kentucky, 2010).

37. Gary Gallagher provides an insightful analysis of *Sommersby* in which he labels this racially enlightened agenda as "post-civil rights" and far less "Lost Cause" than was true for many earlier Southern-based Civil War–era films that he discusses. Gallagher, *Causes Won, Lost, and Forgotten: How Hollywood and Popular Art Shape What We Know about the Civil War* (Chapel Hill: University of North Carolina Press, 2008), 59–62.

38. *Encyclopedia of African American Society*, ed. Gerald D. Jaynes (Thousand Oaks, CA: SAGE, 2005), s.v. "Black Judiciary," 479. See also Eric Foner, ed., *Freedom's Lawmakers: A Directory of Black Officeholders during Reconstruction*, rev. ed. (Baton Rouge: Louisiana State University Press, 1996). The 1867 date for the film's later scenes is established by the year that appears on Jack Sommersby's tombstone at its conclusion.

39. Much of this was based on widely held perceptions of race relations in Appalachia, rather than on the more complex and varied realities chronicled in more recent scholarship on the region. For an overview of that scholarship, see John C. Inscoe, "Race and Racism in Nineteenth-Century Appalachia: Myths, Realities, and Ambiguities," in *Appalachia in the Making: The Mountain South in the Nineteenth Century*, ed. Mary Beth Pudup, Dwight B. Billings, and Altina Waller (Chapel Hill: University of North Carolina Press, 1995), 103–31.

40. See Eric Foner, *Matewan*, in *Past Imperfect: History According to the Movies*, ed. Mark C. Carnes (New York: Henry Holt, 1995), 204–8.

41. John Sayles, *Thinking in Pictures: The Making of the Movie "Matewan"* (Boston: Houghton Mifflin, 1987), 21.

42. Sayles, *Thinking in Pictures*, 21.

43. Roland L. Lewis, *Black Coal Miners in America: Race, Class, and Community Conflict, 1780–1980* (Lexington: University Press of Kentucky, 1987), 141.

44. Lewis, *Black Coal Miners*, 142. Lewis drew much of his account of Chain from the memoir of a UMWA official, Fred Mooney, who fought the "scabs" alongside him at Camp Creek. Fred Mooney, *Struggle in the Coal Fields*, ed. J. W. Hess (Morgantown: West Virginia University Press, 1967), 29–31. See also Joe William Trotter Jr., "The Formation of Black Community in Southern West Virginia Coalfields,"

in Inscoe, *Appalachians and Race*, 295–97; James Green, *The Devil Is Here in These Hills: West Virginia's Coal Miners and Their Battle for Freedom* (New York: Atlantic Monthly Press, 2015), 106, 126; Thomas E. Wagner and Phillip J. Obermiller, *African American Miners and Migrants: The Eastern Kentucky Social Club* (Urbana: University of Illinois Press, 2004), esp. chaps. 1 and 2.

45. Sayles, *Thinking in Pictures*, 50–51.

46. Quotes are drawn from the "Shooting Script," which is fully reproduced as the final section of Sayles, *Thinking in Pictures*.

47. Joe William Trotter Jr., *Coal, Class, and Color: Blacks in Southern West Virginia, 1915–32* (Urbana: University of Illinois Press, 1990), 20–21; David Corbin, *Life, Work, and Rebellion in the Coal Fields: The Southern West Virginia Miners, 1880–1922* (Urbana: University of Illinois Press, 1981), 52–54.

48. Huie's novel was one of two on which Kazan drew for his characters and plot. See chapter 1 for a fuller discussion of both the novels and Kazan's use of them.

49. Nancy L. Grant, *TVA and Black Americans: Planning for the Status Quo* (Philadelphia: Temple University Press, 1990), 14, 49. For other perspectives on the TVA's racial policies, see also Matthew L. Downs, *Transforming the South: Federal Development in the Tennessee Valley, 1915–1960* (Baton Rouge: Louisiana State University Press, 2014), 92–94, 114–19. (Note that Down's focus is limited to northern Alabama.)

50. *The Defiant Ones* (1958) and *To Kill a Mockingbird* (1962) are the only other Hollywood productions of this period that confronted race relations in the South so directly; most treatments of race at the time, such as *Imitation of Life* (1959), *Raisin in the Sun* (1961), and *Lilies of the Field* (1963), were set in other parts of the country. Curiously, none of the scholarly studies of African Americans or the South in film acknowledge *Wild River* and its strong racial component. The only two serious analyses of the film and its racial subtext are Allison Graham, *Framing the South: Hollywood, Television, and Race during the Civil Rights Struggle* (Baltimore: Johns Hopkins University Press, 2001); Chris Cagle, "The Postwar Cinematic South: Realism and the Politics of Liberal Consensus," in *American Cinema and the Southern Imaginary*, ed. Deborah E. Barker and Kathryn Mckee (Athens: University of Georgia Press, 2011).

51. If the racial demographics are off for this particular setting, that doesn't mean that the racial bigotry on display there was not a reality. On racial attitudes in Southern Appalachia during the late nineteenth and early twentieth centuries, see W. Fitzhugh Brundage, "Racial Violence, Lynchings, and Modernization in the Mountain South," in Inscoe, *Appalachians and Race*, 302–16; Inscoe, "Race and Racism in Nineteenth-Century Appalachia."

52. See Janet Burroway, "The Mockingbird Syndrome," *New Letters* 82 (July 2015): 12–17, www.newletters.org/UserFiles/File/Burroway%202.pdf. This article focuses primarily on literary sources (some of which were adapted to film) and gives as much attention to white women serving in such roles as to white men. See also Herman Vera and Andrew M. Gordon, *Screen Saviors: Hollywood Fictions of Whiteness* (Lanham, MD: Rowan and Littlefield, 2003); Matthew W. Hughey, *The*

White Savior Film: Content, Critics, and Consumption (Philadelphia: Temple University Press, 2014).

Chapter Three

1. One of the few historians to attempt to make a clear distinction between guerrilla and irregular warfare, terms that are all too often used interchangeably, is Robert R. Mackey, *The Uncivil War: Irregular Warfare in the Upper South, 1861–1865* (Norman: University of Oklahoma Press, 2004), 5–20. In essence, Mackey sees guerrillas as self-constituted armed men operating independently of any organized or authorized military force, and irregular warfare as a far broader label applied to any unconventional military activity not involving the main armies of either side (6–7). Daniel E. Sutherland, while generally treating the terms "irregular" and "guerrilla" as synonymous, provides a useful categorization for the range of activity and groups to whom the label could be applied. See Sutherland, *A Savage Conflict: The Decisive Role of Guerrillas in the American Civil War* (Chapel Hill: University of North Carolina Press, 2009), x–xii. For an interesting roundtable discussion on warfare, see "Irregular Warfare and Its Impact on the Civil War," *North and South* 11 (May 2009): 45–52, 68–70.

2. J. W. Williamson, *Southern Mountaineers in Silent Films: Plot Synopses of Movies about Moonshining, Feuding and Other Mountain Topics, 1904–1929* (Jefferson, NC: McFarland, 1994), 1–2. Neither version of *Little Shepherd* still exists, and a plot synopsis survives only for the 1920 production (259–60, 290).

3. John Fox Jr., *Blue-Grass and Rhododendron: Out-Doors in Old Kentucky* (New York: Charles Scribner's, 1901), 6–7. On Fox's life and Appalachian writings, see Warren I. Titus, *John Fox, Jr.* (New York: Twayne, 1971); Bill York, *John Fox, Jr.: Appalachian Author* (Jefferson, NC: MacFarland, 2003); Darlene Wilson, "The Felicitous Convergence of Mythmaking and Capital Accumulation: John Fox Jr. and the Formation of An(Other) Almost-White American Underclass," *Journal of Appalachian Studies* 1 (Fall 1995): 17–29; Wilson, "A Judicious Combination of Incident and Psychology: John Fox Jr. and the Southern Mountaineer Motif," in *Confronting Appalachian Stereotypes: Back Talk from an American Region*, ed. Dwight B. Billings, Gurney Norman, and Katherine Ledford (Lexington: University Press of Kentucky, 1999), 98–118; Allen W. Batteau, *The Invention of Appalachia* (Tucson: University of Arizona Press, 1997), 64–74. On the significance of *The Little Shepherd of Kingdom Come* in particular, see Nina Silber, "'What Does America Need So Much as Americans?': Race and Northern Reconciliation with Southern Appalachia, 1870–1900," in *Appalachians and Race: The Mountain South from Slavery to Segregation*, ed. John C. Inscoe (Lexington: University Press of Kentucky, 2001), 254–56.

4. On the lingering effects of Civil War loyalties in the early twentieth century, see John C. Inscoe, "A Northern Wedge in the Heart of Appalachia: Explaining Civil War Loyalties in the Age of Appalachian Discovery, 1900–1920," in *Reconstructing Appalachia: The Civil War's Aftermath*, ed. Andrew Slap (Lexington: University Press of Kentucky, 2010), 240–64.

5. John Fox Jr., *The Little Shepherd of Kingdom Come* (c. 1903; repr., Lexington: University Press of Kentucky, 1987), 150, 190–91.

6. Fox, *Little Shepherd of Kingdom Come*, 24, 150.

7. *Shenandoah* features two brief but generic clashes between Union and Confederate forces, and *Cold Mountain* opens famously with a full re-creation of the siege of Petersburg and the battle of the Crater, where Inman is wounded. The other two films include no battlefield action, conventional or otherwise.

8. Encounters with John Hunt Morgan's cavalry would have taken the form of guerrilla-like skirmishes or raids or pillaging and looting, rather than the far too conventionally staged battle portrayed in the film. On Morgan's activity in Kentucky in 1863 and 1864, see Sutherland, *Savage Conflict*, 221–26; Brian D. McKnight, *Contested Borderland: The Civil War in Appalachian Kentucky and Virginia* (Lexington: University Press of Kentucky, 2006), 199–205.

9. A similar discrepancy between a novel and its film adaptation comes in *The Dollmaker*, discussed in chap. 1, in which the screenwriters opt to return Gertie Nevels and her family to their mountain home in Kentucky at the end of World War II rather than leave them in Detroit, as author Harriette Arnow chose to do at the conclusion of her novel. Thus, it seems that filmmakers, more so than novelists, see their protagonists more happily situated by returning to their highland origins than remaining in the flatland urban settings in which they found themselves at war's end.

10. It's curious to see how often both of these films are categorized as westerns by film historians and by biographers of both McLaglen and James Stewart. Brian Wills references *Little Shepherd of Kingdom Come* only once, in a chapter on "The West's Civil War"; and a biography of Stewart places *Shenandoah* under the category of "The Older West." See Brian Steel Wills, *Gone with the Glory: The Civil War in Cinema* (Lanham, MD: Rowman & Littlefield, 2007), 85; Don Dewey, *James Stewart, A Biography* (Atlanta: Turner, 1996), 426–47. Most notably for *Shenandoah*, see Bruce Chadwick, *The Reel Civil War: Mythmaking in American Film* (New York: Alfred A. Knopf, 2001), 232–33.

11. Stephen B. Armstrong, *Andrew V. McLaglen: The Life and Hollywood Career* (Jefferson, NC: MacFarland, 2011), 137. *Shenandoah* was the sixth highest grossing picture of 1965, a year dominated by blockbusters such as *The Sound of Music*, *Dr. Zhivago*, and the James Bond film *Thunderball*. It was also Stewart's top-grossing film of the 1960s. On the original title, see interview with McLaglen in C. Courtney Joyner, *The Westerners: Interviews with Actors, Directors, Writers and Producers* (Jefferson, NC: McFarland), 71.

12. Marc Eliot, *Jimmy Stewart: A Biography* (New York: Harmony Books, 2006), 355.

13. Gerald Molyneaux, *James Stewart: A Bio-Bibliography* (Westport, CT: Greenwood Press, 1992), 147.

14. Gary W. Gallagher, *Causes Won, Lost, and Forgotten: How Hollywood and Popular Art Shape What We Know about the Civil War* (Chapel Hill: University of North Carolina Press, 2008), 51.

15. Gallagher, *Causes Won, Lost, and Forgotten*, 51–52.

16. On the demographics of this mountain elite, see John C. Inscoe, *Mountain Masters: Slavery and the Sectional Conflict in Western North Carolina* (Knoxville: University of Tennessee Press, 1989), chaps. 1–3; Robert D. Mitchell, "The Settlement Pattern of the Shenandoah Valley, 1790–1860: Pattern, Process, and Structure," in *After the Backcountry: Rural Life in the Great Valley of Virginia, 1800–1900*, ed. Kenneth E. Koons and Warren R. Hofstra (Knoxville: University of Tennessee Press, 2000). See also other essays in Koons and Hofstra, *After the Backcountry.*

17. Chadwick, *Reel Civil War*, 233. Director Andrew V. McLaglen defended the choice of filming location, claiming "there is no place that looks more like Virginia than Oregon."

18. See Stephen L. Longenecker, "The Narrow Path: Antislavery, Plainness, and the Mainstream," in Koons and Hofstra, *After the Backcountry*, 185–93. See also other essays in Koons and Hofstra, *After the Backcountry.*

19. *Friendly Persuasion*, a 1956 adaptation of Jessamyn West's best-selling novel, was just as forthright in dealing with these themes, though it did so through the travails of a Quaker family in Indiana. Brian Wills sees that film as a northern counterpart to *Shenandoah*; the parallels are striking enough to make one wonder how much *Shenandoah*'s original screenplay by James Lee Barrett may have been influenced by *Friendly Persuasion*. See Wills, *Gone with the Glory*, 46–48.

20. IMDb entry on "Shenandoah," under Trivia.

21. For a recent treatment of Robert E. Lee's loyalties and, by extension, those of his fellow Virginians, see Elizabeth R. Varon, "'Save in Defense of My Native State': Robert E. Lee's Decision to Join the Confederacy," in *Secession Winter: When the Union Fell Apart*, ed. Robert J. Cook, William L. Barney, and Elizabeth R. Varon (Baltimore: Johns Hopkins University Press, 2013), 34–57.

22. Among the fullest treatments of conscription and impressment and Southern civilians' reaction to them remains Emory Thomas, *The Confederate Nation, 1861–1865* (New York: Harper & Row, 1979), esp. chaps. 7 and 9; Douglas B. Ball, *Financial Failure and Confederate Defeat* (Urbana: University of Illinois Press, 1991); David Williams and Teresa Crisp Williams, *Plain Folk in the Rich Man's War: Class and Dissent in Confederate Georgia* (Gainesville: University Press of Florida, 2002).

23. The film was adapted into a Broadway musical in 1975, and one of its showstopping musical numbers was a duet between Jennie and Gabriel called "Freedom." A dumbed-down version of the film, the stage production has the two strut across the stage together, singing lyrics such as "Freedom is a notion sweeping the nation, Freedom is a right of all mankind. Freedom ain't a state like Maine and Virginia, Freedom is a state of mind."

24. Jerry Williamson points out that cross-dressing women were a regular feature of "hillbilly" movies from early silent films on. He lists over forty such films under the heading "Hillbilly Gals" in Williamson, *Southern Mountaineers in Silent Films*, 302, and devotes a full section to the topic in the more modern era, called "Cross-Dressers: Who's Wearing the Pants?," in J. W. Williamson, *Hillbillyland: What the Movies Did to the Mountains and What the Mountains Did to the Movies* (Chapel

Hill: University of North Carolina Press, 1995), 235–42, though he makes no mention of Civil War–based films.

25. The literature on Appalachian women engaged in guerrilla warfare is extensive and includes Ralph Mann, "Guerrilla Warfare and Gender Roles: Sandy Basin, Virginia as a Test Case," *Journal of the Appalachian Studies Association* 5 (1993): 59–68; Gordon B. McKinney, "Women's Role in Civil War Western North Carolina," *North Carolina Historical Review* 69 (January 1992): 69–82; William A. Strasser, "'A Terrible Calamity Has Befallen Us': Unionist Women in Civil War East Tennessee," *Journal of East Tennessee History* 71 (1999): 66–88; John C. Inscoe and Gordon B. McKinney, *The Heart of Confederate Appalachia: The Civil War in Western North Carolina* (Chapel Hill: University of North Carolina Press, 2000), chap. 8; Michael Fellman, "Women and Guerrilla Warfare," in *Divided Houses: Gender and the Civil War*, ed. Catherine Clinton and Nina Silber (New York: Oxford University Press, 1992), 147–65.

26. Michael Burrows, *John Ford and Andrew V. McLaglen* (St. Austell, UK: Primestyle, 1970), 20.

27. Bill Cotter, *The Wonderful World of Disney Television* (New York: Hyperion, 1997), 134.

28. M. A. Hancock, *Menace on the Mountain* (Philadelphia: Macrae Smith, 1968). Hancock used initials in place of her first name, on the assumption that male authors garnered more respect from prospective publishers than did females. Background information on Hancock comes from an "Author's Note" in the book and from a newspaper feature story, "She Writes Man-Size Novels: Mary Hancock's Book Sold to Disney Studios," *Gastonia Gazette*, March 15, 1970. I am grateful to Roberta Herrin and Sheila Oliver at East Tennessee State University for sharing information on Hancock with me.

29. Hancock, "Author's Note," *Menace on the Mountain*, 172–73. Hancock's recreation of this historical reality is even more impressive in that she had to rely almost exclusively on firsthand sources, given how little scholarship on the subject there was at the time.

30. "She Writes Man-Sized Novels."

31. Reference is made to his serving in the 18th North Carolina Regiment and having just been part of the battle of Kennesaw, but this is an inaccuracy, given that the 18th was made up primarily of eastern North Carolinians and served in the Virginia theater.

32. On the role of merchants and the impact of the war on the market economy in the mountains, see Inscoe and McKinney, *Heart of Confederate Appalachia*, 167–76. For a more localized treatment of these themes set in an area very much like that in which Hancock set her novel, see Martin Crawford, *Ashe's County's Civil War* (Charlottesville: University Press of Virginia, 2001).

33. According to one source, the last sighting of a panther in the region was in 1914, though it's an issue that has generated considerable debate and speculation through much of the twentieth century. See Nicole Cuthbertson, "Status and History of the Mountain Lion in the Great Smoky Mountains National Park," National Park Service Management Report, No. 15 (1977).

34. For an analysis of twenty-five such narratives published between 1863 and 1915, see John Inscoe, "'Moving through Deserter Country': Fugitive Accounts of Southern Appalachia's Inner Civil War," in *The Civil War in Appalachia: Collected Essays*, ed. Kenneth W. Noe and Shannon H. Wilson (Knoxville: University of Tennessee Press, 1997), 159–86. See also Lorien Foote, *The Yankee Plague: Escaped Union Prisoners and the Collapse of the Confederacy* (Chapel Hill: University of North Carolina Press, 2016).

35. Stoneman's raiders ransacked Asheville on April 28. Other notable activity in late April and throughout May included Capt. Albert Teague's Home Guards (featured in Charles Frazier's *Cold Mountain*), which continued to terrorize Haywood County residents; the Fort Hamby gang, which rampaged throughout Wilkes, Caldwell, and Watauga Counties; and the Adair gang in Rutherford County. See Inscoe and McKinney, *Heart of Confederate Appalachia*, 255–58, 261, 269–71; Steven E. Nash, *Reconstruction's Ragged Edge: The Politics of Postwar Life in the Southern Mountains* (Chapel Hill: University of North Carolina Press, 2016).

36. Hancock quotes a Confederate veteran who returned home to northwestern North Carolina late in the war to find the area in the grip of bushwhacker rule. The man describes the means by which they drove local residents out of their cabin, moved in, and fortified it, stating, "It would have been difficult to have chosen a stronger location, both offensive and defensive. . . . The house was built of logs, two stories high. The robbers cut loopholes for their guns in the upper story. There would be nothing more hazardous than to attempt to reach it. We had no guns of any value to use upon such a fort, such a strong log wall." Hancock, "Author's Note," 173.

37. Guerrilla activity continued west of Asheville in May and June, leading Federal forces from East Tennessee to return to the area to put it down. As late as September 1865, Brig. Gen. Thomas A. Heath reported from Union headquarters of the western North Carolina district "depredations and crimes committed . . . by recent deserters from the Rebel Army." Inscoe and McKinney, *Heart of Confederate Appalachia*, 258, 269.

38. Harry M. Caudill, *Night Comes to the Cumberlands: A Biography of a Depressed Area* (Boston: Little, Brown, 1962), 41–42.

39. Robby Henson, "Back to the Civil War, 'Pharaoh's' Director Knows His History," interview by John Hartl, *Seattle Times*, 1996, www.pbs.org/pharaoh/seattle.htm.

40. Gary Gallagher and Brian Wills offer insightful but very different analyses of *Pharaoh's Army* in their respective books on Civil War films. Gallagher sees it as evidence of the breakdown of the Lost Cause's longtime hold on Hollywood depictions of the war (though he credits it with a stronger anti-Union strain than I see in it); Wills sees it as part of a genre of fairly recent films focusing on home-front struggles in the southern backcountry and on the psychological impact of the war at a personal level. See Gallagher, *Causes Won, Lost and Forgotten*, 62–66; Wills, *Gone with the Glory*, 57–60.

41. McKnight, *Contested Borderland*, 26–28; Earl J. Hess, *The Civil War in the West: Victory and Defeat from the Appalachians to the Mississippi* (Chapel Hill: University of North Carolina Press, 2012), 30–32. Toward the end of 1862 and into

1863, it would be Confederate forces that became the more aggressive and abusive force in terms of informal foraging and more official impressment of mountain civilians along the Kentucky-Virginia border, leading to formal complaints made to the Confederate secretary of war in Richmond. See McKnight, *Contested Borderland*, 119–20.

42. Among the best accounts of military activity in and around the Cumberland Gap early in the war are McKnight, *Contested Borderland*, 73–83, chaps. 6, 7, 8; Hess, *Civil War in the West*, chap. 6; Noel C. Fisher, *War at Every Door: Partisan Politics and Guerrilla Violence in East Tennessee, 1860–1869* (Chapel Hill: University of North Carolina Press, 1997), chap. 4.

43. Caudill, *Night Comes to the Cumberlands*, 41. Caudill acknowledged the limited presence of slaves along the Cumberland Plateau but seemed too quick to attribute the primary differences between the area's Confederate sympathizers and its majority of Unionists to those who owned slaves and those who didn't (37–38). See also McKnight, *Contested Borderland*, chap. 1.

44. Frank Wilkerson, *Recollections of a Private Soldier* (New York: Putnam, 1887), 232–33, quoted in Phillip Shaw Paludan, *Victims: A True Story of the Civil War* (Knoxville: University of Tennessee Press, 1981), 21.

45. Caudill, *Night Comes to the Cumberlands*, 40–41. (This story falls on the same page as that of the ninety-year-old's account of the sinkhole burial, which makes it obvious that Hansen saw it as well.) For a similar such killing of a Confederate home on furlough in Ashe County, North Carolina, and his widow's perpetual retelling of the incident to her children and grandchildren, see John C. Inscoe, "Guerrilla War and Remembrance: Reconstructing a Father's Murder and a Community's Civil War," in Inscoe, *Race, War, and Remembrance in the Appalachian South* (Lexington: University Press of Kentucky, 2008), 322–49.

46. Gallagher, *Causes Lost, Won, and Forgotten*, 65. Gallagher's discussion of the film is part of a chapter subsection called "Hollywood Turns Away from Dixie's Land: The Lost Cause in Crisis."

47. Henson, "Back to the Civil War."

48. Drew Gilpin Faust, *This Republic of Suffering: Death and the American Civil War* (New York: Knopf, 2009), 219–28. Faust cites numerous examples of Southern whites' desecration of Union graves and bodies, including one incident in which a Kentucky man was killed by neighbors for allowing two Union soldiers to be buried on his property (222).

49. In *Un-White: Appalachia, Race, and Film* (Athens: University of Georgia Press, 2019), Meredith McCarroll devotes one of her most inventive chapters to Ada and Ruby, in which she argues that their relationship parallels that of Scarlett O'Hara and Mammy (chap. 2).

50. For Charles Frazier's thoughts on the filming location, see a revealing interview conducted with him by Margaret D. Bauer in "The Way Movies Tell Stories: Putting Charles Frazier's Furniture in Anthony Minghella's Rooms," *North Carolina Literary Review* 22 (September 2013): 142–53.

51. Charles Frazier, *Cold Mountain* (New York: Atlantic Monthly Press, 1997), 265.

52. Gallagher, *Causes Won, Lost, and Forgotten*, 84.

53. See especially Gordon B. McKinney, "Women's Roles in Civil War Western North Carolina," *North Carolina Historical Review* 69 (January 1992): 37–56; Ralph Mann, "Guerrilla Warfare and Gender Roles: Sandy Basin, Virginia, as Test Case," *Journal of the Appalachian Studies Association* 5 (1993): 59–66; Inscoe and McKinney, *Heart of Confederate Appalachia*, chap. 8.

54. Michael Fellman, *Inside War: The Guerrilla Conflict in Missouri during the American Civil War* (New York: Oxford University Press, 1989), 193.

55. On the women of Shelton Laurel, see Paludan, *Victims*, 96–97; James O. Hall, "The Shelton Laurel Massacre: Murder in the North Carolina Mountains," *Blue & Gray* (February 1991): 20–26; Inscoe, "Unionists in the Attic: The Shelton Laurel Massacre Dramatized," in Inscoe, *Race, War, and Remembrance*, 282–302. On other such incidents, see Muriel Sheppard, *Cabins in the Laurel* (Chapel Hill: University of North Carolina Press, 1935), 64; Margaret Walker Freel, *Unto the Hills* (Andrew, NC: Privately printed, l976), 139–40; Inscoe and McKinney, *Heart of Confederate Appalachia*, 194–96.

56. Wilma Dykeman, *The Tall Woman* (New York: Holt, Rinehart, and Winston, 1962), 30–31.

57. For a very different interpretation of the abuse of women in the film, see Anna Creadick's comments in "Roundtable Discussion of *Cold Mountain*, the Film," *Appalachian Journal* 31 (Spring/Summer 2004): 330–31, 347–48. For deeper analyses of Sally Swanger and the after-effects of her torture, see Vicki Sigmon Collins, *The Silent Appalachian: Wordless Mountaineers in Fiction, Film, and Television* (Jefferson, NC: McFarland, 2017), 99–103.

58. I have dealt with this segment of the novel in an environmental context in an essay titled "The Strength of the Hills: Representations of Appalachian Wilderness as Civil War Refuge," in *The Blue, the Gray, and the Green: Toward an Environmental History of the Civil War*, ed. Brian Allan Drake (Athens: University of Georgia Press, 2015), 114–43.

59. Mary Bell to Alfred Bell, May 22, 1862, Alfred Bell Papers, Duke University Library, Durham, NC, quoted in John C. Inscoe, "Coping in Confederate Appalachia: Portrait of a Mountain Woman and Her Community at War," *North Carolina Historical Review* 69 (October 1992): 388–414.

60. Williamson, *Hillbillyland*, 242.

61. Quote from "Voice from Cherokee County," *North Carolina Standard* (Raleigh), August 19, 1863, quoted in Inscoe and McKinney, *Heart of Confederate Appalachia*, 187.

62. Adam Goodheart, "Trail of Tears," review of *Thirteen Moons*, by Charles Frazier, *New York Times Book Review*, October 9, 2006, 14.

63. Goodheart, "Trail of Tears," 14.

Chapter Four

1. On early nineteenth-century manifestations of feuding, see especially Henry D. Shapiro, *Appalachia on Our Mind: The Southern Mountains and Mountaineers in the American Consciousness, 1870 1920* (Chapel Hill: University of North Carolina Press,

1978), 102–12; T. R. C. Hutton, *Bloody Breathitt: Politics and Violence in the Appalachian South* (Lexington: University Press of Kentucky, 2013), chap. 7.

2. On Clay County, see Dwight B. Billings and Kathleen M. Blee, *The Road to Poverty: The Making of Wealth and Hardship in Appalachia* (New York: Cambridge University Press, 2000); on Breathitt, see Hutton, *Bloody Breathitt*; on the Hatfields and McCoys, see multiple sources listed below.

3. Altina L. Waller, "Feuding in Appalachia: The Evolution of a Cultural Stereotype," in *Appalachia in the Making: The Mountain South in the Nineteenth Century*, ed. Mary Beth Pudup, Dwight B. Billings, and Altina L. Waller (Chapel Hill: University of North Carolina Press, 1995), 347–76; Kathleen M. Blee and Dwight B. Billings, "Where 'Bloodshed Is a Pastime': Mountain Feuds and Appalachian Stereotyping," in *Confronting Appalachian Stereotypes: Back Talk from an American Region*, ed. Dwight B. Billings, Gurney Norman, and Katherine Ledford (Lexington: University Press of Kentucky, 1999), 119–37; Allen W. Batteau, *The Invention of Appalachia* (Tucson: University of Arizona Press, 1990), 57–74. The much-quoted description of the region originated as the title of an essay by Will Wallace Harvey, "A Strange Land and Peculiar People," *Lippincott's Magazine* 12 (October 1873): 429–38.

4. John Fox Jr., *Blue-Grass and Rhododendron: Out-Doors in Old Kentucky* (New York: Charles Scribner's, 1901), 40, quoted in Warren I. Titus, *John Fox, Jr.* (New York: Twayne, 1971), 60.

5. On multicausation of feuding and other forms of violence endemic to the region, see Gordon B. McKinney, "Industrialism and Violence," in *An Appalachian Symposium: Essays Written in Honor of Cratis B. Williams*, ed. J. W. Williamson (Boone, NC: Appalachian State University, 1977), 131–46; Shapiro, *Appalachia on Our Mind*, 102–9; John Ed Pearce, *Days of Darkness: The Feuds of Eastern Kentucky* (Lexington: University Press of Kentucky, 1994), chap. 1; Bruce E. Stewart, ed., *Blood in the Hills: A History of Appalachian Violence* (Lexington: University Press of Kentucky, 2012).

6. Cratis D. Williams, "The Southern Mountaineer in Fact and Fiction," pt. 3, *Appalachian Journal* 3 (Spring 1976): 218. This is part of a four-part series that provides a published version of Williams's otherwise unpublished dissertation (Columbia University, 1961).

7. J. W. Williamson, *Southern Mountaineers in Silent Films: Plot Synopses of Movies about Moonshining, Feuding and Other Mountain Topics, 1904–1929* (Jefferson, NC: MacFarland, 1994), 1–6.

8. On the success of the film, see the biography of its director, Walter Coppedge, *Henry King's America* (Metuchen, NJ: Scarecrow Press, 1986), 48–49; Anthony Harkins, *Hillbilly: A Cultural History of an American Icon* (New York: Oxford University Press, 2004), 143.

9. J. W. Williamson, *Hillbillyland: What the Movies Did to the Mountains and What the Mountains Did to the Movies* (Chapel Hill: University of North Carolina Press, 1995), 177. Williamson devotes an entire section to *Tol'able David*, 177–89. See also Harkins, *Hillbilly*, 142–45.

10. The story, originally published in serial form in the *Saturday Evening Post* in 1917, was reprinted in a 1929 anthology of the best short stories by current writers,

by which time its reputation was based far more on the film than on the fiction. Joseph Hergesheimer, "Tol'able David," in *Notable Short Stories of Today*, ed. Edwin Van B. Knickerbocker (New York: Harper & Row, 1929), 73–101. In an introductory statement, Knickerbocker stated that "Tol'able David" was the basis for "one of the best moving pictures that have yet been filmed in this country" (73).

11. Coppedge, *Henry King's America*, 48.

12. Coppedge, 36–37.

13. Coppedge, 48. Coppedge draws on detailed memories of both local residents and film crew members of a very positive experience shared by both groups during the weeks spent filming in Virginia (46–49).

14. Quoted in Williams, "The Southern Mountaineer in Fact and Fiction," 104.

15. Jerry Williamson, noting a pattern among cinematic portrayals of mountain men who bow, up to a point, to the will of wise mothers, includes this film and others—such as *Sergeant York*—in a chapter of *Hillbillyland* he titles "Mama's Boys" (chap. 7).

16. Titus, *John Fox, Jr.*, 94–95. On the outdoor drama, go to "Trail of the Lonesome Pine: The Official Outdoor Drama of Virginia," www.trailofthelonesomepine.com.

17. Titus, *John Fox, Jr.*, chap. 3.

18. Two full-length biographies of Fox are Titus, *John Fox, Jr.*; Bill York, *John Fox, Jr.: Appalachian Author* (Jefferson, NC: McFarland, 2003). See also Darlene Wilson, "A Judicious Combination of Incident and Psychology: John Fox Jr. and the Southern Mountaineer Motif," in Billings, Norman, and Ledford, *Confronting Appalachian Stereotypes*, 98–118; Batteau, *Invention of Appalachia*, 57–74.

19. Titus, *John Fox, Jr.*, 58–59, 92–94. Fox argued that feuding was among the factors that most distinguished Kentucky mountaineers from those in other parts of Southern Appalachia. See, most notably, his essays, "The Southern Mountaineer" and "The Kentucky Mountaineer," in Fox, *Blue-Grass and Rhododendron*.

20. On Fox and *The Little Shepherd of Kingdom Come*, see Williams, "The Southern Mountaineer in Fact and Fiction," pt. 3, 216–19.

21. For the fullest descriptions of the silent film versions of the novel, see Williamson, *Southern Mountaineers in Silent Films*, 160–61, 218–19, 276. See also IMDb entries on each.

22. Harold N. Pomainville, *Henry Hathaway: The Lives of a Hollywood Director* (Lanham, MD: Rowman & Littlefield, 2016), 68. For the fullest description of the film's production, as recounted by Hathaway himself, see Rudy Behlmer, ed., *Henry Hathaway: A Director Guild of America Oral History* (Lanham, MD: Scarecrow Press), chap. 13.

23. Williamson, *Southern Mountaineers in Silent Films*. In an appendix in which Williamson lists these films by place and subject, "Feuding" makes up the largest single topical category, with approximately ninety-five such films made between 1905 and 1928. Just over half fall under the subcategorization of "Romeo and Juliet love stories"; the rest are labeled "all other feud stories" (301).

24. John Ed Pearce, foreword to John Fox Jr., *The Trail of the Lonesome Pine* (Lexington: University Press of Kentucky, 1984, ca. 1908), x–xi; Titus, *John Fox, Jr.*, 96.

25. Williamson, *Southern Mountaineers in Silent Films*, 15.

26. Williamson, 15.

27. Williamson, 301; the only category larger than "Feuds" is "Moonshining," with nearly 180 entries.

28. On Alberta Hannum, see Williams, "The Southern Mountaineer in Fact and Fiction," pt. 4, 345–46.

29. Altina L. Waller, *Feud: Hatfields, McCoys, and Social Change in Appalachia* (Chapel Hill: University of North Carolina Press, 1988), 69. Waller's book, which lays out the Roseanna and Johnse episode on pages 66–69, is the most authoritative account of the Hatfield-McCoy feud. Other full-scale narratives of the history or legend of the feud include Virgil Carrington Jones, *The Hatfields and the McCoys* (Chapel Hill: University of North Carolina Press, 1948); Otis K. Rice, *The Hatfields and the McCoys* (Lexington: University Press of Kentucky, 1978); Pearce, *Days of Darkness,* 57–74.

30. Waller, *Feud,* 69.

31. Quoted in A. Scott Berg, *Goldwyn: A Biography* (New York: Riverhead Books, 1989), 445.

32. The reference here is to an actual incident, though it didn't happen until 1888, eight years after the romance recounted here. A group of Hatfields did indeed attack Randall McCoy's cabin, and in the ensuing skirmish, shots fired by Johnse and his cousin Ellison Mounts (called Mounts Hatfield) wounded Roseanna's mother—and killed one of their sons and their oldest daughter. Jones, *Hatfields and McCoys,* 98–102; Waller, *Feud,* 180–81; Pearce, *Days of Darkness,* 67–69.

33. Waller, *Feud,* chap. 2.

34. Cartoon versions include "A Feud There Was," Warner Bros., 1938; "The Martins and the Coys," Walt Disney, 1946. TV movies include a less than memorable ABC production *Hatfields and McCoys* (1975), featuring Jack Palance as Anse Hatfield and Steve Forrest as Randall McCoy; and an even worse low-budget feature film, *The Hatfields and McCoys: Bad Blood,* released a week after the miniseries aired in 2012.

35. Mary McNamara, review of *Hatfields & McCoys, Los Angeles Times,* May 28, 2012.

36. *Entertainment Weekly,* June 15, 2018, 46–47. One viewer titled his online review on IMDb "Cowboy Costner" (May 31, 2012): "Costner is back where he does best—in the west"; and went on to enthuse: "There is plenty of action and drama. There is romance, and some good old western shooting and riding." In an interview on a *Wall Street Journal* blog on how realistic the miniseries was, Altina Waller made the point more critically: "In some ways the portrayal of mountain people in the post–Civil War era is realistic in that it was a rural culture where everyone knew each other on a face to face basis. But this movie makes Appalachian culture more like the Wild West without cowboys and Indians." She then goes on to single out the town scenes and saloons as the most flagrant examples of that. Interview reprinted in the *Appalachian Journal* 40 (Fall 2012/Winter 2013): 21–23.

37. Waller, *Feud,* 35–36.

38. Waller, 2.

39. Note this more factual version of Mounts's fate than that portrayed in *Roseanna McCoy.*

40. For the fullest accounts of stereotypical treatments of feuding mountaineers beyond films, see Shapiro, *Appalachia on Our Mind*; Harkin, *Hillbilly.*

41. See Blee and Billings, "Where 'Bloodshed Is a Pastime,'" 130–33, in which five popular "myths" regarding the Kentucky feuds of the late nineteenth century include "Myth #5: Women Were Behind/Outside the Conflict."

42. Blee and Billings, "Where 'Bloodshed Is a Pastime,'" 133.

Chapter Five

1. David E. Whisnant, *All That Is Native and Fine: The Politics of Culture in an American Region* (Chapel Hill: University of North Carolina Press, 1983), xiii.

2. Whisnant, *All That Is Native and Fine,* xiii.

3. On the attention of philanthropic and other benefactors redirected from the South's emancipated slave population in the 1860s and 1870s to Appalachian residents during the 1890s and beyond, see James C. Klotter, "The Black South and White Appalachia," *Journal of American History* 66 (March 1980): 8332–49; Nina Silber, "'What Does America Need So Much as Americans?': Race and Northern Reconciliation with Southern Appalachia," in *Appalachians and Race: From Slavery to Segregation in the Mountain South,* ed. John C. Inscoe (Lexington: University Press of Kentucky, 2001), 245–58.

4. The term "benevolent worker" seems to stem from Henry D. Shapiro, *Appalachia on Our Mind: The Southern Mountains and Mountaineers in the Southern Consciousness, 1870–1920* (Chapel Hill: University of North Carolina Press, 1978), esp. chaps. 2 and 6. The scholarship on these women, both as individuals and as a group, has been extensive ever since. For a recent sample, see several articles in a special issue of the *Appalachian Journal* 37 (Spring/Summer 2010), which focuses on women in and of Appalachia.

5. These films were based respectively on C. S. Forester, *The African Queen* (1935); Alan Burgess, *The Small Woman* (1956); Margaret Landon, *Anna and the King of Siam* (1944); Rumer Godden, *Black Narcissus* (1939); and Katherine Hulme, *The Nun's Story* (1956).

6. John M. Talmadge, *Corra Harris, Lady of Purpose* (Athens: University of Georgia Press, 1968), 10.

7. Biographies of Harris include Talmadge, *Corra Harris*; Catherine Oglesby, *Corra Harris and the Divided Mind of the New South* (Gainesville: University of Florida Press, 2008); and several essays, most notably Donald Mathews, "Corra Harris (1869–1935): The Storyteller as Folk Preacher," in *Georgia Women: Their Lives and Times,* ed. Ann Short Chirhart and Betty Wood (Athens: University of Georgia Press, 2009), 1:341–69.

8. Corra Harris, *A Circuit Rider's Wife* (Philadelphia: Henry Altemus, 1910), 116.

9. Harris, *Circuit Rider's Wife,* 116.

10. Talmadge, *Corra Harris,* 84.

11. Oglesby, *Corra Harris and the Divided Mind*, 29–31, 115–16; Talmadge, *Corra Harris*, 10–11, 46–47.

12. Mathews, "Corra Harris," 349.

13. Mathews, 341.

14. Talmadge, *Corra Harris*, 143.

15. Frank Thompson, "Georgians Who Made Film History: Comic Actor Oliver Hardy and Screenwriter Lamar Trotti" (Atlanta Historical Society Presentation, 1986), 8.

16. Walter Coppedge, *Henry King's America* (Metuchen, NJ: Scarecrow Press, 1986), 153.

17. Thompson, "Georgians Who Made Film History," 14–15.

18. Frank Thompson, ed., *Henry King, Director: From Silents to 'Scope* (Los Angeles: Directors Guild of America, 1995), 157. The book is a compilation of interviews with King, who directed over a hundred films between 1919 and 1962, including *Tol'able David* (1921), discussed in chapter 4.

19. Thompson, *Henry King, Director*, 158.

20. Marshall's nonfiction account of her mother's experience appears in Catherine Marshall, *Dearest Mother, Dearest Friend: Godly Inspiration from the Journals and Letters of Catherine Marshall* (Nashville, TN: J. Countryman, 2002), 15–16.

21. Catherine Marshall, *Christy* (New York: McGraw Hill, 1967), 5–6. Oddly, Marshall used the fictional names for places and people used in the novel in this otherwise factual prologue.

22. Marshall, *Christy*, 7.

23. Catherine Marshall, *A Man Called Peter: The Story of Peter Marshall* (New York: McGraw-Hill, 1951). She ultimately wrote more than twenty works of fiction and nonfiction. *A Man Called Peter* was made into a film in 1955, starring Jean Peters as Catherine and Richard Todd as Peter.

24. Marshall, *Dearest Mother, Dearest Friend*, 15–16. On Guerrant and his schools, see Mark Huddle, "Home Missions Revisited: Edward O. Guerrant and the 'Discovery' of Appalachia," in Edward O. Guerrant, *The Galax Gatherers: The Gospel among the Highlanders* (Knoxville: University of Tennessee Press, 2005), xi–xl; J. Gray McAllister and Grace Owings Guerrant, *Edward O. Guerrant: Apostle to the Southern Highlanders* (Richmond, VA: Richmond Press, 1950).

On a personal note, my maternal grandmother also heard Guerrant speak in Montreat several years after Leonora Whitaker did, and was likewise inspired to become a teacher at two of his schools in Kentucky. For an interview in which she describes her experience, see John C. Inscoe, ed., "Memories of a Presbyterian Mission Worker in the Kentucky Mountains, 1918–1921: An Interview with Rubie Ray Cunningham," *Appalachian Journal* 15 (Winter 1988): 144–60.

25. There are multiple websites devoted to *Christy: The Musical*, as there are to both the book and the various TV versions, on which some of the following information is drawn. See also the entry on "Christy" in *Encyclopedia of Appalachia*, ed. Rudy Abramson and Jean Haskell (Knoxville: University of Tennessee Press, 2006), 1699–1700; Susan Sawyer, "The Filming of Christy," *It Happened in Tennessee* (Guilford, CT: Globe Pequot Press, 2002), 100–103. On the novel's critical and popular

reception, see Emily Satterwhite, *Dear Appalachia: Readers, Identity, and Popular Fiction Since 1878* (Lexington: University Press of Kentucky, 2011), chap. 4.

26. Sawyer, "Filming of *Christy*," 101–2.

27. This film is also known as *Christy: The Movie*. See "Resurrecting Christy," *Christian Teens Weekly*, April 2001, reproduced on the most comprehensive of several websites devoted to "Christy" in all its various manifestations: http://tvshow_christy.tripod.com, cited hereafter as christy.tripod. See also www.christyfest.org.

28. Historian Durwood Dunn confirmed in conversation with me that family feuds would have been fairly rare in this area of Tennessee. See also Altina L. Waller, "Feuding in Appalachia: The Evolution of a Cultural Stereotype," in *Appalachia in the Making: The Mountain South in the Nineteenth Century*, ed. Dwight B. Billings, Mary Beth Pudup, and Altina L. Waller (Chapel Hill: University of North Carolina Press, 1995), 347–76; Waller's entry on "Feuds" in Abramson and Haskell, *Encyclopedia of Appalachia*, 1592–93; John Alexander Williams, *Appalachia: A History* (Chapel Hill: University of North Carolina Press, 2002), 192–93, see esp. map of feuding areas, 193.

29. These include women like Katherine Pettit, May Stone, Ethel DeLong Zande, and Cora Wilson Stewart, all of whom founded or supervised schools in Kentucky; Mary Sloop and Lucy Morgan in North Carolina; and Martha Berry in Georgia.

30. While Green is given sole credit for writing the pilot, it is worth noting that three of the four writers of the subsequent series were also women—Green, Dawn Prestwich, and Nicole Yorkin—who together were part of the writing team of such TV dramas as *L.A. Law*, *Chicago Hope*, *Pickett Fences*, and *Judging Amy*.

31. Interviews and running commentary on the film by Maggie Greenwald and David Mansfield appear on the DVD of *Songcatcher* (Lionsgate, 2003). Both also noted that they used the original notations by Mrs. Campbell and Cecil Sharp in their arrangements of the fourteen ballads performed in the film.

32. Quote is from Greenwald's commentary on the DVD of *Songcatcher*.

33. They are Lily Penleric; two settlement house teachers, her sister Elna Penleric and Harriet Tolliver; and three mountain women or girls, Viney Butler, Deladis Slocum, and Alice Kincaid. The only comparable male roles are those of Tom Bledsoe and Fate Honeycutt.

34. They include writer Emma Bell Miles; anthropologist Ellen Churchill Semple; teachers Katherine Pettit and Lucy Morgan; musicologist Dorothy Scarborough, who was the first to record this music with a Dictaphone in 1930; and Maude Karples, Sharp's assistant. See Betty Smith, review of *Songcatcher*, written and directed by Maggie Greenwald, *Appalachian Journal* 30 (Winter/Spring 2003): 248–53; Arthur Krim, "Appalachian Songcatcher: Olive Dame Campbell and the Scotch-Irish Ballad," *Journal of Cultural Geography* 24 (Fall/Winter 2006): 91–112.

35. It is surprising that no one has produced a full biography of either John or Olive Dame Campbell, despite the fact that their extensive papers are held by the Southern Historical Collection at UNC–Chapel Hill; we do, however, have Olive's biography of John: Olive Dame Campbell, *The Life and Work of John C. Campbell*, ed. Elizabeth M. Williams (Lexington: University Press of Kentucky, 2017). Among the best treatments of her are Krim, "Appalachian Songcatcher"; Whisnant, *All*

That Is Native and Fine, chap. 2, 103–80; Olive Dame Campbell, *Appalachian Travels: The Diary of Olive Dame Campbell*, ed. Elizabeth M. Williams (Lexington: University Press of Kentucky, 2012); Jane S. Becker, *Selling Tradition: Appalachians and the Construction of an American Folk, 1930–1949* (Chapel Hill: University of North Carolina Press, 1998); and scattered references in Henry D. Shapiro, *Appalachia on Our Mind: The Southern Mountains and Mountaineers in the American Consciousness, 1870–1920* (Chapel Hill: University of North Carolina Press, 1978).

36. Smith, review of *Songcatcher*, 249. Another anachronism noted by several online reviewers is that the first scene, showing Penleric's arrival in western North Carolina, is set against a backdrop of kudzu, which was only introduced into the American South from Japan in the 1930s. See, for example, the entry for *Songcatcher* on IMDb.

37. Shapiro, *Appalachia on Our Mind*, 137.

38. Cratis D. Williams, *The Southern Mountaineer in Fact and Fiction*, ed. Martha H. Pipes for *Appalachian Journal* (Boone, NC: Belk Library, 2011), 144, CD-ROM.

39. Jerry Williamson makes a similar point, though he does so by focusing more on the manly nature of mountain women in film in what is surely one of his most original and provocative chapters. Williamson, "Hillbilly Gals," in *Hillbillyland: What the Movies Did to the Mountains and What the Mountains Did to the Movies* (Chapel Hill: University of North Carolina Press, 1995), 225.

Chapter Six

1. Much of the work came to a head at a symposium called "Appalachia & Wales: Coal and After Coal," held at Appalachian State University in October 2010, which launched Tom Hansell's documentary film in 2016 and the subsequent book drawn from it, *After Coal: Stories of Survival in Appalachia and Wales* (Morgantown: West Virginia University Press, 2018).

2. Hansell, *After Coal*, 20–21.

3. Helen M. Lewis, "Interview with Dai Francis," E. L. Uhry Collection, Appalachian State University. See also Helen M. Lewis, "Industrialization, Class, and Regional Consciousness in Two Highland Societies: Wales and Appalachia," in *Cultural Adaptation to Mountain Environments*, ed. Patricia D. Beaver and Burton L. Purrington (Athens: University of Georgia Press, 1984), 50–70. The only full monograph to directly compare the two regions is Roger Fagge, *Power, Culture and Conflict in the Coalfields: West Virginia and South Wales, 1900–1922* (Manchester: Manchester University Press, 1996).

4. Crandall A. Shifflett, *Coal Towns: Life, Work, and Culture in Company Towns of Southern Appalachia, 1880–1960* (Knoxville: University of Tennessee Press, 1991), xi, 1–3. The only exception Shifflett acknowledges is a single chapter, titled "Coal, Culture, and Community: Life in the Company Towns," in Ronald D. Eller's *Miners, Millhands, and Mountaineers: The Industrialization of the Mountain South, 1880–1930* (Knoxville: University of Tennessee Press, 1982). A recent and very welcome oral history of black coal communities in Harlan County, Kentucky, is Karida L.

Brown, *Gone Home: Race and Roots through Appalachia* (Chapel Hill: University of North Carolina Press, 2018).

5. Fagge, *Power, Culture and Conflict*, 5.

6. These lines are part of a rousing speech made at a university debate club by David Fenwick, the protagonist of *The Stars Look Down*.

7. Michael Brooke, "King Coal: A Century of Coal-Mining on Screen," BFI ScreenOnline, www.screenonline.org.uk/film/id/1373461/index.html. Other British productions tell stories set in Welsh and English coal mining communities whose miners and mining issues vary in terms of their centrality to plot and character. These include *The Corn Is Green* (1945); *Sons and Lovers* (1960), adapted from D. H. Lawrence's novel; *Brassed Off* (1996); and *Billy Elliot* (2000). The emphasis on music is striking in these films. Like *The Proud Valley*, both *The Corn Is Green* and *Brassed Off* prominently feature male choirs, and *Billy Elliot*'s protagonist is a young ballet dancer.

8. Scott Allen Nollen, *Paul Robeson: Film Pioneer* (Jefferson, NC: McFarland, 2010), 125.

9. Cronin's second and even more successful novel, *The Citadel* (1937), was more autobiographical, and recounted the frustrations and ultimate disillusionment of a young doctor whose first experience was treating work-related respiratory ailments in a Welsh coal-mining town. It was adapted as a film in 1938; the British production starred Robert Donat, Rosalind Russell, and Ralph Richardson, and was directed by King Vidor.

10. Reed went on to direct such prominent films as *Odd Man Out* (1947), *The Third Man* (1949), *Our Man in Havana* (1959), and *Oliver!* (1968). Two biographies of Reed provide full accounts of the production of *The Stars Look Down*: Nicholas Wapshott, *The Man Between: A Biography of Carol Reed* (London: Chatto & Windus, 1990), 122–34; Peter William Evans, *Carol Reed* (Manchester: Manchester University Press, 2005), 30–39.

11. Geoff Brown, "*The Stars Look Down*," BFI ScreenOnline, www.screenonline.org.uk/film/id/491824/index.html; Pauline Kael, *5001 Nights at the Movies* (New York: Holt, Rinehart and Winston, 1982), 554–55.

12. "*The Stars Look Down*," IMDb, www.imdb.com/title/tt0031976/.

13. Paul Robeson, *Here I Stand* (Boston: Beacon Press, 1958), 54.

14. Susan Robeson, *The Whole World in His Hands: A Pictorial Biography of Paul Robeson* (Secaucus, NJ: Citadel Press, 1981), 94.

15. Paul Robeson Jr., *The Undiscovered Paul Robeson: An Artist's Journey, 1898–1939* (New York: John E. Wiley, 2001), 330. There are differing accounts as to who suggested the film's final title. Sheila Tully Boyle and Andrew Bunie, *Paul Robeson: The Years of Promise and Achievement* (Amherst: University of Massachusetts Press, 2001), offers the fullest account of the film's origins and production, and states that it was the director, Pen Tennyson, who first suggested that the film be called *The Proud Valley* (413).

16. Boyle and Bunie, *Paul Robeson*, 417–18; Martin Duberman, *Paul Robeson* (New York: New Press, 1989), 646n46.

17. Susan Robeson, *Whole World in His Hands*, 94.

18. *Afro-American*, May 24, 1941.

19. Tag Gallagher, *John Ford: The Man and His Films* (Berkeley: University of California Press, 1986), chap. 7; Mason Wiley and Damien Bona, *Inside Oscar: The Unofficial History of the Academy Awards* (New York: Ballentine Books, 1986), 120–22.

20. It also won Oscars for supporting actor Donald Crisp, for cinematography, and for set design, and was nominated in five other categories. Perhaps its chief distinction in film history lies in the fact that it won these awards over what's now generally considered one of the greatest films ever made, Orson Welles's masterpiece, *Citizen Kane*.

21. Dave Kehr, "John Ford's Portraits of Loss and Redemption," review of new DVD edition of *How Green Was My Valley*, *New York Times*, February 8, 2013.

22. Quote by David Thomson in Gallagher, *John Ford*, 183–84.

23. Quoted in Wiley and Bona, *Inside Oscar*, 120.

24. The mother is played by Nancy Collins, who made an especially strong impression onscreen. A native of the Rhondda valley, she had never acted until Robeson discovered her there; the role launched her into a notable film career lasting many years. Boyle and Bunie, *Paul Robeson*, 418.

25. John Sayles, *Thinking in Pictures: The Making of the Movie "Matewan"* (Boston: Houghton Mifflin, 1987), 9–10.

26. Sayles, *Thinking in Pictures*, 33–34.

27. Sayles provides a detailed discussion of the strategies used in scouting locations, particularly relevant to Appalachian locales, in *Thinking in Pictures*, 54–57, 66–68.

28. Sayles's *Thinking in Pictures* includes the full shooting script of the film. Quoted lines from the film are drawn both from this script and directly from the film itself.

29. For a full treatment of the agency and the racial context of its activity, see T. R. C. Hutton, "Sleuthing for Mr. Crow: Detective William Baldwin and the Business of White Supremacy," *Journal of Southern History* 85 (May 2019): 285–320.

30. "A Conversation between Eric Foner and John Sayles," in *Past Imperfect: History according to the Movies*, ed. Mark C. Carnes (New York: Henry Holt, 1995), 11–12; Sayles, *Thinking in Pictures*, 21–22. Other films written and directed by Sayles that reflect this emphasis on ensemble storytelling include *The Return of the Secaucus Seven* (1979), *Eight Men Out* (1988), *City of Hope* (1991), and *Lone Star* (1996).

31. Matewan was indeed part of the Tug River valley, in what had been Logan County until newly formed Mingo County split away from it in 1895. This was where the Hatfield-McCoy feud played out over the latter part of the nineteenth century, and it remained the home base of the Hatfield family, which rose to further prominence in state and local politics in the early twentieth century, including Sid Hatfield, who fired the opening shots of the Matewan massacre. For the fullest account of the feud, see Altina Waller, *Feud: Hatfields, McCoys, and Social Change in Appalachia, 1860–1900* (Chapel Hill: University of North Carolina Press, 1988). On the later political clout of the Hatfield family, see Rebecca J. Bailey, *Matewan before the Massacre: Politics, Coal, and the Roots of Conflict in a West Virginia Min-*

ing Community (Morgantown: West Virginia University Press, 2008), esp. chap. 2; James R. Green, *The Devil Is Here in These Hills: West Virginia's Coal Miners and Their Battle for Freedom* (New York: Atlantic Monthly Press, 2015).

32. Rebecca Bailey provides the most detailed description and timeline of the massacre as the prologue to her book, *Matewan before the Massacre*, 1–8; see also Green, *The Devil Is Here*, 206–13; David Alan Corbin, *Life, Work, and Rebellion: The Southern West Virginia Miners, 1880–1922* (Urbana: University of Illinois Press, 1981), chap. 8.

33. For more on Few Clothes and the racial context of *Matewan*, see chapter 2.

34. Loretta Lynn, with George Vecsey, *Loretta Lynn: Coal Miner's Daughter* (Chicago: Henry Regnery, 1976). It reached No. 1 on the *New York Times* Best Sellers list, the first book by a country music star to do so.

35. See chapter 1 for a discussion of York's and his community's involvement in holding the filmmakers to a high standard of realism in that film's portrayal of southern mountaineers.

36. Details of the production come primarily from interviews with Loretta Lynn, Sissy Spacek, and Michael Apted; from a backstory feature on the DVD of the film; and from Mark Emerson and Euge E. Pfaff Jr., *Country Girl: The Life of Sissy Spacek* (New York: St. Martin's Press, 1988), 73–88.

37. Loretta Lynn, interview by Michael Apted, special feature on DVD of film.

38. Lynn devoted two chapters to her future husband, his family, his character (she calls him "rough and tough, but a softie"), and their courtship in her autobiography, most of which the film re-created fairly faithfully. Lynn and Vecsey, *Coal Miner's Daughter*, chaps. 6 and 7.

39. Lynn and Vecsey, *Coal Miner's Daughter*, 65.

40. Lynn devoted several pages of her autobiography to her father's last days, and his funeral and burial. Lynn and Vecsey, *Coal Miner's Daughter*, 64–67.

41. Hickam has laid these circumstances out in multiple forms, including in an essay, "How I Came to Write the Memoir, *Rocket Boys*," on his website, homerhickam.com, and later in a published booklet, *From Rocket Boys to October Sky* (Huntsville, AL: Privately published, 2013).

42. Hickam, *From Rocket Boys to October Sky*, 21.

43. Hickam, 22.

44. Hickam, 30, 37; interview with director Joe Johnston, feature on DVD of *October Sky*.

45. Homer H. Hickam Jr., *Rocket Boys: A Memoir* (New York: Delacorte Press, 1998), 1. The paperback edition of the book took the title of the film, *October Sky*.

46. Miss Riley's relationship with Homer brings to mind that of a teacher in Emlyn Williams's stage play *The Corn Is Green*, filmed in 1945 with Bette Davis as Miss Moffat (and again in 1979 as a TV movie with Katharine Hepburn in the part), who establishes a school for local children in a Welsh mining town over the objections of a local squire, who fears the subversive influences of education on his future miners. She takes on the special quest of getting one very bright young man out of the mine by prepping him for entrance exams at Oxford University. It's curious that teachers don't factor as similar catalysts of escape in more of these films, either British or Appalachian-based.

47. Hickam, *From Rocket Boys to October Sky*, 33.

48. Excerpt from book review in *Publisher's Weekly* quoted in Hickam, "How I Came to Write the Memoir, *Rocket Boys*."

49. In *From Rocket Boys to October Sky*, Hickam states that the mine was closed in 1978, and he never makes any attempt to point out or explain the discrepancy with the film's claim that it closed in 1965 (107).

50. Quoted in David Remnick, "The Talk of the Town: Dignity and the Fourth," *New Yorker*, July 10, 2017, 24.

Index

Page numbers in *italics* indicate photographs.

FSC
www.fsc.org
MIX
Paper from
responsible sources
FSC® C008955